AA004026

MMEDIA 2017

The Ninth International Conferences on Advances in Multimedia

April 23 - 27, 2017

Venice, Italy

MMEDIA 2017 Editors

Marco Martalò, SMARTEST Research Center, E-Campus University, Italy & Department of Information Engineering, University of Parma, Italy

Riccardo Raheli, Department of Information Engineering, University of Parma, Italy

Hiroshi Ishikawa, Information and Communication Systems, Faculty of System Design, Tokyo Metropolitan University, Japan

Shohei Yokoyama, Faculty of Informatics, Shizuoka University, Japan

Masaharu Hirota, National Institute of Technology, Oita College, Japan

Printed from e-media with permission by:

Curran Associates, Inc.
57 Morehouse Lane
Red Hook, NY 12571

Some format issues inherent in the e-media version may also appear in this print version.

Copyright© (2017) by International Academy, Research, and Industry Association (IARIA)
Please refer to the Copyright Information page.

Printed by Curran Associates, Inc. (2017)

International Academy, Research, and Industry Association (IARIA)
412 Derby Way
Wilmington, DE 19810

Phone: (408) 893-6407
Fax: (408) 527-6351

petre@iaria.org

Additional copies of this publication are available from:

Curran Associates, Inc.
57 Morehouse Lane
Red Hook, NY 12571 USA
Phone: 845-758-0400
Fax: 845-758-2633
Email: curran@proceedings.com
Web: www.proceedings.com

TABLE OF CONTENTS

MMEDIA 1: MULTIMEDIA SERVICES

The Research of Critical Success Factors for Performance-oriented Electronic Support Systems - Resource-Based View 1
J. Lee, W. Yan, C. Yu

3D Model Representations and Transformations in the Context of Computer-Aided Design: A State-of-the-Art Overview 10
C. Schinko, U. Krispel, E. Eggeling, T. Ullrich

MMEDIA 2: MULTIMEDIA APPLICATIONS

Investigating the Use of Semi-Supervised Convolutional Neural Network Models for Speech/Music Classification and Segmentation 16
D. Doukhan, J. Carrive

Adaptive Queue Management Scheme for Flexible Dual TCP/UDP Streaming Protocol 20
A. Dhamodaran, K. Gatimu, B. Lee

Improving Feature Extraction Accuracy for Skin Analysis 26
W. Kim, H. Kim, E. Hwang

MMEDIA 3 / SBD I: SOCIAL AND BIG DATA I

A Data Model for Integrating Data Management and Data Mining in Social Big Data 32
H. Ishikawa, R. Chbeir

Examination of Best-time Estimation using Interpolation for Geotagged Tweets 38
M. Endo, S. Ohno, M. Hirota, Y. Shoji, H. Ishikawa

Classification of Unlabeled Deep Moonquakes Using Machine Learning 44
S. Kikuchi, R. Yamada, Y. Yamamoto, M. Hirota, S. Yokoyama, H. Ishikawa

MMEDIA 4 / SBD II: SOCIAL AND BID DATA II

Analysis of Spatial and Temporal Features to Classify the Deep Moonquake Sources Using Balanced Random Forest 51
K. Kato, R. Yamada, Y. Yamamoto, M. Hirota, S. Yokoyama, H. Ishikawa

Measurement-based Cost Estimation Method of a Join Operation for an In-Memory Database 57
T. Tanaka, H. Ishikawa

A Proposal of Activation Mechanism for User Communication based on User Behavior Analysis on Wedding Community Sites 67
T. Hayashi, Y. Wang, Y. Kawai, K. Sumiya

A Node Access Frequency based Graph Partitioning Technique for Efficient Dynamic Dependency Analysis 73
K. Kusu, I. Kume, K. Hatano

MMEDIA 5 / STCD I: MODELS AND ALGORITHMS FOR SPATIALLY AND TEMPORALLY CORRELATED DATA I

A Message Passing Approach for Decision Fusion of Hidden-Markov Observations in the Presence of Synchronized Attacks 79
A. Abrardo, M. Barni, K. Kallas, B. Tondi

MMEDIA 6 / STCD II: MODELS AND ALGORITHMS FOR SPATIALLY AND TEMPORALLY CORRELATED DATA II

Modelling Temporal Structures in Video Event Retrieval using an AND-OR Graph 85
M. Boer, C. Escher, K. Schutte

Resolution Enhancement of Incomplete Thermal Data of Earth by Exploitation of Temporal and Spatial Correlation 89
P. Addesso, M. Longo, R. Restaino, G. Vivone

Extraction of Periodic Features from Video Signals 95
D. Alinovi, R. Raheli

Author Index

MMEDIA 2017

Forward

The Ninth International Conferences on Advances in Multimedia (MMEDIA 2017), held between April 23-27, 2017 in Venice, Italy, was an international forum for researchers, students, and professionals where to present recent research results on advances in multimedia, and in mobile and ubiquitous multimedia. MMEDIA 2017 brought together experts from both academia and industry for the exchange of ideas and discussions on future challenges in multimedia fundamentals, mobile and ubiquitous multimedia, multimedia ontology, multimedia user-centered perception, multimedia services and applications, and mobile multimedia.

The rapid growth of information on the Web, its ubiquity and pervasiveness, makes the www the biggest repository. While the volume of information may be useful, it creates new challenges for information retrieval, identification, understanding, selection, etc. Investigating new forms of platforms, tools, principles offered by Semantic Web opens another door to enable human programs, or agents, to understand what records are about, and allows integration between domain-dependent and media dependent knowledge. Multimedia information has always been part of the Semantic Web paradigm, but it requires substantial effort to integrate both.

The new technological achievements in terms of speed and the quality expanded and created a variety of multimedia services such as voice, email, short messages, Internet access, m-commerce, mobile video conferencing, streaming video and audio. Large and specialized databases together with these technological achievements have brought true mobile multimedia experiences to mobile customers. Multimedia implies adoption of new technologies and challenges to operators and infrastructure builders in terms of ensuring fast and reliable services for improving the quality of web information retrieval. Huge amounts of multimedia data are increasingly available. The knowledge of spatial and/or temporal phenomena becomes critical for many applications, which requires techniques for the processing, analysis, search, mining, and management of multimedia data

The conference had the following tracks:

- Multimedia Applications
- Multimedia Services
- SBD: Social and Big Data
- STCD: Models and Algorithms for Spatially and Temporally Correlated Data

We take here the opportunity to warmly thank all the members of the MMEDIA 2017 technical program committee, as well as all the reviewers. The creation of such a high quality conference program would not have been possible without their involvement. We also kindly thank all the authors that dedicated much of their time and effort to contribute to MMEDIA

2017. We truly believe that, thanks to all these efforts, the final conference program consisted of top quality contributions.

We also gratefully thank the members of the MMEDIA 2017 organizing committee for their help in handling the logistics and for their work that made this professional meeting a success.

We hope that MMEDIA 2017 was a successful international forum for the exchange of ideas and results between academia and industry and to promote further progress in the field of multimedia. We also hope that Venice, Italy provided a pleasant environment during the conference and everyone saved some time to enjoy the unique charm of the city.

MMEDIA 2017 Committee

MMEDIA Steering Committee

Jean-Claude Moissinac, TELECOM ParisTech, France
Daniel Thalmann, Nanyang Technological University, Singapore

MMEDIA Industry/Research Advisory Committee

Trista Chen, Trista Chen Consulting, USA
Alexander C. Loui, Kodak Alaris Inc., USA
Dimitrios Liparas, Information Technologies Institute (ITI) - Centre for Research & Technology Hellas (CERTH), Greece
Siyu Tang, Alcatel-Lucent Bell Labs - Antwerp, Belgium
Giuseppe Amato, CNR-ISTI, Italy

MMEDIA 2017
Committee

MMEDIA Steering Committee

Jean-Claude Moissinac, TELECOM ParisTech, France
Daniel Thalmann, Nanyang Technological University, Singapore

MMEDIA Industry/Research Advisory Committee

Trista Chen, Trista Chen Consulting, USA
Alexander C. Loui, Kodak Alaris Inc., USA
Dimitrios Liparas, Information Technologies Institute (ITI) - Centre for Research & Technology Hellas (CERTH), Greece
Siyu Tang, Alcatel-Lucent Bell Labs - Antwerp, Belgium
Giuseppe Amato, CNR-ISTI, Italy

MMEDIA 2017 Technical Program Committee

Vladimir Alexiev, Ontotext AD, Bulgaria
Giuseppe Amato, CNR-ISTI, Italy
Stylianos Asteriadis, University of Maastricht, Netherlands
Ramazan S. Aygun, University of Alabama in Huntsville, USA
Jenny Benois-Pineau, University of Bordeaux, France
Fernando Boronat Seguí, Universitat Politecnica de Valencia, Spain
Pierre Boulanger, University of Alberta, Canada
Dumitru Dan Burdescu, University of Craiova, Romania
Nicola Capuano, University of Salerno, Italy
Shannon Chen, Facebook, USA
Trista Chen, Trista Chen Consulting, USA
Luis A. da Silva Cruz, University of Coimbra, Portugal
Vlastislav Dohnal, Masaryk University, Czech Republic
Marcio Ferreira Moreno, IBM Research, Brazil
Daniela Giorgi, Institute of Information Science and Technology - National Research Council of Italy, Italy
William Grosky, University of Michigan-Dearborn, USA
Jun-Won Ho, Seoul Women's University, South Korea
Yin-Fu Huang, National Yunlin University of Science and Technology, Taiwan
Eenjun Hwang, Korea University, South Korea
Hiroshi Ishikawa, Tokyo Metropolitan University, Japan
Hermann Kaindl, Vienna University of Technology, Austria
Dimitris Kanellopoulos, University of Patras, Greece

Sokratis K. Katsikas, Norwegian University of Science & Technology (NTNU), Norway
Panos Kudumakis, Queen Mary University of London, UK
Marco La Cascia, Università degli Studi di Palermo, Italy
Jin-Jang Leou, National Chung Cheng University, Taiwan
Anthony Y. H. Liao, Asia University, Taiwan
Guo-Shiang Lin, Da-Yeh University, Taiwan
Dimitrios Liparas, Information Technologies Institute (ITI) - Centre for Research & Technology Hellas (CERTH), Greece
Alexander C. Loui, Kodak Alaris Inc., USA
Sathiamoorthy Manoharan, University of Auckland, New Zealand
Vasileios Mezaris, CERTH-ITI, Greece
Jean-Claude Moissinac, TELECOM ParisTech, France
Mario Montagud Climent, Universitat Politècnica de València (UPV), Spain
Jose G Moreno, Paul Sabatier University - Toulouse III, France
Shashikant Patil, SVKMs NMIMS Mumbai, India
Riccardo Raheli, University of Parma, Italy
Chaman Lal Sabharwal, Missouri University of Science & Technology, USA
Heiko Schuldt, University of Basel, Switzerland
Christine Senac, IRIT Laboratory (Institut de recherche en Informatique de Toulouse), France
Cristian Stanciu, University Politehnica of Bucharest, Romania
Tamas Sziranyi, MTA SZTAKI, Budapest, Hungary
Siyu Tang, Alcatel-Lucent Bell Labs - Antwerp, Belgium
Anel Tanovic, University of Sarajevo, Bosnia and Herzegovina
Georg Thallinger, Joanneum Research, Austria
Daniel Thalmann, Nanyang Technological University, Singapore
Dian Tjondronegoro, Queensland University of Technology, Australia
Chien-Cheng Tseng, National Kaohsiung First University of Science and Technology, Taiwan
Tayfun Tuna, University of Houston, USA
Paula Viana, School of Engineering - Polytechnic of Porto and INESC TEC, Portugal
Huiling Wang, Tampere University of Technology, Finland
Riaan Wolhuter, Stellenbosch University, South Africa
Shigang Yue, University of Lincoln, UK
Sherali Zeadally, University of Kentucky, USA
Pavel Zemcik, Brno University of Technology, Czech Republic
Ligang Zhang, Centre for Intelligent Systems - Central Queensland University, Brisbane, Australia

Copyright Information

For your reference, this is the text governing the copyright release for material published by IARIA.

The copyright release is a transfer of publication rights, which allows IARIA and its partners to drive the dissemination of the published material. This allows IARIA to give articles increased visibility via distribution, inclusion in libraries, and arrangements for submission to indexes.

I, the undersigned, declare that the article is original, and that I represent the authors of this article in the copyright release matters. If this work has been done as work-for-hire, I have obtained all necessary clearances to execute a copyright release. I hereby irrevocably transfer exclusive copyright for this material to IARIA. I give IARIA permission or reproduce the work in any media format such as, but not limited to, print, digital, or electronic. I give IARIA permission to distribute the materials without restriction to any institutions or individuals. I give IARIA permission to submit the work for inclusion in article repositories as IARIA sees fit.

I, the undersigned, declare that to the best of my knowledge, the article is does not contain libelous or otherwise unlawful contents or invading the right of privacy or infringing on a proprietary right.

Following the copyright release, any circulated version of the article must bear the copyright notice and any header and footer information that IARIA applies to the published article.

IARIA grants royalty-free permission to the authors to disseminate the work, under the above provisions, for any academic, commercial, or industrial use. IARIA grants royalty-free permission to any individuals or institutions to make the article available electronically, online, or in print.

IARIA acknowledges that rights to any algorithm, process, procedure, apparatus, or articles of manufacture remain with the authors and their employers.

I, the undersigned, understand that IARIA will not be liable, in contract, tort (including, without limitation, negligence), pre-contract or other representations (other than fraudulent misrepresentations) or otherwise in connection with the publication of my work.

Exception to the above is made for work-for-hire performed while employed by the government. In that case, copyright to the material remains with the said government. The rightful owners (authors and government entity) grant unlimited and unrestricted permission to IARIA, IARIA's contractors, and IARIA's partners to further distribute the work.

The Research of Critical Success Factors for Performance-oriented Electronic Support Systems - Resource-Based View

Lee, Jhen-Shien
Department of Information
Cathay Bank
Taipei, Taiwan
email: lucifer9978@gmail.com

Yen, Wan-Hsuan
Dept. of Technology Application & Human Resource Development
NTNU
Taipei, Taiwan
email: gordonwyen@gmail.com

Yu, Chin-Cheh
Dept. of Technology Application & Human Resource Development
NTNU
Taipei, Taiwan
email: jackfile991@gmail.com

***Abstract*—Intensive competition has driven enterprise to look for more effective methods to increase performance. The Electronic Performance Support System (EPSS) has been proposed to provide instant performance whenever and wherever needed. However, due to its difference to traditional e-learning mindset, the adoption and design of EPSS is still at the early stage. This research aims to find the critical success factors of EPSS adoption through Resource-Based View (RBV). Six companies that adopted EPSS were interviewed and the success factors were identified. The results show that organizational needs, knowledge management and renewal, training materials and top management support are among the most cited factors for success. Finally, specific recommendations for companies in different adoption phases are given for better success rate.**

Keywords- electronic performance support system (EPSS); performance support (PS); performance centered design (PCD); resource-based view (RBV); critical success factor (CSF).

I. Introduction

With the advancement of the current market, the importance of human resource and its productivity can not be over emphasized. Business owners, human resource development specialists, and information technology professionals are putting their best efforts to enhance the competence and performance of modern workers. However, traditional training and developing concepts still focus on making "teaching" and "learning" more effective, even though this may take a longer time and the transfer from learning to workplace may not always be efficient, requiring numerous repetitions and a lot of practice.

The idea of Performance Support System (PSS) aims at solving this very issue. It improves workers' behavior, then their performance, by providing the needed instruction and information at the right place and the right time. Ideal performance support is to provide workers mandatory information or instruction whenever and wherever needed, without the workers having to memorize numerous rarely-used data or processes. It can also shorten the training period, as workers can get immediate support after taking their positions.

Gangano [33] stressed the necessity to align the learning activity with the performance. Many professionals have claimed Electronic PSS (EPSS) can effectively improve individual's efficacy and organization's competing ability. Many real world cases have also demonstrated how the performance support system integrates various resources and helps employees fulfill job requirements. [13][21][30]

EPSS has served as software a tool to help workers complete their jobs even before the millennial [27]. With the rise of the Internet, it has become natural to use networks as media to deliver training. However, with the fast changing pace and the increasing competition, modern workers need faster and more precise information to help them handle the tasks. Since these tasks and the circumstances might change from time to time, the need for a fast transformation from various customer demands and complicated knowledge to a satisfactory result is growing quickly. As a result, the development of PSS has regained attention and a performance centered design methodology is also being emphasized.

Along with the advancement of wireless and networking technology, Mobile Performance Support System (MPSS) extends the applicable circumstance without being limited to a workstation, like traditional EPSS. The increment of bandwidth allows more data to be transmitted simultaneously, which makes the support and simulation more vivid to reduce the transfer gap between knowing and doing.

The progress of technology and the need to catch up with the market demand both trigger the ongoing interests of PSS. On the other hand, the obvious different approach from traditional instruction design --- learner-centered or instructor-centered --- to performance-centered design not only constrains the available resources from the market, but also requires a paradigm shift for the professionals involved in the field.

This paper is structured as follows. In Section II, the earlier research results about the definition and utilization of Critical Success Factor (CSF) along with the evolving of electronic PSS are presented to set the foundation of the importance of this research. The research method, including the background of interviewees and the categorized interview content, are presented in Section III. The reflection on the six cases presented and the suggestion for application are discussed in Section IV. The conclusion is in Section V.

II. LITERATURE REVIEW

A. Critical Success Factor

In order to help organizations adopt the new tool and widely utilize it so that efficiency can be increased, fulfillment of the critical factors for successful adoption are needed. Critical success factors are the items that have positive effects on the operation while also increasing the competing ability for the company. Critical success factors vary under different circumstances.

The idea dates back to Commons' "Limited Factor" [9] which applies it on management and negotiation. Barnard [3] adopted the idea and stated "Strategic Factors", which are factors people are looking for when making an analysis during decision processes. Daniel [10] considered "Success Factors" as elements filtered by three to six critical criteria that vary from domain to domain. These elements are influential to the success or failure of the industry and companies need to put more resources on such impactful areas. The optimization of the above elements can make companies more successful.

Leslie and Richard [18] proposed eight critical success factors for the adoption of information technology. Imtiaz et al. [16] summarized 15 factors by reviewing articles from 1999 to 2012. Upon the research, they hypothesized 7 factors such as: Top Management Support, Leadership, Clear Goals, Team Capability, Effective Communication, Customer/User Involvement, and Adequate Requirement have a strong effect on the success of IT (Information Technology) projects.

B. Resource-based View

To better link the critical success factors for performance support system and the assessment of readiness for enterprises, we utilized Resource-based View (RBV) to analyze the factors. RBV refers to the fact that competitive advantages of a firm lie primarily in the application of a bundle of valuable, tangible or intangible resources at the firm's disposal [23][26][29]. Barney [4] re-categorized resources from the viewpoints of owned or held by organizations. He then labeled Physical Capital Resources, Human Capital Resources, and Organizational Capital Resources. A subsequent distinction made by Amit and Schoemaker [2] was that the encompassing construct previously called "resources" could be divided into resources and capabilities. In this respect, resources were tradable and non-specific to the firm, while capabilities were firm-specific and used to engage the resources within the firm. Such implicit processes were used to transfer knowledge within the firm [15][19].

Wu [31] suggested resources should be categorized as tangible capital and intangible capital which can be measured by a dollarized value, while capabilities can be categorized as organizational capability and individual capability, which help organizations become more competitive by better proceeding resources. Bharadwaj [6] considered IT as an organizational capability and classified as IT infrastructure, human IT resources, and IT-enabled intangibles. He also found firms with high IT capability tend to outperform the firms with low IT capability.

C. EPSS

The operation of business rates effectiveness and efficiency highly. It is no surprise the call for "learning when working" and "just in time support" is vastly required by managers. Business owners and managers always want to put their resources on the most rewarding area, which reflects the earlier development of EPSS than E-Learning [27].

Gery [13] proposed EPSS as an integrated electronic environment available to each employee. It was structured to provide immediate, individualized on-line access to the full range of information, software, guidance, advice and assistance, data, images, tools, and assessment and monitoring systems to permit job performance with minimal support and intervention by others. Raybould [34] gave a shorter definition: a computer-based system that improves worker productivity by providing on-the-job access to integrated information, advice, and learning experiences. Bezanson [5] provided a definition linked to the application usability and organizational results: A performance support system provides just-in-time, just enough training, information, tools, and help for users of a product or work environment, to enable optimum performance by those users when and where needed, thereby also enhancing the performance of the overall business.

EPSS shifts the idea of worker as "people who accept training" to "people who need support when doing their jobs". It centers on the tasks on hand. EPSS responds to questions and requirements when workers are facing new or complicated situations. A well-designed EPSS can provide on-time support such as suggestions and aids, blend supports within the environment, and utilizes technology when needed [7].

Raybould [25] further suggested EPSS should support all aspects that might affect workers' productivity among the whole production process and embed knowledge seamlessly. He considered EPSS as an Electronic infrastructure that can obtain, store, and distribute knowledge capital between the organization and the individual so workers can achieve the desired performance level within the shortest period with the lowest level of other people's support. The top five perceived benefits of EPSS are: decreased information overload and paper documentation, reduced training time, increased productivity, improved job performance, and enhanced employee empowerment [8]. Chang [8] claimed it reduced external support by 80% and saved half of the training time.

With the huge progress of wireless and networking technology, the flexibility of data transmission today is far beyond the imagination of the nineties. The advantages of adopting mobile technology include flexibility, speed, and more efficient networking, which allow access to large numbers of staff throughout the world and a more efficient working environment, with less manual paperwork – work can be done faster, more flexibly, and with greater levels of accessibility. Even more important are more efficient training, saving time to inform staff about new products and processes and saving of time and money [24].

Ahmad and Orton [1] considered MPSS has high potential to improve performance, especially for the works in isolated time and location. To ensure MPSS is being optimized for the workplace performance, contextual knowledge is mandatory regarding the ease-to-use and the design. MPSS is the combination of communication device and EPSS [28]. It utilizes mobile devices and applications to facilitate the performance of the job. Tamez [28] proposed the model of mobile phones as performance support systems (Figure 1).

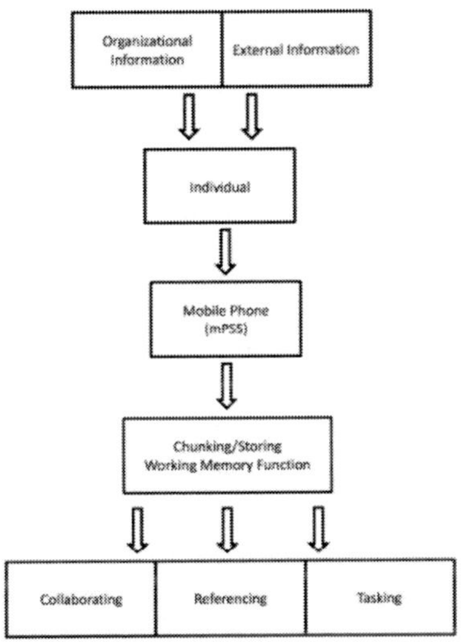

Figure 1. Model of mobile phones as performance support systems [28]

D. *Comparison between EPSS and E-Learning*

E-Learning and blended learning have already been well-known and widely adopted methods to train and develop workers. However, most 'learning' activities require workers to be away from their work, which not only reduces their time on the job, but also increases the difficulty for workers to apply their learning, because of the difference of circumstances and the delay of time from learning to application [22]. Accordingly, more emphasis is put on support performance and learning at the workplace. This approach not only allows workers to work and learn at the same time without being limited by time and space, but also learning at the real working environment and under the needed situation to achieve the optimal result.

Gottfredson and Mosher [14] stated that, in order to make a learning system more complete, it was inevitable to include PS, since "appliance" was the most important issue among the five learning needs. Although PS had its training possibility, its biggest value resided in solving professional problems and not in education [12].

The idea of designing EPSS comes from Performance Centered Design (PCD). With PCD in mind, the user interface is structured to execute job assignments and the activities should also focus on optimizing possible performances by considering the context and assignments. Empirical results showed that using PCD for advanced technology training can be more effective at preparing learners with self-oriented learning and improve or adapt the varying working environment than traditional classroom training [17]. Yu and Yen [32] stated the specialty of PS was to let workers learn the exact amount rather than a lot, at the exact time rather than early.

To achieve this desired result, McGraw [20] proposed the process of PCD: (1) Identify Requirements, (2) Analyze Requirements and Reengineered Process, (3) Develop Visual Prototype of Key Functions/Screens, (4) Conduct Formative Usability Evaluation, (5) Refine Requirements, (6) Design User Interface Screens, (7) Develop User Interface Screens, (8) Conduct Summative Usability Evaluation.

The central focus should include: User Characteristics, Cognitive Needs, Performance Needs, Performance problems, Training Issues, System Functionality, and Attitudes [20].

There have already been several cases utilizing EPSS in the western world which brought sound results. The application situation varies from healthcare usage to fast food chains. The purpose of it can also be very different, from coast security to car manufacturing. However, the application is still not too widely explored in Asia. To retrieve the critical success factors, further research should be conducted.

III. Research Method

We chose semi-structured interviews to understand the strategy used by case companies as well as their consideration to extract the possible success factors for adopting EPSS. This method provides a framework of data collection and also gives the possibility to reveal more in-depth information. The interview guide is designed based on RBV and earlier researches to cover the resource and ability required to successfully adopt EPSS within the organization. The interview is recorded with the permission of the interviewee and the transcript is reviewed with the original interviewee to ensure correctness. The approved transcript is then coded for categorization and analyses.

Six case companies were interviewed in this research. As we looked for the successfully adopted cases, only the companies with EPSS in place for more than one year are considered. Since EPSS is not a common tool used yet, the cases are chosen by snow-bowling. To really extract the success factors of EPSS, the decision maker or the professionals who are highly connected to the adoption/usage of EPSS are interviewed. Shown in Table I below are the backgrounds of the case companies and interviewees.

TABLE I. BASIC INFORMATION OF CASE COMPANIES AND INTERVIEWEES

Basic Information	Company Symbol					
	A	*B*	*C*	*D*	*E*	*F*
Industry	E-learning system	OEM of IT product	Information Service	Human Resource Service	OEM of IT/Telecom product	Digital Contents
Fouding time	2000	1984	1979	1997	2001	2000
EPSS adoption years	2 years	6 years	5 years	16 years	7 years	2 years
Title of interview-ee	Manager	Senior Director	Group Leader	Consultant	OD and HR System Manager	General Manger
Deprtment of interviewee	Sales and Marketing	Research Engineering	Training and Development	Consulting	Human Resource	General Manager's Office
Gender	Male	Female	Male	Male	Male	Male
Seniori-ty	3 years	11 years	11 years	1 year	9 years	14 years

A. *Analysis*

We categorize the transcripts into four constructs: tangible assets, intangible assets, individual capability and organizational capability. The constructs and the coding are listed below in Table II.

TABLE II. CODING TABLE OF CSF OF EPSS

Constructs	Axial Coding	Optional Coding
Tangible Assets	A01 IT Infrastructure	A0101 Organizational Needs
		A0102 Individual Mobile Device Needs
	A02 Quality of IT System	A0201 Easy-to-use
		A0202 IT Security
Intangible Assests	B01 Knowledge Assets	B0101 Need Assessment and Planning
		B0102 Knowledge Management and Renewal
Individual Capability	C01 Promotion and Training	C0101 Seminars
		C0102 Training Materials
	C02 Willingness and Motivation	C0201 Communication
		C0202 Compensation
Organizational Capability	D01 Change Management	D0101 Culture and Environment
		D0102 Top Management Support

1) Tangible Assets Construct: This construct is set to evaluate the effect of tangible assets owned by the organization on the adoption of EPSS. We can further label them into two categories: IT Infrastructure and Quality of IT System. These tangible assets include hardware and software such as Internet structure, system platform, device and carriers. Networking technology, cooperation between hardware and software, quality of the system and IT security all affect the success or failure of the adoption.

a) IT Infrastructure (A01): Whether the infrastructure provided by the organization can pass the minimum requirement and whether the device used by the individual is suitable will affect the ease to get online and reduce the barrier to support users.

- Organizational Needs (A0101): Most interviewees considered having networking environment, servers, and personal computers as basic requirements to support the adoption of EPSS.
  'A server is needed for sure, if there is no server, then there must be a self-built or cloud server in place. There must be databases and relating servers as well. People can then access relevant learning materials.'(S01-03-10)
  'IT infrastructure needs to be provided such as computers, networks, servers, and application softwares'(S02-02-09)
  'Networks, softwares, and infrastructures need to be provided'(S03-02-08)
  'I reviewed the system requirement and it is not too hard to achieve. Basically a server is still needed.'(S04-03-09)
  'The basic computers, databases, and server network are "musts". With the basis of the hardware, all personal data must be loaded onto the system so the rights of people can be changed accordingly.'(S05-03-06)
- Individual Mobile Device Needs (A0102): With the advanced of wireless technology, many interviewees also mentioned that the adoption of mobile devices is more and more popular.
  Because our company emphasize the potential of mobile technology, we wish there were some wireless network device or the normal users can own something like laptops, pads, or smartphones to allow them to connect to the net as well.'(S01-03-12)
  'Every member of the staff has a PC and a workstation according to their job nature, so they can access the network anytime they want.' (S02-02-09)
  'Laptops, tablets, and even cell phones should always work since you should be able to use it no matter where and when' (S03-02-08)
  'Since it is basically operated under a PC, as long as you have PC, you are able to log in and operate.' (S04-03-10)
  'I think those sales persons cannot even work without tablets. In addition, if it is not connected to the network, it is as if the device is not functioning . That's why all the sales persons are equipped with network connecting tablets' (S06-05-09)

b) Quality of IT system (A02): The design of the system should consider user's needs and also the security of enterprise IT system. A well-designed system can reduce the learning curve while also preventing major risks of the enterprise IT system.

- Easy-to-use (A0201): Most interviewees mentioned, the user interface should consider the factors of easy-to-operate and easy-to-understand, so users can quickly understand and achieve expected goals.
  'When dealing with a more complicated case, the sales team and customer support team can have timely support from the system. It is like having an expert system.' (S01-02-05)
  'We need to make them feel the developers really knew the demands and are great help.' (S02-04-19)
  'Need to fill the job needs of users which can really help users during their design times. Need to be sensitive to needs, ... Need to have passion to serve.' (S02-04-17)
  'Easy-to-use and also the user's habit should be considered. How to make people develop such habit is also quite important.' (S04-05-19)
  'I think if we consider mere local office, the biggest issue might be in language as the system is mainly displayed in English which brings more difficulties to us.' (S04-05-18)
  '(When filling out system requirement form,) sometimes the coordinator only cares about whether the form is completely filled while IT people only care about whether I completed all the specs required by the user. However, this system will be used under different kinds of circumstances. Whether these possibilities and twists are considered or not is a big issue.' (S05-09-19)
  'It needs to be an easy-to-use system. Easy-to-use means, the function and usability fits the needs of their company. You should not develop something of non-value.' (S06-06-11)
- IT security (A0202): Some interviewees considered management of access rights and the control of IT security are both important topics need to be paid attention to.
  'We operate under flexible hours and the employees can connect back to the office through VPN. That's why IT security is a must for us.' (S02-02-09)
  'We need to consider IT security when using the system to help on assignments' (S03-02-08)
  'Talking about security, we will regulate different rights according to different purposes and requirements. Take PS as an example, all of our company's platform can let employees log in with their employee ID. The HR system manager has additional ID so he can use another identity to manage the system.' (S05-04-07)
  'That system has its own password. In our company, each different system requires control and certificate whenever people try to log in.' (S05-04-08)
  'I think, in order to make EPSS valuable, it must be connected to the network, be it intranet or internet. However, if the network is connected, it is unavoidable to have security issues. This is always a challenge to a big company and people will likely stick with intranet only.' (S06-02-03)

2) Intangible Assets Construct: This construct refers to how the intangible assets owned by an organization affect the implementation of EPSS. The knowledge base itself, the updates of the content and knowledge management and integration can all influence the success rate of the system. The relating transcripts are listed below:

a) Knowledge Assets (B01): There must be a fit between the task and the aid provided to make the system really helpful. The integration of knowledge management and the construction of knowledge database can also help others maximize the benefits of knowledge.

- Need for Assessment and Planning (B0101): Most interviewees stated that it is necessary to analyze the goal of users to provide information that fits the circumstance and really have the links with users. Only through the value of the system is maximized.
  'The key learning needs for the new sales person is on how to get new accounts. If we can provide new information about our product and also the knowledge of the competitor (through the system), then the sales can utilize the more up-to-date information.' (S01-01-04)
  'Each department needs different things. Since they have different requirements, thus they need different tools for each of them. The system used here will not be provided to all other units.' (S02-02-07)
  'Needs analysis is mandatory when adopting a system. During needs analysis, different processes will be analyzed. (For instance,) if the system is for the use of HR, then the process of HR is analyzed.' (S05-06-13)
  'The idea is, when the employee has some questions, then he or she does not need to ask anyone but can get the correct answer from the system.' (S06-02-01)
- Knowledge Management and Renewal (B0102): Most interviewees mentioned the company will reorganize data into useful information along with the evolving of time, so the system users can obtain a more suitable knowledge.
  'We will update the system through time. We usually check every six months to see if it is necessary to update.' (S02-02-10)
  'We will review the content and take out the outdated material and purchase new material that fits our current needs.' (S03-03-09)
  'The reference materials, such as system databases will be updated whenever there is a need. I think it will be updated for sure. I am just not certain how often.' (S03-03-10)
  'We update the system regularly ever since it was developed.' (S04-02-06)
  'In the beginning we set up only one universal database for all managers. Since 2007, we began setting up new management competence for different management levels, which meant we changed and improved the system by the requirement of the company.' (S05-05-08)
  'If it is not updated , then I bet it will soon be forgotten like an unmaintained website. As a result, I always think the best chance resides in a mobile solution, as it is portable and can trigger more interests to update. I think only the combination of mobile devices, content of

mobile spirit and structure of wiki can construct a continuous updated EPSS. If a company can do this, this will be a great help to that company.' (S06-03-04)

3) Individual Capability Construct: This construct refers to the human resource and capability of the organization to the effect of successful adoption of EPSS. The perception of people and how enterprises help people to use the system to obtain the required skill and ability are all related. These include the seminar of system being placed, training materials for users, surveys and feedback collection from users.

a) Promotion and Training (C01): Proper training and promotion can increase familiarity of employees with the new system, reduce trial and error so users can smoothly use the system to help their job.

- Seminars (C0101): When using systems from vendors, seminars can make employees better understand the idea and relating policy about the new system.
  'We are sales people. Not only do we use this system but also sell this system. As a result, we got an idea of how this works when we took product training.' (S01-04-18)
  'For the customer, we still need to tell them how this system works to make it easy for them.' (S01-04-19)
  'The vendor will host seminars to demonstrate how to use this system prior to implementation' (S03-03-13)
  'There will be a public announcement when the system is put online. Afterwards, we will set mandatory classes for different groups of people according to the different fields of each system' (S05-07-14)
- Training Materials (C0102): For global companies, using digital training materials can help employees get used to the new system without being limited by time and space.
  'It all depends on the complexity of the system. If it is quite complicated, then there will be training sessions. However, if the system is not that complicated, a handbook or SOP will be enough. Besides, we have all those on-line as well.' (S02-03-13)
  'We will host seminars and aid with some relating documents. Vendors will prepare their presentation and email to us.' (S03-04-15)
  'Relating introduction and demo, it can be found within the intranet.' (S04-04-15)
  'We will try to put some idea of SOP inside the system. There will be explanations on how to use the system within the system itself. Users can then check the use of different function when they want to.' (S05-07-15)

b) Willingness and Motivation (C02): The employee is one of the most valuable assets of an organization. Performance of employees is key to the competitively of a firm. An implementation strategy and optimization system that adjust according to the feedback from users can help increase willingness to use the system while, suitable compensation can boost motivation even further.

- Communication (C0201): Interviewees responded that user feedbacks are critical factors that drive system adjustment. Regular communication and collecting feedbacks can make the system even better.
  'Not only do we listen to employees, but also to customers and adjust our system accordingly.' (S01-04-15)
  'We do user survey every six month.' (S02-03-11)
  'Our survey aims at department and not just at the managers. All levels are welcome.' (S02-03-12)
  'We will regularly ask, at least once a year, about the satisfaction with the system.' (S03-03-11)
  'When purchasing a new system, we will go back and ask which should be preserved and which should be thrown away.' (S03-03-12)
  'I know they will adjust the system and have a certain way to measure it.' (S04-04-14)
  'All of our systems have a service window. For instance, there is (the contact window's) information within the system. If you have any opinion about the system, you can contact the corresponding person and all feedback from user will be taken into consideration.' (S05-05-10)
  'We will consider the impact and priority first, then we arrange time for the modification.' (S05-05-11)
  'The feature of the mobile world is "fast", so you cannot put a system there and never change a thing forever. For instance, one of our customer's systems has new material every week. When there are needs for adjustment, one perspective is from the management view and the other is from the survey, looking at what the sales person's needs as what they can do for the next stage, no matter the function or the content.' (S06-03-05)
- Compensation (C0202): Most interviewed companies used and consider it is a more effective way to compensate rather than to punish employees to motivate them to adopt the new system.
  'We used compensation to encourage employees using the system and the effect is not too bad.' (S04-04-17)
  'The culture of our company is open policy: If the system is not used by someone, we will not force him/her nor punish him/her.' (S02-04-16)
  'We will use event or reward gift to motivate employees and we don't have any punishment policy. However, there are something an employee has to do otherwise he or she will not be able to do his/her job properly.' (S03-04-19)
  'From our own experience, if there is no special incentive, then the utilization rate will be lower. Unless this system fits perfectly with the users need when designing, then there is no need for special promotion.' (S06-05-09)
  'We need to encourage content generation and the use of the contents. In the end, if there is content but no one is using it, the content will simply be a waste. That's why I think knowledge management was in the situation of no user. This situation is improved with wiki. As a result, I think it is important to include a broad encouraging initiative so we can have the content coming out continuously.' (S06-05-08)

4) Organizational Capability Construct: This construct refers to the effect on change management within the organization to the adoption of EPSS. We discussed the influence from operation, organizational environment and degree of digitalization. Factors including supervisor support, management ideas, and organization culture all affect the success rate of a system.

a) Change Management (D01)

- Culture and Environment (D0101): The interviewed companies usually face change with an open attitude, while not forcing employees to follow.
  'The company is not a forceful entity that is driven by the boss. I think it is because of the differences between cultures. There is no special mechanism. If someone thinks something is needed to be done then just go ahead and do it. If there is something that needs to be fixed, then just have it fixed.' (S02-04-15)
  'There are some systems that, if you don't use them, you are not able to complete your job properly. As a result, you must go consult someone and learn.' (S03-04-18)
  'Since our company belongs to Hi-Tech industry, we are highly digitalized. There is no need for special training about how to use computer and we can figure it out pretty much by just looking at it.' (S03-04-15)
  'To make it a habit, you internalize it.' (S03-05-22)
- Top Management Support (D0102): Interviewees think the supportive gesture taken by high level managers can help promote overly and change the atmosphere of the company.
  'This is the policy of our company, since we are going to sell this as well. It is a decision from the boss himself, thus his support is a really big driver for this.' (S01-04-17)
  'Top managers surely communicated with the directors and managers of my department already. We need to have top management support to continue on this.' (S03-04-14)
  'Emphasize from top management level is the most critical factor. He or she needs to personally link to your projects.' (S03-05-20)
  'They are totally supportive of the decision of the company. However, the support might come in a different size and shape. One of the most common ways is he will tell us what might make the system even better.' (S05-07-16)
  'The support from top management is surely important. If there is no command from the top management, normally no one will care for this thing.' (S06-04-06)

These CSFs are summarized according to the response of case companies. As we can see by the numbers of being mentioned: all six companies view IT infrastructure a must and all data need to be able to be accessed through networks. In addition, the management and especially the updates of the knowledge content are also important for all responders.

Almost all companies reported training materials and top management support are critical to the success of the adoption of EPSS. While seminars, communication, need for assessment and planning, and individual mobile device needs follow on the most counted list.

IV. Discussion and Conclusion

With RBV, a framework to analyze the CSFs of enterprise adopting EPSS is proposed. Out of the four constructs, "Intangible Assets" is considered the most critical one by the average counting of its items. All six companies highlight the belonging factor "Knowledge Management and Renewal". This coincides with the trend of modern "Knowledge Economy Era". In this era, the creation and storage of knowledge and skill is crucial. This critical asset can create wealth of individual to nation as well as drive economy activity. Knowledge becomes a strategic resource of enterprises and its management is important. All innovation relies heavily on knowledge, thus the content of the platform must be rich and relative to facilitate users to obtain suitable information and access to relating knowledge. Employees can then handle their own task and extend their professions at the same time. As a result, the efficiency of a person is increased and, in sum, the organization's performance is also increased.

Since EPSS is the system that helps workers when they are in need, the system itself needs to be kept up-to-date at least to the status-quo to be effective. "Need Assessment and Planning" is also an important factor under that construct as the system needs to really solve the problems of users. This will also affect the willingness and the culture, as one of the most obvious cases is a person might not even work well without the help of the system, such as transcript S03-04-18.

On the other hand, the axial "IT Infrastructure" under the construct "Tangible Assets" is also critical based on the response of the interviewees. The proper setup of server and network is the foundation, while suitable mobile flexibility should be provided to employees. The mention of server and networking in "Organizational Needs" does not bring too much information to us as most companies have the infrastructure in place, be it self-constructed or hosted by vendors. On the other hand, whether mobile network can be accessed and utilized truly depends on the policy and strategy of the company. Some companies even provide mobile devices intentionally to help their employees.

The axial "Quality of IT System" was mentioned by fifty percent of the interviewees. Although both Easy-to-use and IT security are important issues, the influence from them seems to be moderate compared to the other factors. This might be because these factors are less relative to a specific system, but rather an integration of consideration of a whole.

From the aspect of "Capability", interviewees mentioned the axial "Promotion and Training" most frequently. Both "Seminars" and "Training Materials" are referred to as CSFs by more than 60% interviewees. This reminds us although EPSS system tries to reduce the workers' down time due to the necessity for off-site training, it is still unavoidable to employ mandatory opportunities. However, one must be very careful when designing the course and system as this extra learning due to the additional system should not reduce the productivity of employees when considering all the pros and cons. If the system builds in itself self-guided or clear instruction, then this could reduce the needed time and effort to utilize the system.

While "Seminars" and "Training Materials" both have an effect on communication between providers and users, the factor "Communication" covers more aspects than that. To make the system best serve the employees, feedbacks from employees should also be considered. To collect feedback from users for the regular modification or purchase of the new system is a common practice among the interviewees.

An organization that does well on both side communications can make known the purpose and benefits of the change, while also collecting opinions from the field more quickly. Elving [11] stated, "Communication is vital to the effective implementation of organizational change" and the adoption of a new system is certainly one kind of change. Prior to the introduction of the system, it is better to consider the communication policies and programs to achieve the best result.

Last but not least, the support from top management is also vastly mentioned within the survey. The support can help on various aspects, such as monitoring the progress and motivating the involvement of employees. If there is a communication problem among different departments or internal communities, the help from top management can also facilitate the discussion and agreement among groups.

Most companies responded that they took a step-by-step approach such that, once the adoption project gains the approval from managers, a small group will first adopt as trial. Once the benefits of the system emerge, the necessity for the vast promotion will decrease significantly while other departments would eager to adopt the system as well.

To recommend companies to successfully adopt EPSS in the future, we propose the following suggestions:

1) Companies considering but not yet adopting EPSS:

- Draft proposal: Evaluate the needs of the organization and compare the status quo of the company to the CSFs. If the benefit is better than the effort, construct the proposal in an easy to understand way and gain the support from top management.
- Search for external support: Project team should consult other companies who already adopted the system to learn from their experience and current situation. It can also try the vendors system for further evaluation about the cost and benefit of in-house development or external procurement.

2) Companies just adopted EPSS:

- Focus area of the project team: The project team needs to ensure it has sufficient representatives from key departments such as IT, HR, and top managers. The project team can then evaluate which will be the quickest area for rewards and focus on realizing the benefit.
- Complete promotion and reward: The communication for the users and managers should be considered and well-prepared for better integration between them. Proper reward can boost awareness and motivate the early adopters.

3) Companies using EPSS:

- Management of knowledge assets: A continuous improvement mechanism needs to be put in place and executed so that not only the users feel that the information is beneficial and helpful today but also increase the habit to look it up when difficulties arise.
- Follow-up of the usage and effect of the system: The comparison of performance and behavior change do not always require much to trace. A simple indicator can be used to examine the possible effect of EPSS. The result can also provide another source of improvement for a more beneficial system.

One of the limitations of this research is that the sample size is small and the surveyed industry is concentrated since EPSS is yet at its starting stage in Taiwan. Due to the industry nature of the island and the characteristic of the applied system itself, there are more applications in high knowledge density places such as high tech and consulting industry than the others. Whether the CSFs are identical to those of other industries is yet to be understood.

The other direction for the future approach is to add the quantitative aspect for more depth to the research. Although the number of counting is used as an index of relative importance but it might not truly reflect the real impact of such factor. If a weighting system can be considered to calibrate the response, the final result could be more indicative to the key factors of successful implementation.

As an organization is a holistic entity where each part is connected to one another, the CSFs are also not isolated either. For instance, with the "Top Manager Support", it is easier to fulfill "Organizational Needs" and the resource for "Seminars" and "Training Materials" are easier to obtain as well. With the better usage of the system, "Communication" for the better modification of the system will raise the tendency to "Knowledge Management and Renewal". This shows all the CSFs are not just critical solely but will have effect on one another. One should consider a more thorough planning when implementing EPSS to increase the possibility of successful adoption.

REFERENCES

[1] N. Ahmad, and P. Orton, Smartphones Make IBM Smarter, But Not As Expected. Training & Development, journal of the American Society for Training & Development, vol. 64, no. 1, 46-50, 2010.

[2] R. Amit, and R. Schoemaker, Strategic assets and organizational rent, Strategic Management Journal, vol. 14, no. 1, pp. 33-46, 1993

[3] C. S. Barnard, Organization and Management. Cambridge, Harvard University Press, 1948.

[4] J. Barney, Firm resources and sustained competitive advantage. Journal of Management, vol. 17, no. 1, pp. 99-120, 1991.

[5] W. Bezanson, Performance Support Solutions: Achieving Goals Through Enabling User Performance. Trafford Publishing, 2006

[6] A. S. Bharadwaj, A resource-based perspective on information technology capability and firm performance: an

empirical investigation. MIS Quarterly, vol.24, pp.169-196, 2000

[7] L. A. Brown, Designing and developing electronic performance systems. Boston, MA: Digital Press. American Journal of Small Business, vol. 8, no. 3, pp. 49-57, 1996.

[8] C. Chang, The relationship between the performance and the perceived benefits of using an electronic performance support system (EPSS). Innovations in Education & Teaching International, vol. 41, no. 3, pp. 343-363, 2004

[9] J. R. Commons, Institutional economics. New York: Macmillan, 1934

[10] D.W. Daniel, Management Information Crisis. Havard BusinessReview, pp. 111-121, 1961

[11] W. Elving, The role of communication in organisational change, Corporate Communications: An International Journal, vol. 10, no. 2, pp. 129-138, 2005.

[12] E. Gal, and R. Nachmias, Implementing on-line learning and performance support using an EPSS. Interdisciplinary Journal of E-Learning and Learning Objects, vol. 7, pp. 213-224, 2011.

[13] G. Gery, Electronic performance support systems. Cambridge, MA: Ziff Institute, 1991.

[14] C. Gottfredson, and B. Mosher, Innovative Performance Support: Strategies and Practices for Learning in the Workflow, McGraw Hill Professional, 2010.

[15] D.G. Hoopes, T.L. Madsen, and G. Walker, Guest Editors' Introduction to the Special Issue: Why is There a Resource-Based View? Toward a Theory of Competitive Heterogeneity. Strategic Management Journal, vol. 24, pp. 889–902, 2003.

[16] M.A. Imtiaz, A.S. Al-Mudhary, M.T. Mirhashemi, R. Ibrahim, Critical Success Factors of Information Technology Projects, International Journal of Social, Behavioral, Educational, Economic, Business and Industrial Engineering, vol. 7, no. 12, pp. 2880-2884, 2013.

[17] D. Keegan, and N. Mileva, Mobile learning performance support system for vocational education and training, Bulgaria, University of Plovdiv and Spain, the UNED, 2010

[18] W. Leslie, and S. Richard, The role of the CIO and IT function in ERP. Communications Of The ACM, vol. 43, no. 4, pp.32-38, 2000.

[19] R. Makadok, Toward a Synthesis of the Resource-Based View and Dynamic-Capability Views of Rent Creation. Strategic Management Journal, vol. 22, no.5, pp. 387–401, 2001.

[20] K. McGraw, The performance-centered design and development methodology. New Work: Cognitive Technologies, Inc., 2009

[21] S. E. McKenney, Computer support for science education materials developers in Africa: Exploring potentials. USA: University of Twente, 2001.

[22] K. O'Leonard, Performance support systems. CA: Bersin & Associates, 2005.

[23] E.T. Penrose, The Theory of the Growth of the Firm, New York: Wiley, 1959.

[24] K. Peters, m-Learning: Positioning educators for a mobile, connected future. International Review ofResearch in Open and Distance Learning, vol. 8, no.2, 2007. Retrieved Mar, 2017, From: http://www.irrodl.org/index.php/irrodl/article/viewArticle/350/894.

[25] B. Raybould, Performance support engineering: An emerging development methodology for enabling organizational learning. Innovations in Education and Training International, vol. 32, no. 1, pp. 65-69, 1995

[26] D.P. Rumelt, Towards a Strategic Theory of the Firm. Alternative theories of the firm; 2002, vol. 2 pp. 286–300, Elgar Reference Collection. International Library of Critical Writings in Economics, vol. 154. Cheltenham, U.K. and Northampton, Mass.: Elgar; distributed by American International Distribution Corporation, Williston, Vt., 1984.

[27] K. Ruyle, EPSS : A 20-Year Retrospective. Performance Xpress , ISPI, 2004.

[28] R. Tamez,, A Model for Mobile Performance Support Systems as Memory Compensation Tools, Learning and Performance Quarterly, vol. 1, no. 3, pp. 19-30, 2012.

[29] B. Wernerfelt, The Resource-Based View of the Firm. Strategic Management Journal, vol. 5, no. 2, pp. 171–180, 1984.

[30] M. Wild, Designing and evaluating an educational performance support system. British Journal of Educational Technology, vol. 31, no. 1, pp. 5-20, 2000.

[31] S. H. Wu, Thenature of the strategy, 3rd ed., Taipei, Face Publishing, 2000

[32] C. Yu, and W. Yen, Performance Centered Design for Training Resource: The Development and Application of Electronic Performance Support Systems and Mobile Performance Support Systems, T&D Fashion, vol. 158, pp. 1-29, 2013.

[33] S. Gangano, Using performance–based learning to drive business outcome, paper presented at American Society of Training and Developing International Conference and Exhibition, Denver, CO, 2012

[34] B. Raybould, An EPSS Case Study: Prime Computer. Paper presented at the Electronic Performance Support Conference, Atlanta, GA, 1991.

3D Model Representations and Transformations in the Context of Computer-Aided Design: a State-of-the-Art Overview

Christoph Schinko, Ulrich Krispel, Eva Eggeling, and Torsten Ullrich
Institute of Computer Graphics and Knowledge Visualization, Graz University of Technology
& Visual Computing, Fraunhofer Austria Research GmbH, Austria
email: { christoph.schinko, ulrich.krispel, eva.eggeling, torsten.ullrich } @fraunhofer.at

Abstract—**Within a virtual world, either in virtual reality or in a simulation environment, the digital counterparts of real objects are described by mathematical and computational models. Depending on the purpose, the field of application, and the used toolchain a wide variety of model representations is established. As a consequence, conversion methods and transformation algorithms are becoming increasingly important. This article gives a state of the art overview on model representations and on the most important transformation techniques.**

Keywords–3D Model Representations; 3D Transformations

I. Introduction

Many different ways of model descriptions are available, tailored to the requirements in their respective areas of research. In the context of Computer-Aided Design (CAD), the model description of a digital counterpart of a real object is called a shape description. At this point, it is important to emphasize that there are differences in the process of shape perception between human beings and computers. For a computer, the task of shape classification heavily depends on the underlying description. Even after successfully classifying shapes, a computer is yet not aware of the meaning of shape, as discussed by Sven Havemann et al. in their work [1]. For the description of shape, it is important to be aware of these differences, even if shape classification is not in the context of this article.

The following sections describe the model representations (Section 2), transformation (Section 3) and Level-of-Detail (Section 4) techniques, as well as semantic enrichment methods (Section 5).

II. Model Representations

In dictionaries, shapes are described by words forming a textual definition. For a human being, this description is sufficient enough to easily recognize the described shape when seeing it. The precondition for this accomplishment of the human brain is a basic understanding of the terms and definitions used in the description. From a computer science point of view, this definition is of a rather abstract nature representing a difficult basis for creating detectors. A computer program relies on more formal, mathematical definitions. In the context of CAD and Computer-Aided Manufacturing, a shape model has to be complete and has to comprehend all needed information. For these purposes, volumetric and boundary-/surface-based representations are used.

A. Point Sets

Points are a basic primitive to describe the surface of a shape [2]. A point set is a list of points defined in a coordinate system. While points are not the primitive of choice when using 3D modeling software to create shapes, they are widely used by 3D scanners due to the nature of their measurements. A point set is the outcome when measuring a large number of points on an object's surface.

For rendering approaches of point sets, the literature survey by Markus Gross and Hanspeter Pfister offers in-depth explanation [3]. The creation of another shape representation from point set data is called shape reconstruction.

B. Polygonal Faces

A very common representation to describe a shape's surface is to use a mesh of polygonal faces. The accuracy of the representation heavily depends on the shape's outline and is directly affected by the number of faces. A cylinder, for example, cannot be accurately represented by planar faces – it can only be approximated. This limitation is often outweighed by its advantages in the field of CAD:

- Computer graphics hardware is tailored towards processing polygonal faces – especially triangles. This is the reason why many of the other shape representations are converted into polygonal meshes prior to rendering.
- A lot of tools and algorithms exist to create, process and display polygonal objects [4] [5].

The data structures for storing polygonal meshes are numerous. In a very simple form, a list of coordinates (x,y,z) representing the vertices of the polygons can be used. The de-facto standard data interface between CAD software and machines (e.g. milling machines, 3D printers, etc.) is the stereolithography file format (STL). It simply consists of a triangle list specifying its vertices. While this data structure is sufficient for some manufacturing purposes, it may not satisfy the needs of a 3D modeler for editing. More sophisticated data structures reproducing hierarchical structures (groups, edges, vertices) and adding additional attributes like normals, colors and texture coordinates provide a remedy. The problem of traversing a mesh can be tackled by introducing vertex-, face- and half-edge-iterators. A half-edge is a directed edge with references to its opposite half-edge, its incident face, vertex and next half-edge. By defining operations using this data structure, it is possible to conveniently traverse a mesh [6].

C. Parametric Surface Representations

A parametric representation of a shape's surface is defined by a function $f : \Omega \rightarrow S$ mapping a 2D parameter domain $\Omega \subset \mathbb{R}^2$ to the surface $S = f(\Omega) \subset \mathbb{R}^3$. As any surface can be approximated by polynomials, the concept of polynomial surface patches has gained currency in the CAD domain [7] [8].

The idea is to split the function domain into smaller regions. Each surface patch, henceforth called patch, is described by a distinct parametric function approximating the local geometry of the patch [9].

1. Bézier Surfaces

A Bézier surface is a three-dimensional surface generated from the Cartesian product of two Bézier curves [10]. A Bézier surface of degree (m, n) is defined as a parametric function $f(u, v) = \sum_{i=0}^{m} \sum_{j=0}^{n} b_{ij} B_i^m(u) B_j^n(v)$. It is evaluated over the unit square $(u, v) \in [0, 1] \times [0, 1]$ with the control points b_{ij} using the Bernstein polynomials $B_i^n(t) = \binom{n}{i} t^i (1-t)^{n-i}$ of degree n, for $t \in [0, 1]$.

In CAD, Bézier surfaces are often used in the form of bi-cubic Bézier patches, i.e., a set of 4×4 points represents the control mesh and is responsible for the shape of the surface. In all cases, Bézier curves and surfaces have important properties:

- A Bézier surface fulfils the partition of unity property, i.e., $\sum_{i=0}^{m} \sum_{j=0}^{n} B_i^m(u) B_j^n(v) = 1$, thus the relationship between a Bézier surface and its control mesh is invariant under affine transformations.
- A Bézier surface is contained within the convex hull of its control mesh and the four corner points of the control mesh are interpolated by the Bézier surface.
- A Bézier surface exhibits four boundary curves being Bézier curves themselves and their control points are the boundary points of the control mesh.
- The control points do not exert local control alone. Moving a single control point affects the whole surface. Geometric continuity (e.g. G^1, G^2) between patches can only be achieved by satisfying constraints on the control points' positions.

2. Rational Bézier Surfaces

The idea behind rational Bézier surfaces is to add adjustable weights to extend the design space of shapes [11]. In contrast to a Bézier Surface, which can only approximate spheres and cylinders, the rational Bézier Surfaces can describe them exactly – a very important property in CAD. A rational Bézier surface of degree (m, n) is defined with the control points b_{ij}, the weights w_{ij}, and the Bernstein polynomials $B_i^m(u)$ and $B_j^n(v)$ as

$$f(u, v) = \frac{\sum_{i=0}^{m} \sum_{j=0}^{n} w_{ij} b_{ij} B_i^m(u) B_j^n(v)}{\sum_{i=0}^{m} \sum_{j=0}^{n} w_{ij} B_i^m(u) B_j^n(v)}.$$

3. B-spline Surfaces

B-spline surfaces exhibit advantages when joining patches under continuity requirements. Let $m, n, k, l \in \mathbb{N}$ with $n \geq k$ and $m \geq l$. Then, a B-spline surface of degree (l, k) is defined as $f(u, v) = \sum_{i=0}^{m} \sum_{j=0}^{n} d_{ij} N_i^l(u) N_j^k(v)$, with the basis functions $N_i^0(t) = 1, \text{if } t_i \leq t < t_{i+1}; \text{and } 0, \text{otherwise}$ and $N_i^r(t) = \frac{t - t_i}{t_{i+r} - t_i} N_i^{r-1}(t) + \frac{t_{i+1+r} - t}{t_{i+1+r} - t_{i+1}} N_{i+1}^{r-1}(t)$ for $1 \leq r \leq n$ and a nondecreasing sequence of knots, a so-called knot vector, $T = \{t_0 \leq \cdots \leq t_n \leq \cdots \leq t_{n+m+1}\}$.

It can be evaluated over $(u, v) \in [u_l, u_{m+1}[\times [v_k, v_{n+1}[$ with the control points d_{ij} and the polynomials $N_i^l(u)$ and $N_j^k(v)$. The control points d_{ij} forming the control polygon are called de Boor points. In computer graphics, B-spline surfaces are typically used in the form of bi-cubic B-spline patches with 4×4 control points per patch. B-splines with knots t_i satisfying the condition $t_0 = 0$ and $t_{i+1} = t_i$ or $t_{i+1} = t_1 + 1$, $(i = 0, \ldots, n + m)$ are called uniform B-splines.

B-spline surfaces satisfy properties similar to Bézier surfaces [10]. (1) The relationship between a B-spline surface and its control mesh is invariant under affine transformations. (2) A B-spline surface is contained within the convex hull of its control mesh. (3) In contrast to Bézier surfaces, the control points exert local control – if a control point is moved, only the local neighbourhood is affected and (4) by choosing appropriate knot vectors, a B-spline surface can become a Bézier surface.

4. NURBS Surfaces

The combination of rational Bézier techniques and B-Spline techniques leads to non-uniform, rational B-Splines, NURBS for short [12]:

Let $m, n, k, l \in \mathbb{N}$ with $n \geq k$ and $m \geq l$. Additionally, let $w_{00}, \ldots, w_{mn} \in \mathbb{R}$, u = $(u_0 \ldots u_{m+l+1})^T$ and v = $(v_0 \ldots v_{n+k+1})^T$ be two knot vectors and $d_{00}, \ldots, d_{mn} \in \mathbb{R}^3$. Then, a non-uniform, rational B-spline (NURBS) surface of degree (l, k) is defined as

$$f(u, v) = \frac{\sum_{i=0}^{m} \sum_{j=0}^{n} w_{ij} d_{ij} N_i^l(u) N_j^k(v)}{\sum_{i=0}^{m} \sum_{j=0}^{n} w_{ij} N_i^l(u) N_j^k(v)}.$$

over $(u, v) \in [u_l, u_{m+1}[\times [v_k, v_{n+1}[$ with the control points d_{ij}, the polynomials $N_i^l(u)$ and $N_j^k(v)$, the knot vectors u and v for the de Boor points $d_{00}, \ldots, d_{mn}$ and the weights $w_{00}, \ldots, w_{mn}$. Similar to B-spline patches, NURBS surfaces are commonly used in computer graphics in the form of bi-cubic NURBS patches.

B-spline surfaces and Bézier surfaces are special cases of NURBS surfaces [13]. If all weights are equal, a NURBS surface becomes a B-spline surface. Additionally, when all knot vectors are chosen appropriately, the B-spline surface becomes a Bézier surface.

A common way to model arbitrarily complex smooth surfaces is to use a mesh of bi-cubic NURBS patches. Regular meshes consisting of bi-cubic patches formed by vertices of valence four can be seen as connected planar graphs. A direct consequence of the Euler characteristic for connected planar graphs with the aforementioned properties is that such meshes must be topologically equivalent to an infinite plane, a torus, or an infinite cylinder - all other shapes cannot be constructed unless using trimming or stitching. The resulting surfaces offer precise feature control at the cost of computational complexity due to trimming and stitching [14].

D. Subdivision Surfaces

Subdivision surfaces are the generalization of spline surfaces to arbitrary topology. Instead of evaluating the surface itself, the refinement of the control polygon represents the subdivision surface. There are many different subdivision schemes, e.g., Catmull-Clark [15], Doo-Sabin [16], Loop [17], Kobbelt [18], etc.

The subdivision scheme presented by Edwin Catmull and Jim Clark is a generalization of bicubic B-Spline surfaces to arbitrary topology [15]. The set of 4×4 control points p_{ij}

forms the starting mesh for an iterative refinement process where each step results in a finer mesh.

Subdivision surfaces are invariant under affine transformations. They offer the benefit of being easy to implement and computationally efficient. Only the local neighbourhood is used for the computation of new points. A major advantage of subdivision surfaces is their repeated refinement process – level-of-detail algorithms are always "included" by design.

E. Implicit Surface Representations

In contrast to the parametric surface representations described above, implicit surfaces, are defined as isosurfaces by a function $\mathbb{R}^3 \rightarrow \mathbb{R}$ [19]. Therefore, similar to voxels, a surface is only indirectly specified. A simple 3D example of an implicit surface is the following definition of a torus with major radius R and minor radius r

$$f(x, y, z) = (x^2 + y^2 + z^2 + R^2 - r2)^2 - 4R^2(x^2 + y^2) = 0.$$

Inside and outside of the surface is defined by $f(x, y, z) < 0$, respectively $f(x, y, z) > 0$. While a parametric description of the torus exists, many implicit surfaces do not have a closed, parametric form. In terms of expressiveness, implicit surfaces are more powerful than parametric surfaces [20].

Drawbacks of implicit surfaces are the inherent difficulty of describing sharp features (unless trimming is used) or finding points on the surface. However, this representation has several advantages. Efficient checks whether a point is inside a shape or not are possible. Surface intersections, as well as boolean set operations can also be implemented efficiently. Since the surface is not represented explicitly, topology changes are easily possible.

Implicit surfaces can be described in algebraic form (see the example of the torus), as a sum of spherical basis functions (so called blobby models), as convolution surfaces (skeletons), procedurally, as variational functions, or by using samples. The latter approach directly relates to volumetric shape descriptions.

F. Volumetric Shape Descriptions

Volumetric approaches can be used to indirectly describe a shape's surface. In contrast to surface-based descriptions, they define the surface to be a boundary between the interior and the exterior of a shape. However, the idea behind these approaches is not so much a description of a shape's surface, but a description of the entire volume.

1. Voxels

Data sets originating from measurements do not have continuous values and are limited to the points in space where measurements have been collected. It is very common that data points form a uniform regular grid. Such data points in 3D are known as voxels, a name related to their 2D counterparts: the pixels. Since a voxel represents only a single point on the grid, the space between voxels is not represented. Depending on the area of application, the data point can be multi-dimensional, e.g., a vector of density and color. Due to the fact that position and size of a voxel are pre-defined, voxels are good at representing regularly sampled spaces. The approximation of free-form shapes suffers from this inherent property. Voxel representations do not suffer from numerical instabilities as they are typically defined on an integer grid. A major drawback of voxel representations is the amount of data needed for storage.

Typical use cases are the visualization and analysis of medical data (medical imaging) acquired from sources like Computed Tomography (CT), Magnetic Resonance Imaging (MRI), or 3D ultrasonography.

2. Convex Polytopes

Shapes can be described as geometric objects with flat sides – so called polytopes. They are defined in any dimension as n-dimensional polytopes or n-polytopes. Two-dimensional polygons are called 2-polytopes and three-dimensional polytopes are called 3-polytopes. A special case of a polytope is a convex polytope having the additional property of being a convex set of points in n-dimensional space $\mathbb{R}^n$, respectively in n-dimensional Euclidean space $\mathbb{E}^d$. Convex polytopes can be defined over their convex hull, or by the intersection of half-spaces.

Branko Grünbaum and Geoffrey C. Shephard define a convex polytope as the convex hull of any finite set of points in Euclidean space $\mathbb{E}^n$ ($n \geq 0$) [21]. A set $S \subseteq \mathbb{E}^d$ is convex, if for any pair of points $x, y \in S$, the line segment $\lambda x + (1 - \lambda)y$ with $0 \leq \lambda \leq 1$, lies entirely in S. For any set S, the smallest convex set containing S is called the convex hull of S. A definition relying on the convex hull of a set of points is called a vertex representation.

Convex polytopes can also be defined as the intersection of a finite number of half-spaces [22]. Because of the fact that the intersection of arbitrary half-spaces need not be bounded, this property must be explicitly required. An algebraic formulation for convex polytopes consists of the set of bounded solutions to a system of linear inequalities. Hence, a closed convex polytope can be written as a system of linear inequalities. Open convex polytopes are defined similarly with strict inequalities instead of non-strict ones [23].

A limitation of convex polytopes is the inherent restriction to represent convex geometry only. The representation of non-convex geometry is possible through composition of convex polytopes. Topologically, convex polytopes are homeomorphic to a closed ball.

3. Constructive Solid Geometry

Constructive solid geometry (CSG) is a technique to create complex shapes out of primitive objects. These CSG primitives typically consist of cuboids, cylinders, prisms, pyramids, spheres and cones. Complex geometry is created by instantiation, transformation, and combination of the primitives. They are combined by using regularized Boolean set operations like Union, Difference and Intersection that are included in the representation. A CSG object is represented as a tree with inner nodes representing operators and primitives in the leaves.

In order to determine the shape described by a CSG tree, all operations have to be evaluated bottom-up until the root node is evaluated. Depending on the representation of the leaf geometry, this task can vary in complexity. Some implementations rely on representations that require the creation of a combined shape for the evaluation of the CSG tree, others do not create a combined representation. In that sense, CSG is not as much a representation as it is a set of operations that need to be implemented for the underlying shape representation [24].

However, CSG can also be performed on other shapes and shape representations. Two different approaches can be used to create CSG objects: Object-space approaches and image-space approaches. The main difference between the two approaches is that object-space approaches create shapes, while image-space approaches "only" create correct images.

Object-space CSG approaches using primitives described implicitly can be calculated accurately. Performing CSG on other shape representations (like polygonal meshes) typically introduces accuracy problems, due to the finite precision of floating-point numbers. A common representation used for CSG operations are binary space partitioning (BSP) trees. BSP is a method for subdividing a space into convex cells yielding a tree data structure. This data structure can be used to perform CSG operations using tree-merging as described by Bruce Naylor et al. [25]. The algorithm is relying on accurate information of inside and outside of a shape (or, in case of planes, above and below).

G. Algorithmic/Generative Shape Descriptions

Algorithmic shape descriptions are also called generative, procedural, or parametric descriptions. However, there are differences between the three terms. Parametric descriptions are loop-computable programs (the functions it can compute are the primitive recursive functions), and therefore always terminate [26]. On the other hand, procedural descriptions offer additional features, like infinite loops (the functions it can compute are computable functions), are structured in procedures, and are not guaranteed to terminate. Compared to procedural descriptions, generative descriptions are a more general term, including, for example, functional languages.

In this context, algorithmic descriptions are henceforth referred to as generative descriptions. The process of creating such descriptions is referred to as generative modeling. In contrast to many other descriptions, which are only describing a shape's appearance, generative shape descriptions represent inherent rules related to the structure of a shape. In simple terms, it is a computer program for the construction of the shape. It typically produces a surface-based or volumetric shape description for further use. In the article "Modeling Procedural Knowledge – A Generative Modeler for Cultural Heritage" [27] by Christoph Schinko et al., the authors state that all objects with well-organized structures and repetitive forms can be described in such a way. Many researchers enforce the creation of generative descriptions due to its many advantages [28].

Its strength lies in the compact description compared to conventional approaches, which does not depend on the counter of primitives but on the model's complexity itself [29]. Particularly large scale models and scenes – such as plants, buildings, cities, and landscapes – can be described efficiently. Generative descriptions make complex models manageable as they allow identifying a shape's high-level parameters.

Another advantage is the included expert knowledge within an object description, e.g., classification schemes used in architecture, archaeology, civil engineering, etc. can be mapped to procedures. For a specific object only its type and its instantiation parameters have to be identified. This identification is required by digital library services: markup, indexing, and retrieval [30]. The importance of semantic meta data becomes obvious in the context of electronic product data management, product lifecycle management, data exchange and storage or, more general, of digital libraries.

Generative descriptions have been developed in order to generate highly complex shapes based on a set of formal construction rules. They represent a whole family of shapes, not just a single shape. A specific exemplar is obtained by defining a set of parameters, or a sequence of processing steps: Shape design becomes rule design [31].

Because such descriptions already belong to a specific class of shapes, there is no need for detectors. However, with a generative description at hand, it is interesting to enrich other descriptions and representations. What is the best generative description of one or several given instances of an object class? This question is regarded as the inverse modeling problem [32].

III. Model Transformation

In a product lifecycle, the digital counterpart of a future, real-world object has to pass several stages of a multistep pipeline. First sketches of a product are represented in a different representation than the final CAD production-ready dataset. Furthermore, virtual product tests and simulations require special purpose model representation as well. As a consequence, each transformation between two possible model representations has a field of application. For the most important representations Table I lists the conversion methods and algorithms.

IV. Level-of-Detail Techniques

Managing level of detail is at once a very current and a very old topic in computer graphics. As early as 1976 James Clark described the benefits of representing objects within a scene at several resolutions. Recent years have seen many algorithms, papers, and software tools devoted to generating and managing such multiresolution representations of objects automatically [53].

The idea of "Level of Detail", or LOD for short, is an important topic in computer graphics as it is one of the key optimization strategies that would help 3D graphical programs, such as modelling software to run faster and reliably rendered across all the new and old hardware.

V. Semantic Enrichment

The problem of extracting semantic information from 3D data can be formulated simply as *What is the point?* [54] A-priori it is not clear whether a given point of a laser-scanned 3D scene, for example, belongs to a wall, to a door, or to the ground [55]. To answer this question is called semantic enrichment and it is always an act of interpretation [1].

The idea of generalized documents is to treat multimedia data, in particular 3D data sets, just like ordinary text documents, so that they can be inserted into a digital library. For any digital library to be able to handle a given media type, it must be integrated with the generic services that a DL provides, namely markup, indexing, and retrieval. This defines a digital library in terms of the function it provides [56] [57]. Like any library, it contains meta-information for all data sets. In the simplest case, the metadata are of the Dublin Core type

TABLE I. TRANSFORMATION BETWEEN MODEL REPRESENTATIONS.

Model Transformation from\to	*Point Sets*	*Polygonal Faces*	*Parametric Surfaces*	*Subdivision Surfaces*	*Implicit Surfaces*	*Volumetric Shapes*	*Generative Shapes*
Point Sets		Surface Reconstruction Library [33], Poison Reconstruction [34]	Surface Fitting and Regression [9]	Surface Fitting [35]	Surface Fitting [36]	Direct Evaluation [37]	Generative Fitting [32]
Polygonal Faces	Monte Carlo Sampling [38]		Surface Fitting [39]	Surface Fitting [40] [41]	Variational Interpolation [42]	Scan-line Filling [43]	Generative Fitting [32]
Parametric Surfaces	Monte Carlo Sampling [38]	Triangulation [10] [12]	Conversion [11]	NURBS-compatible Subdivision [44]	Spherical Coordinates [45]	Forward Differencing [46]	Inverse (Procedural) Modeling
Subdivision Surfaces	Point Sampling [38]	Evaluation [47]	NURBS-compatible Subdivision [44]			Evaluation [47] with Forward Differencing [46]	Inverse (Procedural) Modeling
Implicit Surfaces	Point Evaluation [48]	Marching Cubes [49]	Spherical coordinate representations [45]	Interpolation [50]		Voxelization [51]	Inverse (Procedural) Modeling
Volumetric Shapes	Point Sampling / Iso-Surface-Extraction	Marching Cubes [49]	via Marching Cubes	via Marching Cubes	via Marching Cubes		Inverse (Procedural) Modeling
Generative Shapes	Evaluation [28]	Evaluation [28]	Evaluation [28]	Evaluation [28]	Evaluation [28]	Evaluation [28]	Euclides [52]

(title, creator/author, and time of creation, etc.) [58]. This is insufficient for large databases with a huge number of 3D objects, because of their versatility and rich structure. Scanned models are used in raw data collections, for documentation archival, virtual reconstruction, historical data analysis, and for high-quality visualization for dissemination purposes [59]. Navigating and browsing through the geometric models must be possible not only in 3D, but also on the semantic level. The need for higher-level semantic information becomes immediately clear when considering typical questions users might want to ask when a large database of 3D objects is available.

- How many different types of chairs are stored in the library?
- I want to compare the noses of all these statues, can you extract them?
- ...

These questions cannot be answered, if the library simply treats 3D objects as binary large objects (BLOB) as it is done quite often. For a heap of geometric primitives without semantics, it is hard – if not impossible – to realize the mandatory services required by a digital library, especially in the context of electronic data exchange, storage and retrieval.

In the context of CAD, the processes of markup, indexing, and retrieval are a challenge with many open problems [60] [61].

VI. CONCLUSION

Model representations and their transformation into each other have been a challenge in the past and will remain a future challenge as well. The search for a comprehensive model representation combining the advantages of the various, different approaches is still on-going.

ACKNOWLEDGMENT

The authors gratefully acknowledge the support of the Austrian Research Promotion Agency, the Forschungsförderungsgesellschaft (FFG) for the research project AEDA (K-Projekt "Advanced Engineering Design Automation").

REFERENCES

[1] S. Havemann, T. Ullrich, and D. W. Fellner, "The Meaning of Shape and some Techniques to Extract It," Multimedia Information Extraction, vol. 1, 2012, pp. 81–98.

[2] M. Zwicker, M. Pauly, O. Knoll, and M. Gross, "Pointshop 3D: an interactive system for point-based surface editing," Proceedings of 2002 ACM Siggraph, vol. 21, 2002, pp. 322–329.

[3] M. Gross and H. Pfister, Point-Based Graphics. San Francisco, California, USA: Morgan Kaufmann Publishers Inc., 2007.

[4] M. Botsch, L. Kobbelt, and M. Pauly, Polygon Mesh Processing. Natick, Massachusetts, USA: AK Peters, 2010.

[5] M. Attene, D. Giorgi, M. Ferri, and B. Falcidieno, "On converting sets of tetrahedra to combinatorial and pl manifolds," Computer Aided Geometric Design, vol. 26, 2009, pp. 850–864.

[6] M. Botsch, S. Steinberg, S. Bischoff, and L. Kobbelt, "Openmesh – a generic and efficient polygon mesh data structure," Proceedings of OpenSG Symposium, vol. 1, 2002, pp. 1–5.

[7] G. Farin, Curves and Surfaces for Computer Aided Geometric Design, G. Farin, Ed. Academic Press Professional, Inc., 1990.

[8] H. Pottmann and S. Leopoldseder, "Geometries for CAGD," Handbook of 3D Modeling, G. Farin, J. Hoschek, and M.-S. Kim (editors), vol. 1, 2002, pp. 43–73.

[9] J. Hoschek and D. Lasser, Grundlagen der Geometrischen Datenverarbeitung (english: Fundamentals of Computer Aided Geometric Design), J. Hoschek and D. Lasser, Eds. Teubner, 1989.

[10] H. Prautzsch, W. Boehm, and M. Paluszny, Bézier and B-Spline Techniques, H. Prautzsch, W. Boehm, and M. Paluszny, Eds. Springer, 2002.

[11] G. Aumann and K. Spitzmüller, Computerorientierte Geometrie (english: Computer-Oriented Geometry), G. Aumann and K. Spitzmüller, Eds. BI-Wissenschafts-Verlag, 1993.

[12] L. Piegl and W. Tiller, The NURBS book, L. Piegl and W. Tiller, Eds. Springer-Verlag New York, Inc., 1997.

[13] J. Fisher, J. Lowther, and C.-K. Shene, "If you know b-splines well, you also know NURBS!" Proceedings of the 35th SIGCSE technical symposium on Computer science education, vol. 35, 2004, pp. 343–347.

[14] G. Farin, NURBS for Curve and Surface Design from Projective Geometry to Practical Use, G. Farin, Ed. AK Peters, Ltd., 1999.

[15] E. Catmull and J. Clark, "Recursively generated B-spline surfaces on arbitrary topological meshes," Computer-Aided Design, vol. 10, 1978, pp. 350–355.

[16] D. Doo and M. Sabin, "Behavior of Recursive Division Surfaces near Extraordinary Points," Computer Aided Design, vol. 10, no. 6, 1978, pp. 356–360.

[17] C. Loop, "Smooth Subdivision Surfaces Based on Triangles," Master's Thesis, University of Utah, USA, vol. 1, 1987, pp. 1–74.

[18] L. Kobbelt, "Interpolatory Subdivision on Open Quadrilateral Nets with

Arbitrary Topology," Computer Graphics Forum, vol. 15, no. 3, 1996, pp. 409–420.

[19] E. Sultanow, "Implizite Flächen (english: Implicit surfaces)," Technical Report at Hasso-Plattner-Institut, vol. 1, 2004, pp. 1–11.

[20] A. Knoll, Y. Hijazi, C. Hansen, I. Wald, and H. Hagen, "Interactive Ray Tracing of Arbitrary Implicits with SIMD Interval Arithmetic," Proceedings of IEEE Symposium on Interactive Ray Tracing, vol. 7, 2007, pp. 11–18.

[21] B. Grünbaum and G. C. Shephard, "Convex polytopes," Bull. Lond. Math. Soc., vol. 1, 1969, pp. 257–300.

[22] U. Krispel, T. Ullrich, and D. W. Fellner, "Fast and Exact Plane-Based Representation for Polygonal Meshes," Proceeding of the International Conference on Computer Graphics, Visualization, Computer Vision and Image Processing, vol. 8, 2014, pp. 189–196.

[23] W. Thaller, U. Krispel, R. Zmugg, S. Havemann, and D. W. Fellner, "Shape Grammars on Convex Polyhedra," Computers & Graphics, vol. 37, 2013, pp. 707–717.

[24] Y. Hijazi, A. Knoll, M. Schott, A. Kensler, C. Hansen, and H. Hagen, "CSG Operations of Arbitrary Primitives with Interval Arithmetic and Real-Time Ray Casting," Scientific Visualization: Advanced Concepts, vol. 978-3-939897-19-4, 2010, pp. 78–89.

[25] B. Naylor, J. Amanatides, and W. Thibault, "Merging bsp trees yields polyhedral set operations," SIGGRAPH Comput. Graph., vol. 24, no. 4, 1990, pp. 115–124.

[26] U. Schöning, Theoretische Informatik - kurz gefasst, 5th ed. Heidelberg: Spektrum Akademischer Verlag, 2008.

[27] C. Schinko, M. Strobl, T. Ullrich, and D. W. Fellner, "Modeling Procedural Knowledge – a generative modeler for cultural heritage," Proceedings of EUROMED 2010 - Lecture Notes on Computer Science, vol. 6436, 2010, pp. 153–165.

[28] U. Krispel, C. Schinko, and T. Ullrich, "A Survey of Algorithmic Shapes," Remote Sensing, vol. 7, 2015, pp. 12 763–12 792.

[29] R. Berndt, D. W. Fellner, and S. Havemann, "Generative 3D Models: a Key to More Information within less Bandwidth at Higher Quality," Proceeding of the 10th International Conference on 3D Web Technology, vol. 1, 2005, pp. 111–121.

[30] D. W. Fellner and S. Havemann, "Striving for an adequate vocabulary: Next generation metadata," Proceedings of the 29th Annual Conference of the German Classification Society, vol. 29, 2005, pp. 13–20.

[31] U. Krispel, C. Schinko, and T. Ullrich, "The Rules Behind – Tutorial on Generative Modeling," Proceedings of Symposium on Geometry Processing / Graduate School, vol. 12, 2014, pp. 21–249.

[32] T. Ullrich and D. W. Fellner, "Generative Object Definition and Semantic Recognition," Proceedings of the Eurographics Workshop on 3D Object Retrieval, vol. 4, 2011, pp. 1–8.

[33] R. B. Rusu and S. Cousins, "3D is here: Point Cloud Library (PCL)," in IEEE International Conference on Robotics and Automation (ICRA), Shanghai, China, May 9-13 2011.

[34] M. Kazhdan, M. Bolitho, and H. Hoppe, "Poisson Surface Reconstruction," in Symposium on Geometry Processing, A. Sheffer and K. Polthier, Eds. The Eurographics Association, 2006.

[35] K.-S. D. Cheng, W. Wang, H. Qin, K.-Y. K. Wong, H. Yang, and Y. Liu, "Fitting Subdivision Surfaces to Unorganized Point Data using SDM," Proceedings of 12th Pacific Conference on Computer Graphics and Applications, vol. 1, 2004, pp. 16–24.

[36] P. Keller, O. Kreylos, E. S. Cowgill, L. H. Kellogg, and M. Hering-Bertram, "Construction of Implicit Surfaces from Point Clouds Using a Feature-based Approach," in Scientific Visualization: Interactions, Features, Metaphors, ser. Dagstuhl Follow-Ups, H. Hagen, Ed. Dagstuhl, Germany: Schloss Dagstuhl–Leibniz-Zentrum fuer Informatik, 2011, vol. 2, pp. 129–143.

[37] S. Muraki, "Volumetric shape description of range data using “blobby model”," SIGGRAPH Comput. Graph., vol. 25, no. 4, Jul. 1991, pp. 227–235.

[38] P. Cignoni, M. Callieri, M. Corsini, M. Dellepiane, F. Ganovelli, and G. Ranzuglia, "Meshlab: an open-source mesh processing tool," in Sixth Eurographics Italian Chapter Conference, 2008, pp. 129–136.

[39] W. Ma and J. P. Kruth, "Nurbs curve and surface fitting for reverse engineering," The International Journal of Advanced Manufacturing Technology, vol. 14, no. 12, 1998, pp. 918–927.

[40] X. Ma, S. Keates, Y. Jiang, and J. Kosinka, "Subdivision surface fitting to a dense mesh using ridges and umbilics," Computer Aided Geometric Design, vol. 32, 2015, pp. 5–21.

[41] D. Panozzo, M. Tarini, N. Pietroni, P. Cignoni, and E. Puppo, "Automatic construction of quad-based subdivision surfaces using fitmaps," IEEE Transactions on Visualization & Computer Graphics, vol. 17, no. undefined, 2011, pp. 1510–1520.

[42] G. Yngve and G. Turk, "Robust creation of implicit surfaces from polygonal meshes," IEEE Transactions on Visualization and Computer Graphics, vol. 8, no. 4, 2002, pp. 346–359.

[43] A. Kaufman, "An Algorithm for 3D Scan-Conversion of Polygons," in EG 1987-Technical Papers, A. Kaufman, Ed. Eurographics Association, 1987.

[44] T. J. Cashman, U. H. Augsdörfer, N. A. Dodgson, and M. A. Sabin, "Nurbs with extraordinary points: High-degree, non-uniform, rational subdivision schemes," ACM Trans. Graph., vol. 28, no. 3, Jul. 2009, pp. 46:1–46:9.

[45] C. Ünsalan and A. Erçil, "Conversions between parametric and implicit forms using polar/spherical coordinate representations," Comput. Vis. Image Underst., vol. 81, no. 1, 2001, pp. 1–25.

[46] A. Kaufman, "Efficient algorithms for 3d scan-conversion of parametric curves, surfaces, and volumes," in Proceedings of the 14th Annual Conference on Computer Graphics and Interactive Techniques, ser. SIGGRAPH '87, 1987, pp. 171–179.

[47] W. Ma, "Subdivision surfaces for cad?an overview," Computer-Aided Design, vol. 37, no. 7, 2005, pp. 693–709.

[48] P. Ning and J. Bloomenthal, "An evaluation of implicit surface tilers," IEEE Computer Graphics and Applications, vol. 13, no. 6, 1993, pp. 33–41.

[49] E. V. Chernyaev, "Marching Cubes 33: Construction of topologically correct isosurfaces," Technical Report CN/95-17, 1995.

[50] X. Jin, H. Sun, and Q. Peng, "Subdivision interpolating implicit surfaces," Computers & Graphics, vol. 27, no. 5, 2003, pp. 763–772.

[51] N. Stolte and A. Kaufman, "Novel techniques for robust voxelization and visualization of implicit surfaces," Graphical Models, vol. 63, no. 6, 2001, pp. 387–412.

[52] C. Schinko, M. Strobl, T. Ullrich, and D. W. Fellner, "Scripting technology for generative modeling," International Journal on Advances in Software, vol. 4, no. 3-4, 2011, pp. 308–326.

[53] D. Luebke, M. Reddy, A. Cohen, Jonathan D. abd Varshney, B. Watson, and R. Huebner, Level of Detail for 3D Graphics, 1st ed. Heidelberg, Germany: Morgan Kaufmann, 2002.

[54] S. Biasotti, B. Falcidieno, D. Giorgi, and M. Spagnuolo, Mathematical Tools for Shape Analysis and Description. Morgan & Claypool Publishers, 2014.

[55] M. Attene, F. Robbiano, M. Spagnuolo, and B. Falcidieno, "Characterization of 3d shape parts for semantic annotation," Computer-Aided Design, vol. 41, 2009, pp. 756–763.

[56] D. W. Fellner, "Graphics Content in Digital Libraries: Old Problems, Recent Solutions, Future Demands," Journal of Universal Computer Science, vol. 7, 2001, pp. 400–409.

[57] D. W. Fellner, D. Saupe, and H. Krottmaier, "3D Documents," IEEE Computer Graphics and Applications, vol. 27, no. 4, 2007, pp. 20–21.

[58] Dublin Core Metadata Initiative, "Dublin Core Metadata Initiative," http://dublincore.org/ [retrieved: Feb. 2017], 1995.

[59] V. Settgast, T. Ullrich, and D. W. Fellner, "Information Technology for Cultural Heritage," IEEE Potentials, vol. 26, no. 4, 2007, pp. 38–43.

[60] C. Schinko, T. Vosgien, T. Prante, T. Schreck, and T. Ullrich, "Search & retrieval in cad databases – a user-centric state-of-the-art overview," Proceedings of the International Joint Conference on Computer Vision, Imaging and Computer Graphics Theory and Applications (GRAPP 2017), vol. 12, 2017, pp. 306–313.

[61] H. Laga, M. Mortara, and M. Spagnuolo, "Geometry and context for semantic correspondences and functionality recognition in man-made 3d shapes," ACM Transactions on Graphics, vol. 32, 2013, p. 150ff.

Investigating the Use of Semi-Supervised Convolutional Neural Network Models for Speech/Music Classification and Segmentation

David Doukhan and Jean Carrive
French National Institute of Audiovisual (Ina)
Paris, France
Email: ddoukhan@ina.fr, jcarrive@ina.fr

***Abstract*—A convolutional neural network architecture, trained with a semi-supervised strategy, is proposed for speech/music classification (SMC) and segmentation (SMS). It is compared to baseline machine learning algorithms on three SMC corpora and demonstrates superior performances, associated to perfect media-level speech recall scores. Evaluation corpora include speech-over-music segments with durations varying between 3 and 30 seconds. Early SMS results are presented. Segmentation errors are associated to musical genres not covered in the training database, and/or with close to speech acoustic properties. These experiments are aimed to help the design of novel speech/music annotated resources and evaluation protocols, suited to TV and radio stream indexation.**

***Keywords*–Speech/music discrimination; Audio segmentation; Convolutional Neural Networks; Music Information Retrieval; Multimedia Indexation.**

I. Introduction

Speech/Music classification (SMC) task consists in predicting if a given audio excerpt contains speech or music. The excerpts are supposed to be pure and contain either speech or music. Classified excerpts may have variable durations. Longer excerpt durations are known to make classification tasks easier. Speech excerpts are generally defined as containing *spoken speech*: this includes speech alone, superposed voices, and speech over music. Music excerpts are defined as containing instruments, instruments mixed with lyrics, or *a cappella* vocals. These technologies attracted much interest for the management of large multimedia collections: selection of optimal audio compression strategy at Swedish radio [1], as well as tag correction in Deezer's catalog [2].

Speech/Music segmentation (SMS) task consists in splitting audio streams into pure speech and pure music segments [3]. SMS algorithms are often based on frame-level SMC procedures, followed by a post-processing step (mean filtering, dynamic programming, etc.). SMS is a pre-processing stage required for several higher level indexation tasks such as speech and speaker recognition, song and musical genre recognition. Consequently, their development has received considerable attention from speech analysis and music information retrieval communities, illustrated by several evaluation campaigns, e.g. ESTER [4], Albayzín-2014 [5] or MIREX 2015 [6].

This paper presents the ongoing research on SMC and SMS tasks carried out at French National Institute of Audiovisual (Ina). Ina is a public institution in charge of the preservation, digitization, distribution and dissemination of the French audiovisual heritage. Ina's archives represent 70 years of radio and 60 years of TV programs, for a total of 15 million hours. The integration of SMS technologies in Ina workflows would allow a fast localization of interest areas within audio recordings, and address several identified needs. SMS may help speeding up media descriptions processes, which are performed manually by professional archivists. Manual media description is expensive, and associated to variable levels of detail: TV broadcast news are described with greater details than early radio collections. Consequently, SMS may ease the browsing and exploitation of under-documented archive contents. Latest identified use-case is music track segmentation, aimed at detecting and measuring the duration of musical tracks, in order to calculate the amount of royalties to be paid to rights collection societies.

The work presented in this paper is a preliminary study on SMC and SMS issues, using Convolutional Neural Networks (CNN). It is motivated by the excellent results reported with these architectures on MIREX 2015 SMC and SMS tasks, consisting in classifying 30-seconds long pure music and pure speech audio files. MIREX 2015's best SMC results were obtained using CNNs trained using fully supervised procedures: a MFC-based model with 1 convolutionnal layer [7], and a CQT-based model with 3 convolutionnal layers [8]. The main contribution of this paper is the description of MFC-based CNN's performances on publicly available datasets, using shorter audio segments (from 3 to 30 seconds), as well as speech-over-music excepts. Another major contribution is the proposal of an unsupervised SMC training strategy used in the first layer of the network, allowing to obtain visually relevant audio classification features.

This paper is structured as follows. Section II describes the audio feature extraction process. Section III describes the proposed CNN architecture and training strategy. Section IV and V describe the corpora used for SMC evaluation, and the corresponding results. Section VI describes the early results obtained on the SMS task. Section VII provides a summary of the results obtained, and introduces our future work.

II. Feature extraction and normalization

Audio excerpts are downsampled to 16KHz mono signals. Mel-frequency cepstrums (MFC) corresponding to 40 Mel bands are extracted from 20 ms frames, sampled with a 10 ms time step. Adjacent frames are concatenated using a contextual length varying between 1 (no context, 40 dimensions) and 50 (context of 500 ms, 2000 dimensions).
The resulting features are firstly normalized at the media level through a cepstral mean subtraction and a standard deviation division process. Similarly to *patch normalization* procedures, mean and standard deviation are also computed for each feature vector, and used to perform local mean subtraction and standard deviation division process.

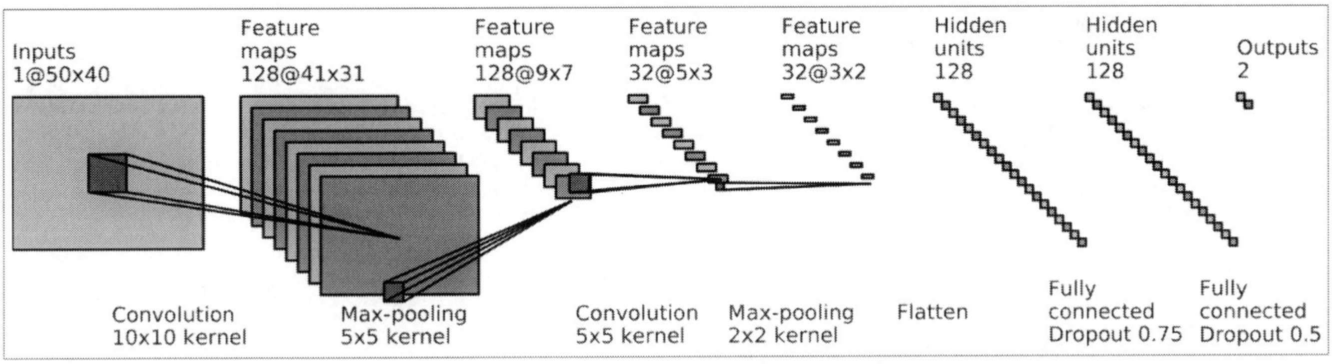

Figure 1. Proposed convolutional neural network architecture for frame-level speech/music classification

III. Semi-Supervised Convolutional Neural Network Model

CNNs are a type of feed-forward artificial neural network, in which the response of neurons to stimuli is triggered by convolution operations [9]. The weights are organized into a set of *filters* allowing the detection of localized spatio-temporal patterns, behaving like task-oriented feature extractors. Pattern shift and space invariance is achieved through the use of *pooling* operations.

In the scope of this study, several CNN architectures and training strategies were implemented using Tensorflow [10] and compared using variable number of convolutional and densely connected layer, filter shapes, pooling strategies, regularization methods. Figure 1 shows the structure of the CNN model associated to the best performances, reported in the next sections.The model input is composed of 50 MFC frames, corresponding to a 500 milliseconds temporal resolution. The frames are first processed by two convolutional layers (128 10×10 and 32 5×5 filters) reduced by max-pooling layers (5×5 and 2×2). These layers are followed by two densely connected layers of 128 neurons, which are associated to dropout rates of 0.75 and 0.5 [11]. Rectified linear unit (ReLU) activation functions are used between layers. The output layer is composed of two neurons, normalized using a softmax function, corresponding to the detection of music or speech. The first convolutional layer of the network is trained using an unsupervised procedure based on Spherical K-Means and ZCA whitening [12], with K being the number of filters of the first layer. Filters obtained through this procedure are associated to unit l^2 norm, which avoids irregular neural response magnitude, and prevents overfitting. First layer's filters are associated to visually relevant features (vertical, horizontal and diagonal patterns) illustrated by figure 2. Visual relevance of these shapes is also a desirable property (see [2] for filter shapes associated to fully supervised regularization strategies). The first layer stays constant during the training procedure, and remaining layers are trained using supervised Adaptive Moment Estimation (Adam) gradient descent optimization algorithm [13], for a maximal amount of 30 *epochs*, and are stopped when the accuracy on the training set reaches 99.9%.

IV. Speech/Music classification corpora

Three publicly available SMC corpora were used, each of them being associated to specific speaking styles, musical genres, and track durations.

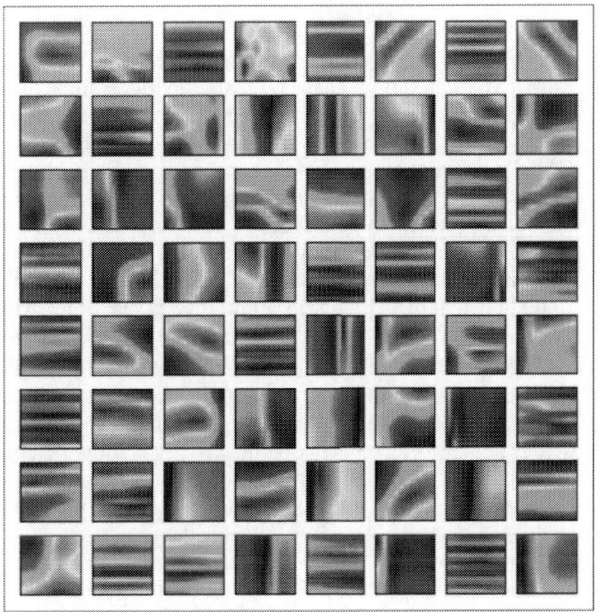

Figure 2. 10×10 Filters used in the first layer of the CNN

GTZAN music/speech collection [14] contains 120 tracks, each 30 seconds long. It contains 60 examples of speech and 60 examples of music. Speech samples cover various languages, accents and contexts: comic, radio, films, interviews, dialogues, advertisements, news, story-telling, etc. Music samples include several genres, including vocals without instruments.

Scheirer-Slaney Music/Speech corpus [15] contains 240 15-seconds tracks. These excerpts were collected from radio streams, which is a context representative of Ina's use case. It is composed of 140 examples of speech (English and Spanish) and 100 examples of music (with and without vocals). An interesting feature of this corpus is that 60 speech examples correspond to speech-over-music, which is supposed to increase the difficulty of classification and segmentation tasks.

Music, Speech, and Noise Corpus (MUSAN) [16] contains about 60 hours of speech and 42 hours of music. 20 hours of the speech material are full audiobook chapters, read in 12 languages, and correspond to clean read speech. The 40 remaining hours of speech material are composed of US government hearings, committees and debates, containing background noise (noisy spontaneous and prepared speech). Music material is provided with annotations related to performers and musical genres. 3 seconds long segments were extracted from MUSAN corpus through a procedure aimed at measuring the ability of the models to discriminate speech versus music on small segments and providing controlled variations on the training and testing examples. MUSAN's speech material is composed of 2 randomly selected segments per track in US government material, and 3 segments per audiobook, amounting to 1024 segments, for a duration of 9 minutes for each speech category. Music material is composed of some 6 randomly extracted segments per artist, amounting to 924 segments obtained from 252 different artists. Automatic energy-based procedures were designed to discard empty segments, as well as segments with less than one second of activity.

V. Speech/Music classification evaluation

CNN performances are estimated on SMC corpora and compared to baseline machine learning algorithms provided in `Scikit-learn` toolbox [17]: Support Vector Machines (SVM) with RBF kernel, and Gaussian Mixture Models (GMM) with diagonal covariance matrices and varying number of gaussians (32 to 512). Models are evaluated using input vectors corresponding to concatenated MFC frames, with contextual length varying between 1 (no context) and 50 (context of 500 milliseconds). Best results are obtained using the highest contextual length, which was limited to 50 in order to allow acceptable temporal resolution in following segmentation tasks (10 milliseconds time step and 500 milliseconds context).

Effectiveness is reported at the *frame level* and at the *media level*. Frame-level decisions are based on the raw instantaneous predictions of SMC models obtained for each input vector (500 milliseconds context). The frame-level decision correspond to the class (speech or music) with highest probability. Media-level decisions are based on the products across all frame-level probabilities per class obtained for an audio excerpt (100 frame-level predictions per second). Best instantaneous frame-level estimates does not necessarily produce best media-level estimates, nor best segmentations. SMC performances reported are those associated to the models achieving the best media-level performances, which is more representative of the final use-case.

Models are compared using a 5-fold cross-validation process. Effectiveness is described using speech, music and mean recalls, providing a description of the most frequent classification errors. MUSAN corpus evaluations are carried out using constraints on cross-validation, in order to group subtracks corresponding to a same performer in the same folds. These constraints avoid testing a model on a track produced by a performer found in the model's training set. Similar constraints are applied for segments obtained from the same audio-book or us-government track.

Tables I, II and III report the results obtained on GTZAN, Scheirer-Slaney and MUSAN corpora. All classification algorithms achieve 100% correct media-level classification rate on GTZAN corpora. This better media-level recall is probably due to the duration associated to GTZAN samples (30 seconds, instead of 15 in Scheirer-Slaney and 3 in MUSAN). For all other tasks, CNN models achieve better classification results

TABLE I. Speech/Music classification results obtained on GTZAN corpus [14] using 120 30-seconds long excerpts

Algorithm	*Frame-level Recall*			*Media-level Recall*		
	Speech	Music	Mean	Speech	Music	Mean
GMM	89,18	84,05	86,61	100	100	100
SVM	95,64	91,06	93,35	100	100	100
CNN	98,16	96,25	**97,21**	100	100	100

TABLE II. Speech/Music classification results obtained on Scheirer-Slaney corpus [15] using 240 15-seconds excerpts

Algorithm	*Frame-level Recall*			*Media-level Recall*		
	Speech	Music	Mean	Speech	Music	Mean
GMM	85,28	81,03	83,15	99,29	98,00	98,64
SVM	93,01	89,62	91,32	98,54	98,00	98,27
CNN	93,79	91,79	**92,79**	100	98,00	**99,00**

TABLE III. Speech/Music classification results obtained on MUSAN corpus [16] using 1948 3-seconds long excerpts

Algorithm	*Frame-level Recall*			*Media-level Recall*		
	Speech	Music	Mean	Speech	Music	Mean
GMM	97,32	95,04	96,18	99,41	97,17	98,29
SVM	97,17	94,5	95,84	99,8	97,41	98.6
CNN	99,36	98,85	**99,11**	100	99,46	**99,73**

than GMM and SVM, both at the frame and media level. For all of these methods, frame-level recall is higher for speech than for music, as several music frames are incorrectly predicted as speech. CNN predictions are associated to a perfect media-level speech recall score for all corpora. CNN produces only 2 classification errors on Scheirer-Slaney corpus, and 5 on MUSAN corpus. Manual analysis of these errors shows vocal singing excerpts without instrumental accompaniment, or singing style close to regular speech, that are predicted as speech. An additional error found in Scheirer-Slaney corpus corresponds to a pure music track incorrectly classified as speech. This is explained by the presence of 3 training samples containing the same music track with superposed speech, learned as speech excerpts. Frame-level results obtained on Scheirer-Slaney corpus are worse than those obtained on other corpora, since this corpus contains speech-over-music excerpts, harder to discriminate than pure speech or pure music segments. Best frame-level results are obtained on MUSAN corpus; this may be explained by the low variability observed within its speech material.

VI. Speech/Music segmentation evaluation

This section reports the early results obtained on the SMS task, using the CNN architecture associated to the best SMC performances. CNN model was trained using GTZAN, Scheirer-Slaney and MUSAN corpora described in the last sections, corresponding to about 3 hours of annotated material. Raw frame-level music and speech probabilities are obtained using a step size of 10 milliseconds. Viterbi algorithm is used to infer the most likely state sequence (speech or music) from these raw estimates, allowing to increase the robustness of CNN's predictions.

MIREX 2015 speech/music detection training examples material [6] was used for this evaluation (the training examples material is different from MIREX evaluation material which is not public). It contains about 5 hours of radio streams, corresponding to 4 hours of music, 1 hour of speech, 7 minutes of speech-over-music, and 6 minutes of other phenomena (pauses, applause, etc.). It is split into 7 tracks associated

TABLE IV. SPEECH/MUSIC SEGMENTATION RESULTS OBTAINED ON MIREX 2015 TRAINING EXAMPLES MATERIAL

Radio Stream Genre	*Raw Frame-level Recall*			*Frame-level Recall after Viterbi post-processing*		
	Speech	Music	Mean	Speech	Music	Mean
Classical	91.30	97.66	94.48	100	100	100
Country	92.94	73.45	83.19	96.82	88.55	92.69
Ethnic	95.15	71.49	83.32	99.18	79.26	89.22
Irish	95.08	88.32	91.70	99.38	96.50	97.94

to specific musical genres. Two tracks contain instrumental classical music. Three files contain ethnological recordings, including shamanic singing and psalms. One contains country music and blues, including *a cappella* singing. Last track contains Irish folk music. Table IV reports frame-level results obtained for all of these genres. Results for frames not associated to speech or music are not reported. Perfect results are obtained for material associated to instrumental classical music, which is the easiest category, well represented in our training database. Errors found in ethnological recordings are mostly associated to shamanic psalms, not covered in our training set, which are detected as speech. Errors found in the country music material are mostly associated to *a cappella* singing detected as speech. This source of error is coherent with studies reporting similar acoustic properties in country singer's speech and singing [18].

VII. DISCUSSION AND FUTURE WORK

This study presents the use of a CNN architecture on several SMC tasks and on a SMS task. The proposed model shows clear advantages over SVM and GMM, both at the *frame level* and at the *media level*. All speech segments used in classification evaluations, with to durations between 3 and 30 seconds, are correctly classified. The proposed semi-supervised training procedure allows to obtain slightly better SMC results than fully supervised approaches on MUSAN corpus (not reported in last sections), resulting in a reduction of two media-level errors over 1948 samples. This trend needs to be confirmed using harder SMC evaluation protocols, as well as larger evaluation corpora.

Errors related to music excerpts, recognized as speech, are mostly associated to *a cappella* or predominant vocals, and singing styles close to regular speech (hip hop, shamanic psalms, country vocals, opera *recitative* style, etc.). Scheirer-Slaney corpus is the only classification corpus used in this study including speech-over-music samples, resulting in the lowest frame-level classification results. These findings suggest to constitute training and evaluation corpora containing these difficult musical genres, and to systematically integrate speech-over-music samples in our future evaluation procedures.

Work in progress covers the constitution of a representative music segment dataset, with annotated variations related to genre, singing style, performer, and track identification. The use of speech databases containing speaker identities, and speaking styles annotations is required to improve control over our next evaluations. This issue may be partly addressed using a 2290-speaker corpus realized at Ina [19]. The hardest issue is the design of models able to discriminate speech-over-music and music, especially for music having vocal acoustic properties close to regular speech (hip hop, eletro, etc.). This will be addressed through data augmentation strategies, here consisting in artificially superposing speech to music [20]. The last issue is the constitution of a music track segmentation corpus, including early challenging archive documents representative of the diversity of Ina's collections [21].

REFERENCES

[1] L. Ericsson, "Automatic speech/music discrimination in audio files," Skolan för datavetenskap och kommunikation, Kungliga Tekniska högskolan, 2010.

[2] R.-L. Jimena, R. Hennequin, and M. Moussallam, "Detection and characterization of singing voice using deep neural networks," UPMC-Paris, 2015.

[3] Y. Lavner and D. Ruinskiy, "A decision-tree-based algorithm for speech/music classification and segmentation," EURASIP Journal on Audio, Speech, and Music Processing, no. 1, 2009, p. 239892.

[4] S. Galliano, G. Gravier, and L. Chaubard, "The ester 2 evaluation campaign for the rich transcription of french radio broadcasts." in Interspeech, vol. 9, 2009, pp. 2583–2586.

[5] D. Castán et al., "Albayzín-2014 evaluation: audio segmentation and classification in broadcast news domains," EURASIP Journal on Audio, Speech, and Music Processing, no. 1, 2015, p. 33.

[6] "Mirex 2015 music/speech classification and detection and challenge," visited on 2017-03-07. [Online]. Available: http://www.music-ir.org/mirex/wiki/2015:Music/Speech_Classification_and_Detection

[7] T. Lidy, "Spectral convolutional neural network for music classification," in Music Information Retrieval Evaluation eXchange, 2015.

[8] J. Royo-Letelier, R. Hennequin, and M. Moussallam, "Mirex 2015 music/speech classification," Music Inform. Retrieval Evaluation eXchange (MIREX), 2015.

[9] Y. LeCun and Y. Bengio, "Convolutional networks for images, speech, and time series," The handbook of brain theory and neural networks, vol. 3361, no. 10, 1995, p. 1995.

[10] M. Abadi et al., "Tensorflow: Large-scale machine learning on heterogeneous distributed systems," arXiv preprint arXiv:1603.04467, 2016.

[11] N. Srivastava, G. E. Hinton, A. Krizhevsky, I. Sutskever, and R. Salakhutdinov, "Dropout: a simple way to prevent neural networks from overfitting," Journal of Machine Learning Research, vol. 15, no. 1, 2014, pp. 1929–1958.

[12] A. Coates and A. Y. Ng, "Learning feature representations with k-means," in Neural Networks: Tricks of the Trade. Springer, 2012, pp. 561–580.

[13] D. Kingma and J. Ba, "Adam: A method for stochastic optimization," arXiv preprint arXiv:1412.6980, 2014.

[14] G. Tzanetakis and P. Cook, "Musical genre classification of audio signals," IEEE Transactions on speech and audio processing, vol. 10, no. 5, 2002, pp. 293–302.

[15] E. Scheirer and M. Slaney, "Construction and evaluation of a robust multifeature speech/music discriminator," in Acoustics, Speech, and Signal Processing, 1997. ICASSP-97., vol. 2, 1997, pp. 1331–1334.

[16] D. Snyder, G. Chen, and D. Povey, "Musan: A music, speech, and noise corpus," arXiv preprint arXiv:1510.08484, 2015.

[17] F. Pedregosa et al., "Scikit-learn: Machine learning in python," Journal of Machine Learning Research, vol. 12, 2011, pp. 2825–2830.

[18] R. E. Stone, T. F. Cleveland, and J. Sundberg, "Formant frequencies in country singers' speech and singing," Journal of Voice, vol. 13, no. 2, 1999, pp. 161–167.

[19] F. Salmon and F. Vallet, "An effortless way to create large-scale datasets for famous speakers." in Language Resources and Evaluation Conference, 2014, pp. 348–352.

[20] J. Razik, C. Sénac, D. Fohr, O. Mella, and N. Parlangeau-Vallès, "Comparison of two speech/music segmentation systems for audio indexing on the web," in Proc. Multi Conference on Systemics, Cybernetics and Informatics, 2003.

[21] D. Doukhan and J. Carrive, "Simple neural representations of speech for voice activity detection and speaker tracking in noisy archives," 4th International Conference on Statistical Language and Speech Processing, 2016.

Adaptive Queue Management Scheme for Flexible Dual TCP/UDP Streaming Protocol

Arul Dhamodaran, Kevin Gatimu, and Ben Lee

School of Electrical and Computer Science
Oregon State University
Corvallis, Oregon 97331
Email: {dhamodar, gatimuk, benl}@eecs.orst.edu

***Abstract*—Flexible Dual-TCP/UDP Streaming Protocol (FDSP) is a new method for streaming H.264-encoded High-definition (HD) video over wireless networks. FDSP streaming is done in sequential video segments or chunks called substreams. In FDSP, substream lengths are used to control the amount of Transmission Control Protocol (TCP) data that needs to be sent prior to the playback of that substream. To avoid frequent rebuffering, TCP packets of the next substream are overlapped with the User Datagram Protocol (UDP) packets of the current substream. The TCP threshold parameter determines when to overlap new TCP packets with the current UDP stream. This paper analyzes the TCP threshold parameter in the context of FDSP. Our results show that user Quality of Experience (QoE) can be enhanced by adaptive adjusting of the TCP threshold using the additive-increase/multiplicative-decrease (AIMD) algorithm based on the UDP packet loss rate and the TCP rebuffering.**

Keywords–Bitstream Prioritization; HD Video Streaming; Queue Size; TCP Threshold; FDSP.

I. INTRODUCTION

High-definition (HD) video streaming technologies have fundamentally changed the way multimedia content is consumed. These video streaming applications can be broadly classified into client-server and device-to-device streaming applications. Client-server based streaming applications, such as Netflix, Hulu, Amazon Video, etc., typically involve a streaming server to deliver multimedia content to the end user through the internet. On the other hand, device-to-device wireless HD video streaming is enabled by technologies such as Apple AirPlay®, Google Chromecast®, and Wi-Fi Alliance's Miracast® to facilitate various multi-screen (i.e., N-screen) applications [1]. However, the explosion of wireless enabled devices will strain the bandwidth limits due to the need to support multiple streams in the same network.

All the aforementioned video streaming services and applications rely on either Transmission Control Protocol (TCP) or User Datagram Protocol (UDP) protocol. The client-server streaming techniques rely primarily on HTTP-based streaming, which, in-turn, is based on TCP. On the other hand, device-to-device streaming applications Chromecast and Miracast rely on UDP while Airplay uses TCP for video streaming and screen mirroring applications. However, both TCP- and UDP-based streaming protocols have their own set of challenges. TCP guarantees packet delivery ensuring perfect video frame quality, but suffers from freeze frames during video playback due to packet delay caused by bandwidth bottleneck. Figure 1 illustrates the effect of rebuffering caused by TCP packet delay, which occurs when TCP packets arrive at the receiver after the playout deadline due to network congestion. This delay causes

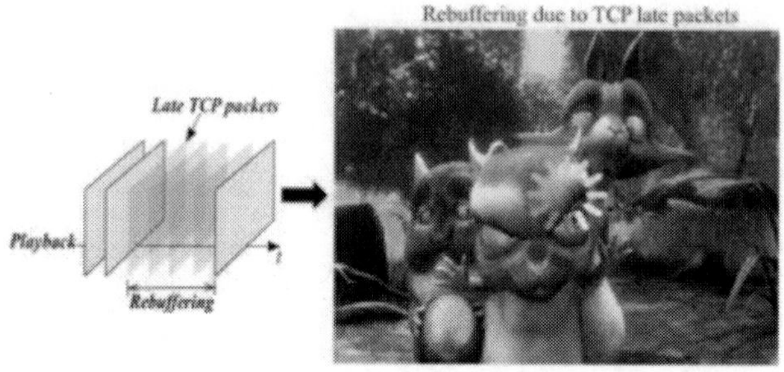

Figure 1. Rebuffering due to late TCP packets.

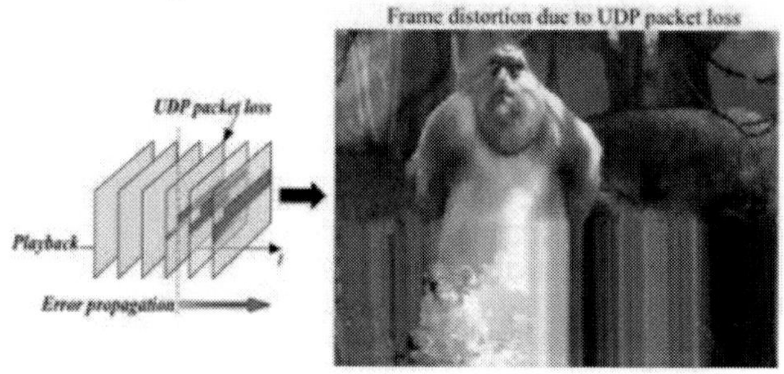

Figure 2. Frame distortion due to UDP packet loss. Note that packet loss also causes frame distortion in subsequent frames due to error propagation.

the received video to freeze frame and stall for more TCP packets to arrive at the receiver before resuming playback. UDP, on the other hand, minimizes delay but suffers from packet loss. Figure 2 illustrates the video quality degradation due to UDP packet loss, which affects not only the frame for which the packet loss occurred but also subsequent frames that use it as the reference frame (referred to as *error propagation*).

In our previous work, a new H.264 based video streaming technique called *Flexible Dual Streaming Protocol* (FDSP) was proposed [2]. FDSP sends packets containing important H.264 video syntax elements (i.e., Sequence Parameter Set (SPS), Picture Parameter Set (PPS), and slice headers) via TCP for guaranteed delivery and the rest of the slice data packets via UDP giving an H.264 decoder a better chance of decoding received video even when packet losses occur. Therefore, FDSP exploits the combined benefits of TCP and UDP by adding reliability to UDP while reducing the latency caused by TCP. This enables FDSP to strike a balance between visual quality and delay by achieving higher video quality than pure-UDP and less rebuffering than pure-TCP.

FDSP was enhanced in [3] using *Bitstream Prioritization* (BP) to reduce the impact of UDP packet loss. This method *statically* chooses the BP metric to classify a select percentage of originally UDP-designated packets from an H.264 bitstream as high priority, which are then transported over TCP for guaranteed delivery. FDSP-BP was further enhanced by introducing Adaptive-BP [4], where the percentage of packets sent over TCP versus UDP is dynamically adjusted based on the estimated rebuffering time for TCP packets and estimated packet loss ratio (PLR) for UDP packets. FDSP with Adaptive-BP further improved the performance by reducing both packet loss and rebuffering time.

FDSP-based streaming is done in sequential video chunks called *substreams*. For each substream, the important syntax elements are sent first via TCP, and then the rest of the data is sent via UDP. Therefore, the substream length determines the amount of TCP data that needs to be sent prior to the playback of that substream. To allow TCP packets to arrive on time, *substream overlapping* is performed where TCP packets for the next substream are sent at the same time as the UDP packets for the current substream. However, an important issue with substream overlapping is the decision on when to insert new TCP packets into the outgoing IP queue of the sender, which is referred to as *TCP Threshold*. In our prior work on FDSP, the TCP threshold was chosen to be fixed at 35% of the maximum IP Queue size [3]. This paper analyzes how varying the TCP threshold affects UDP PLR and TCP rebuffering time and develops an Adaptive TCP Threshold technique to improve user Quality of Experience (QoE).

This paper is organized as follows. Section II discusses other TCP and UDP streaming techniques. An overview of the FDSP streaming method is shown in Section III. Section IV discusses the effects of substream overlapping and TCP threshold. Sections V goes over the experimental setup and Section VI discusses the results of our analysis on how the changes in the TCP threshold affect FDSP streaming. Finally, Section VII concludes the paper.

II. Related Work

Queue management techniques for video streaming applications have been well studied. The two basic approaches proposed for queue management are Random Early Detection (RED) [5] and Blue [6]. Both of these techniques use queue length as an indicator of congestion and use this information to regulate the packet drop rates. Xu *et al.* proposed an active queue management technique for wireless ad hoc networks, called Neighborhood RED (NERD) [7]. This technique uses channel utilization to estimate the queue length to help determine the packet drop probability.

However, all the above queue management techniques are designed for data communication in general, without any consideration for the unique characteristics of video streaming (i.e., multimedia communication). Chen *et al.* proposed an active queue management technique where packets that may potentially be late are actively dropped before they are transmitted to reduce the strain on the network resources and to effectively control the transmission queue length [8]. Shy *et al.* proposed another active queue management (AQM) system, which employs routers that deal with both best-effort traffic flows and multimedia traffic flows [9]. Round trip time (RTT) is used in the packet dropping probability calculations to assure rate reductions in both multimedia and best-effort flows before the queue becomes full.

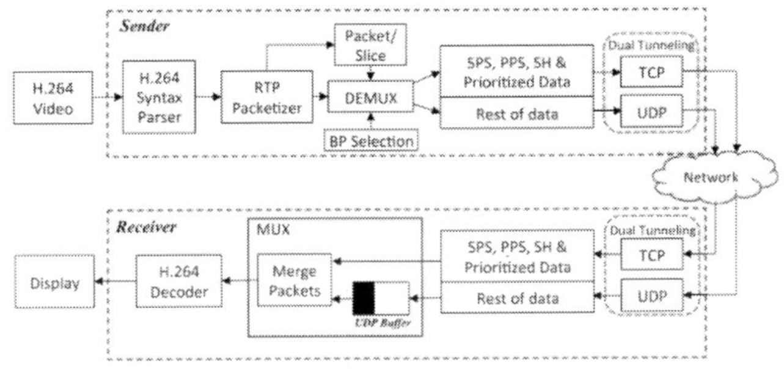

Figure 3. The architecture of FDSP with Adaptive BP [4]

The aforementioned queue management techniques are designed for video streaming systems that are based either on TCP or UDP. Furthermore, all of these systems focus on techniques such as prioritized dropping based on queue length, fairness based scheduling algorithms for packet delay optimization, etc. On the other hand, FDSP is a hybrid streaming protocol that uses both TCP and UDP for video streaming, and thus it presents a unique set of challenges, such as the TCP threshold, that play a crucial role in packet delay optimization. Therefore, this paper expands on the scope of our prior research on FDSP with Adaptive-BP [4] by analyzing the TCP threshold parameter and its impact on UDP PLR and TCP rebuffering.

III. FDSP Overview

FDSP was proposed as a new device-to-device video streaming technique for H.264 content [2]. This section provides a brief overview of its various architectural features and factors affecting video quality (see [2]-[4] for details).

FDSP with Adaptive-BP architecture is shown in Figure 3 [4], which consists of a sender and a receiver. The FDSP sender processes H.264 video data using the *H.264 Syntax Parser* to detect important Network Abstraction Layer (NAL) units, i.e., SPS, PPS, and slice headers (SH). The rest of the NAL units are primarily slice data packets. It also works with the *RTP Packetizer* to encapsulate each NAL unit into the RTP payload format for H.264 video [10]. The *Demultiplexer* (DEMUX) then routes the important NAL units (SPS, PPS, SH, and prioritized I-frame data) through TCP and the rest of the NAL units through UDP. The *BP selection* module sets the BP parameter, which represents the percentage of the I-frame data to be prioritized and sent over TCP. In FDSP with Adaptive-BP, BP is adjusted dynamically based on the estimated available network bandwidth. Finally, *Dual Tunneling* is employed to keep both TCP and UDP sessions active during video streaming.

In the receiver, *Dual Tunneling* is employed to receive packets from both the TCP and UDP streams. The *Multiplexer* (MUX) then discards the late TCP packets and rearranges the TCP and UDP packets based on their RTP timestamps.

During FDSP streaming, the sender first segments the input video into 10 sec. *substreams*, as done in HTTP live Streaming (HLS) [11]. Then, all the TCP packets containing SPS, PPS, SH, and BP prioritized I-frame data for each substream are sent over TCP prior to sending UDP packets containing the slice data. Thus, the receiver must wait for its respective TCP data to arrive before playback. To avoid rebuffering caused by TCP packet delay, the transmission of UDP packets for the current substream is overlapped with the transmission of TCP packets for the next substream (i.e., substream overlapping).

BP is only applied to packets containing I-frame data because they serve as reference frames and any loss in I-frame data leads to error propagation to the entire Group Of Picture (GOP) sequence. If the BP parameter is set to zero, then it defaults to basic FDSP, where SPS, PPS, and slice headers are the only packets that will be sent via TCP. If BP is 25% then a quarter of all I-frame packets would be sent via TCP. Although it is possible to select any distribution of the I-frame to be sent via TCP, a sequential order of I-frame packets are selected to be sent via TCP to achieve better QoE. Increasing BP results in increasing the number of TCP packets, thus increasing the probability of TCP rebuffering, but it reduces UDP packet loss and error propagation due to the proportional reduction in the number of UDP packets.

Since FDSP is a hybrid streaming technique that uses both TCP and UDP protocols, its performance is affected by both packet loss and rebuffering. The various factors that influence packet loss and rebuffering are the BP parameter, the substream length, and substream overlapping. The BP parameter is used to determine the percentage of I-frame packets that are to be sent through TCP. The BP parameter is computed based on TCP round-trip time and UDP packet loss rate, which in turn determines the percentage of TCP versus UDP packets to be sent for each substream. Adaptively adjusting the BP parameter for each substream helps further reduce UDP packet loss while keeping TCP rebuffering time and instances low. The substream length trades off between the likelyhood of rebuffering and the frequency of adaptive BP selection process. Since the BP and substream length have been analyzed in our previous work, this paper focuses on examining how different TCP thresholds affects FDSP video streaming.

IV. Substream Overlapping and TCP Threshold

In FDSP, the important syntax elements for each substream are sent first via TCP, and then the rest of the data is sent via UDP. Therefore, the substream length and the BP parameter determine the amount of TCP data that needs to be sent prior to the playback of that substream. However, rebuffering occurs whenever TCP packets for a substream are not yet all available at the time of playback of that substream. To avoid rebuffering, the TCP packets of the next substream (i.e., substream $i+1$) are overlapped with the UDP packets of the current substream (i.e., substream i).

The important issue with substream overlapping is the decision on when to insert new TCP packets for the next substream into the outgoing IP queue of the sender. This is because inserting TCP packets for the next substream into the queue too soon would interfere with successful UDP packet transmission for the current substream. On the other hand, inserting TCP packets into the queue too late would result in rebuffering. Therefore, substream overlapping is initiated only when the number of packets in the network device's IP queue is below the *TCP Threshold*. Increasing the TCP threshold would result in increased UDP packet loss due to network saturation caused by flooding of TCP packets. On the other hand, decreasing the TCP threshold results in increased TCP rebuffering due to the reduction in the number of new TCP packets being inserted into the queue. The various factors that affect the TCP threshold are: (i) the number of UDP packets in the current substream; (ii) the number of TCP packets in the next substream; (iii) the average queue occupancy; and (iv) the average number of UDP packets per frame. The number of UDP packets for the current substream and the number of TCP packets for the next substream are used to calculate the estimated TCP rebuffering time and the estimated UDP PLR [4]. The average queue occupancy and the average number of UDP packets per frame are used to estimate the number of instances for substream overlapping.

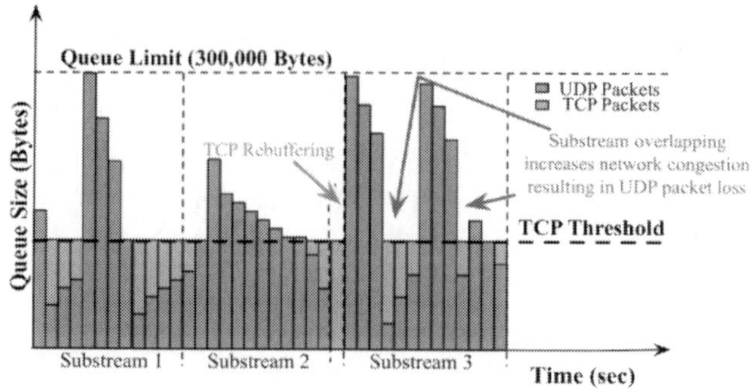

(a) IP queue occupancy for static TCP threshold.

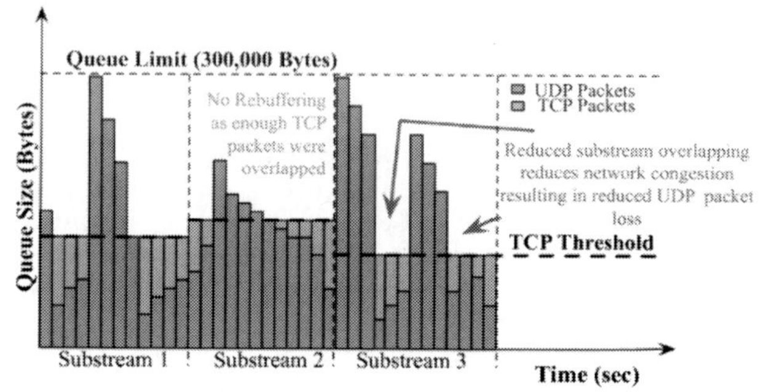

(b) IP queue occupancy for adaptive TCP threshold.

Figure 4. IP queue occupancy example for static vs. adaptive TCP threshold.

Figure 4a shows an example of the IP queue occupancy as a function of time for a static TCP threshold during FDSP streaming. In this example, the TCP threshold is set to 30% of the maximum queue size. For substream 1, the queue size decreases as UDP packets are streamed. When the queue size falls below the TCP threshold, the TCP packets for substream 2 are inserted into the queue. In substream 2, the average number of UDP packets per frame is higher than in substream 1 resulting in reduced opportunities to insert new TCP packets from substream 3, which in-turn increases the probability of TCP rebuffering (indicated by an extra time slot). In substream 3, both the queue occupancy and the average number of UDP packets per frame are high indicating a network congestion. In this scenario, inserting more TCP packets into the queue would exacerbate network congestion and result in UDP packet loss.

Figure 4a clearly shows that having a static TCP threshold is not always optimal for FDSP streaming. Figure 4b shows that adaptively adjusting the TCP threshold can reduce both UDP PLR and TCP rebuffering resulting in better QoE. In this example, the TCP threshold is also set to 30% by default for substream 1, and thus the queue behavior is identical to that of Figure 4a. In substream 2, the average number of UDP packets per frame is higher than substream 1, this reduces the number of TCP packet insertions resulting in increased TCP rebuffering probability. However, since the queue occupancy for substream 2 is not very high, the TCP threshold is increased, which increases the number of TCP packets that can be inserted into the queue and in turn reduces the TCP rebuffering probability.

In substream 3, both the queue occupancy and the average number of UDP packets per frame are very high, indicating network congestion, which in-turn increases UDP packet loss. In Figure 4b, the TCP threshold is decreased for substream 3 to reduce the number of TCP packets inserted into the queue. This in-turn increases the number of UDP packets transmitted, thus reducing UDP PLR. Note that although the TCP threshold is decreased there is no change in the queue level for the first three time slots of substream 3 because there is no substream overlapping. During time slots 4-6, the number of TCP packets inserted into the queue is reduced compared to the case in Figure 4a. This reduction allows for more UDP packets to be transmitted. The increased UDP packet prioritization reduces the queue occupancy levels during time slots 7-9, which reduces the overall UDP packet loss rate for substream 3. This reduction in TCP threshold may increase the TCP rebuffering probability, but there are enough opportunities for TCP overlapping for substream 3 to avoid rebuffering.

A. Adaptive TCP Threshold

The Additive-Increase/Multiplicative-Decrease (AIMD) algorithm is well suited to adaptively adjust the TCP threshold because the TCP threshold is progressively increased, which in-turn increases the number of TCP packets inserted into the queue reducing the likelihood of rebuffering. On the other hand, AIMD prioritizes UDP packets by exponentially reducing the TCP threshold at the first sign of network congestion (based on estimated UDP packet loss). For example, FDSP streaming begins with a default TCP threshold of 30% for the first two substreams. From the third substream on, the TCP threshold is progressively incremented based on the estimated TCP rebuffering probability until UDP packet loss is estimated at which point the TCP threshold is reduced in half. Note that the estimated TCP rebuffering probability and the estimated UDP PLR are computed using TCP round trip time and queue statistics, respectively (for more details please refer to FDSP with Adaptive-BP [4]).

V. Experimental Setup

This section discusses the experimental setup for the analysis of TCP threshold parameters and its impact on both UDP packet loss and TCP rebuffering for FDSP-based video streaming. For our experiments, two full HD (1920×1080 @30fps, 4300 frames) clips from a high-motion (animation) video *Bunny*, and a low-motion (documentary) video *Bears* are used. These clips are encoded using the x264 encoder with an average bit rate of 4 Mbps and four slices per frame.

Our simulation environment is *Open Evaluation Framework For Multimedia Over Networks* (OEFMON) [12], which is composed of a multimedia framework *DirectShow*, and a network simulator *QualNet* 7.3 [13]. OEFMON allows a raw video to be encoded and redirected to a simulated network to gather statistics on the received video. Within OEFMON, an 802.11g ad-hoc network with a bandwidth of 54 Mbps is setup. Note that the version of the Qualnet simulator used for our study only supports the IEEE 802.11g standard. However, the simulation study can easily be adapted to 802.11n by having more background traffic to saturate the network. The network scenario used is an 8-node configuration shown in Figure 5. The distance between each source and destination pair is 5 m and the distance between pairs of nodes is 10 m. These distances were chosen to mimic the proximity of multiple pairs of neighboring streaming devices in an apartment setting. The primary test video is being streamed between nodes 1 and 2, while the remaining three node pairs produces three streams of constant bit rate (CBR) background traffic of 50 Mbps to fully saturate the network.

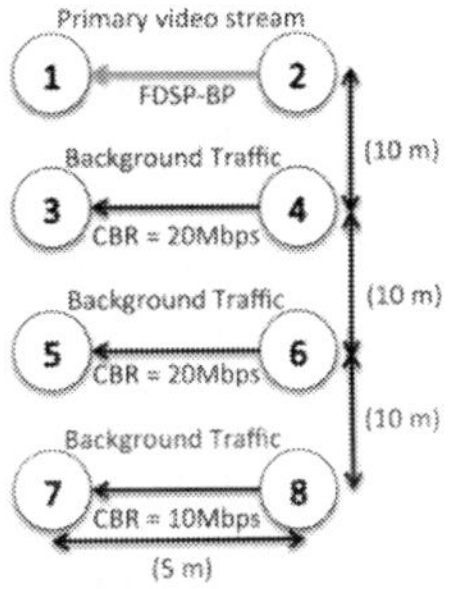

Figure 5. Simulated network scenario.

For the TCP threshold analysis, the primary video is streamed using FDSP with BP of 0% and 100%. These two choices of BP values are based on our prior work [14], which showed that they represent the two extreme effects of FDSP-based streaming, i.e., UDP PLR and TCP rebuffering are maximized at BP of 0% and 100%, respectively, for 10-second substreams. Therefore, the effects of UDP PLR and TCP rebuffering are effectively isolated via their corresponding BP values in order to study how TCP threshold changes affect FDSP streams. For each BP value, 20 different TCP threshold values, ranging from 5% to 100%, are evaluated.

VI. Results

A. Impact of TCP threshold changes on UDP PLR and TCP Rebuffering

Figures 6 and 7 show the effects of the TCP threshold changes on both test videos in a fully congested network with BP of 0% and 100%, respectively. These figures also include the results for pure UDP and pure TCP as a comparison. In a fully congested network scenario, the total TCP rebuffering time incurred by both test videos that are streamed using FDSP with 0% BP decreases as the TCP threshold increases. Conversely, the UDP PLR incurred by both test videos increases as the TCP threshold increases. For example, in the *Bears* video (Figure 6a), TCP thresholds of 10%, 15%, and 20% incur UDP PLRs of 3.8%, 7.4%, and 10.2% and TCP rebuffering times of 43 seconds, 9.8 second, and 1.98 seconds, respectively. Similarly, in the *Bunny* video (Figure 6b), TCP thresholds of 10%, 15%, and 20% incur UDP PLRs of 7.2%, 10.62%, and 12.93% and TCP rebuffering times of 20.21 seconds, 9.64 seconds, and 1.05 seconds, respectively.

In comparison to FDSP with 0% BP streaming, UDP PLR and TCP rebuffering incurred by FDSP with 100% BP in a fully congested network scenario are much more pronounced. For example, in the *Bears* video (Figure 7a), TCP thresholds of 10%, 15%, and 20% incur UDP PLRs of 2.1%, 1.7%, and 2.4% and TCP rebuffering times of 75.1 seconds, 38.95 seconds, and 14.47 seconds, respectively. Similarly, in the *Bunny* video

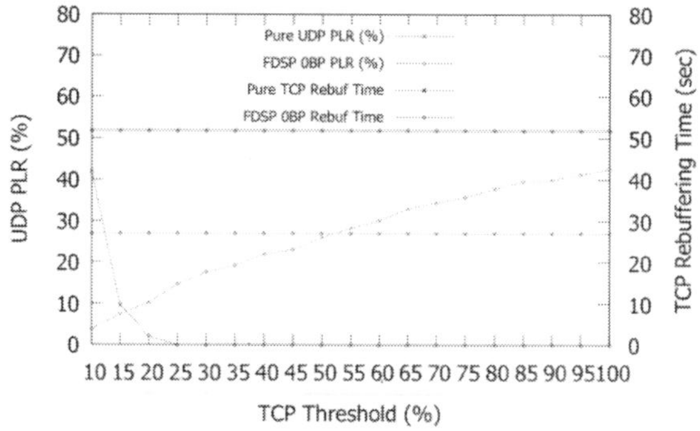

(a) *Bears* video.

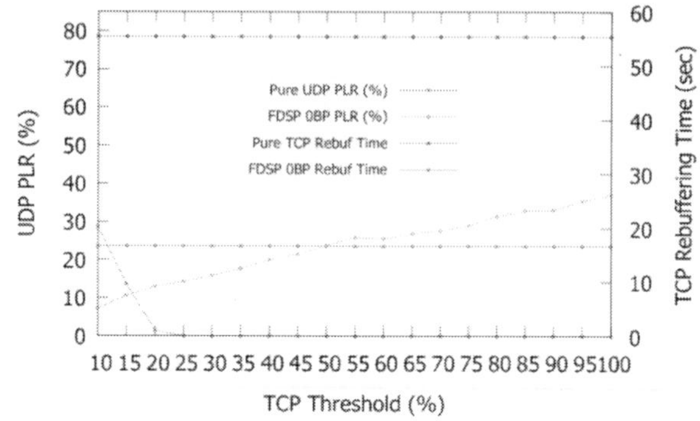

(b) *Bunny* video.

Figure 6. Impact of TCP threshold changes on UDP packet loss and TCP rebuffering in a fully congested network scenario with BP of 0%.

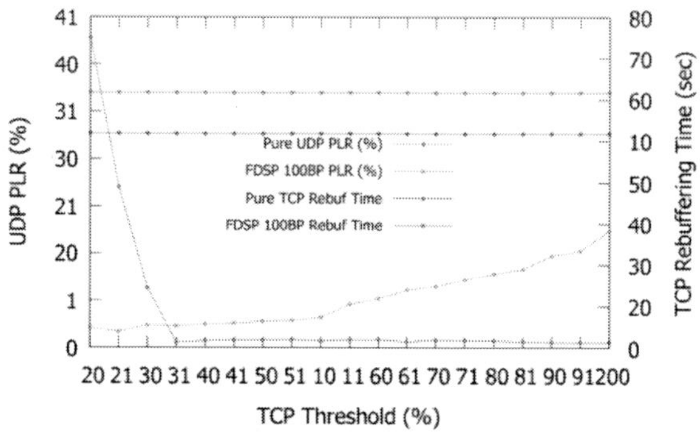

(a) *Bears* video.

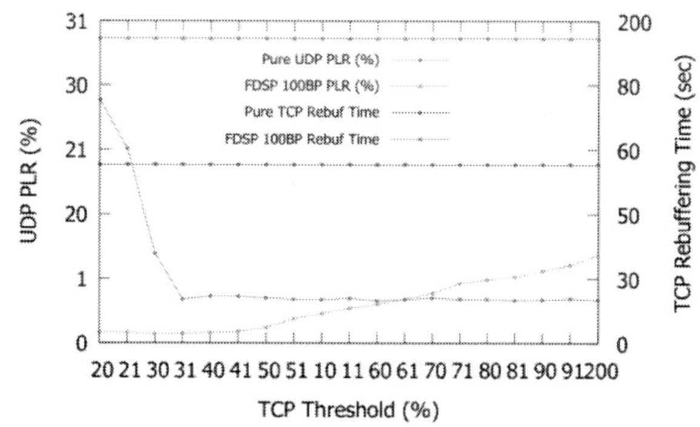

(b) *Bunny* video.

Figure 7. Impact of TCP threshold changes on UDP packet loss and TCP rebuffering in a fully congested network scenario with BP of 100%.

(Figure 7b), TCP thresholds of 10%, 15%, and 20% incur UDP PLRs of 0.8%, 0.81%, and 0.74% and TCP rebuffering times of 75.38 seconds, 60.34 seconds, and 27.63 seconds, respectively. These results show that having a large TCP threshold results in greater opportunities to insert new TCP packets into the IP queue reducing TCP rebuffering time. This, in turn, will cause UDP PLR to increase due to the increase in UDP packet delay resulting in late packets. On the other hand, a smaller TCP threshold results in fewer opportunities to insert TCP packets into the IP queue. This means that fewer TCP packets are sent through substream overlapping and, instead they are buffered in between substreams, thus increasing the total TCP rebuffering time.

The ideal TCP threshold region is the one that minimizes both UDP PLR and TCP rebuffering. For the *Bears* video using FDSP with 0% BP (Figure 6a), the ideal TCP threshold region lies between 15% to 30%. For the *Bunny* video using FDSP with 0% BP (Figure 6b), the ideal TCP threshold region lies between 15% to 25%. Similarly, for the *Bears* video using FDSP with 100% BP (Figure 7a), the ideal TCP threshold region lies between 25 to 50%. For the *Bunny* video with FDSP 100% BP (Figure 7b), the ideal TCP threshold region lies between 25 to 55%. The optimal threshold range for both videos increases as BP increases to accommodate the increase in the number of TCP packets. These results show that the ideal TCP threshold is not constant for all types of videos. Furthermore, the ideal TCP threshold region is affected by the changes in the BP parameter. Hence, the TCP threshold has to be adaptively adjusted for each substream to optimize the substream overlapping and improve FDSP's performance.

B. *Performance of Adaptive TCP Threshold*

Figures 8a and 8b show UDP PLR and TCP rebuffering time for the *Bunny* video streamed based on FDSP with Adaptive-BP using static and adaptive TCP threshold techniques, respectively. Note that the figures are also stacked with plots of the TCP threshold values. These results show that adaptively adjusting the TCP threshold for each substream reduces both UDP PLR and TCP rebuffering time as compared to having a static TCP threshold. For example, using the adaptive TCP threshold scheme incurs only one instance of rebuffering that lasts for 0.83 seconds as compared to the static TCP threshold scheme, which incurs three instances of rebuffering with 0.4 seconds, 1.02 seconds, and 0.12 seconds of rebuffering times. Similarly, the adaptive TCP threshold scheme incurs three instances of UDP packet loss with PLRs of 0.13, 0.04, and 0.08, where as the static TCP threshold scheme also incurs three instances of UDP packet loss but with slightly higher PLRs of 0.13, 0.06 and 0.1. Thus, adaptively adjusting the TCP threshold reduces the TCP rebuffering incurred by 50% and also slightly reduces UDP PLR for the *Bunny* video.

Figures 9a and 9b compare the visual quality of the static and adaptive TCP threshold schemes for frames 2918 and 3391, respectively. These figures clearly show that the adaptive TCP threshold scheme achieves better visual quality than the static TCP threshold scheme by reducing UDP PLR as well as TCP rebuffering time. For frame 2918, the adaptive TCP

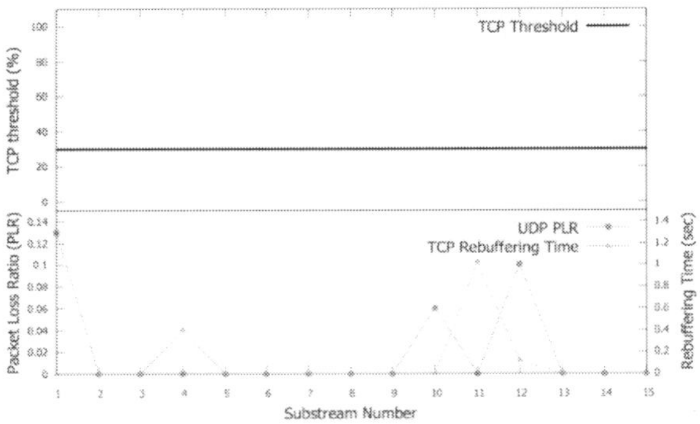

(a) Static TCP threshold results.

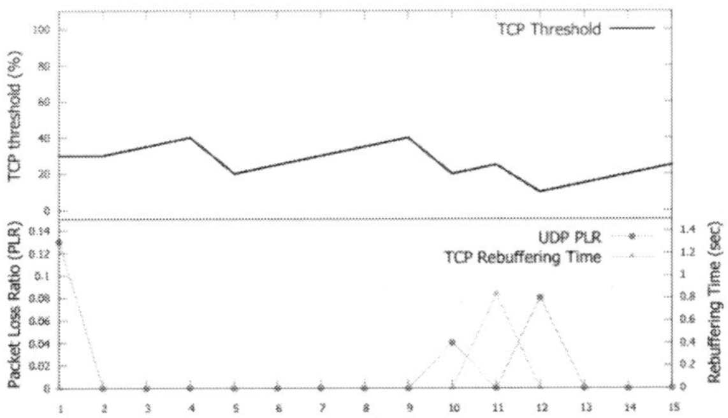

(b) Adaptive TCP threshold results.

Figure 8. Comparison of static vs. adaptive TCP threshold performance of *Bunny* video with Adaptive-BP.

threshold scheme incurs no packet loss resulting in perfect frame quality. For frame 3391, adaptively adjusting the TCP threshold results in slightly lower packet loss as compared to using a static TCP threshold value even though the difference in visual quality is marginal.

These results clearly show that the adaptive TCP threshold scheme reduces both UDP PLR and TCP rebuffering time as compared to the static TCP threshold scheme resulting in better end user QoE.

VII. Conclusion and Future Work

This paper studied the effects that different TCP threshold values have on video streaming in the context of Flexible Dual-TCP/UDP Streaming Protocol (FDSP). Our analysis showed that TCP threshold has a direct effect on both TCP rebuffering and UDP PLR. Our results showed that adaptively adjusting the TCP threshold using an AIMD algorithm reduces both packet loss ratio and rebuffering time, and leads to a better overall video streaming experience. As future work, we plan to study the impact of UDP packet loss and TCP rebuffering on end user Quality of Experience for FDSP streaming.

(a) Video quality comparison of Frame 2918.

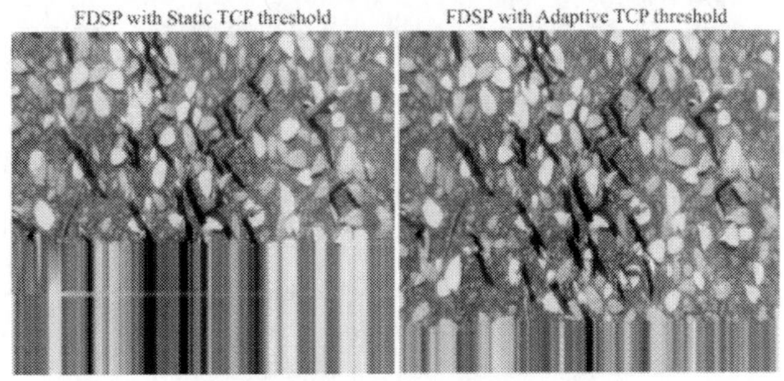

(b) Video quality comparison of Frame 3391.

Figure 9. Visual quality comparison of static vs. adaptive TCP threshold for frames 2918 and 3391.

References

[1] C. Yoon, T. Um, and H. Lee, "Classification of n-screen services and its standardization," in 14th International Conference on Advanced Communication Technology (ICACT), 2012, pp. 597–602.

[2] J. Zhao, B. Lee, T.-W. Lee, C.-G. Kim, J.-K. Shin, and J. Cho, "Flexible dual tcp/udp streaming for h.264 hd video over wlans," in Proc. of the 7th International Conference on Ubiquitous Information Management and Communication (ICUIMC '13). New York, NY, USA: ACM, 2013, pp. 34:1–34:9.

[3] M. Sinky, A. Dhamodaran, B. Lee, and J. Zhao, "Analysis of H.264 bitstream prioritization for dual TCP/UDP streaming of HD video over WLANs," in 2015 IEEE 12th Consumer Communications and Networking Conference (CCNC 2015), Las Vegas, USA, Jan. 2015, pp. 576–581.

[4] A. Dhamodaran, M. Sinky, and B. Lee, "Adaptive bitstream prioritization for dual tcp/udp streaming of hd video," in The Tenth International Conference on Systems and Networks Communications (ICSNC 2015), Barcelona, Spain, November 2015, pp. 35–40.

[5] S. Floyd and V. Jacobson, "Random early detection gateways for congestion avoidance," IEEE/ACM Transactions on Networking, vol. 1, no. 4, Aug 1993, pp. 397–413.

[6] W.-C. Feng, K. G. Shin, D. D. Kandlur, and D. Saha, "The blue active queue management algorithms," IEEE/ACM Transactions on Networking, vol. 10, no. 4, Aug 2002, pp. 513–528.

[7] K. Xu, M.Gerla, L. Qi, and Y. Shu, "Enhancing tcp fairness in ad hoc wireless networks using neighborhood red," in Proceedings of MOBICOM, San Diego, CA USA, sept 2003, pp. 16–28.

[8] J. Chen and V. C. M. Leung, "Applying active queue management to link layer buffers for real-time traffic over third generation wireless networks," in Wireless Communications and Networking, 2003. WCNC 2003. 2003 IEEE, vol. 3, March 2003, pp. 1657–1662 vol.3.

[9] M.-L. Shy, S.-C. Chen, and C. Ranasingha, "Router active queue management for both multimedia and best-effort traffic flows," in Multimedia and Expo, 2004. ICME '04. 2004 IEEE International Conference on, vol. 1, June 2004, pp. 451–454 Vol.1.

[10] Y.-K. Wang, R. Even, T. Kristensen, and R. Jesup, "RTP Payload Format for H.264 Video," RFC 6184 (Proposed Standard), Internet Engineering Task Force, May 2011.

[11] R. Pantos and W. May, "HTTP Live Streaming," Apr. 2014, iETF Draft, URL: https://developer.apple.com/streaming/ [Accessed: 2017-03-03].

[12] C. Lee, M. Kim, S. Hyun, S. Lee, B. Lee, and K. Lee, "OEFMON: An open evaluation framework for multimedia over networks," Communications Magazine, IEEE, vol. 49, no. 9, Sep. 2011, pp. 153–161.

[13] QualNet 7.3 User's Guide, Scalable Network Technologies, Inc., 2016.

[14] M. Sinky, A. Dhamodaran, B. Lee, and J. Zhao, "Analysis of H.264 Bitstream Prioritization for Dual TCP/UDP Streaming of HD Video Over WLANs," in IEEE 12th Consumer Communications and Networking Conference (CCNC 2015), Las Vegas, USA, Jan. 2015, pp. 576–581.

Improving Feature Extraction Accuracy for Skin Analysis

Woogeol Kim, Hyungjoon Kim, Eenjun Hwang
School of Electrical Engineering
Korea University
Anam-Dong, Seongbuk-Gu, Seoul, Republic of Korea
E-mail: {woogulzzang, hyungjun89, ehwang04}@korea.ac.kr

Abstract— **In this paper, we revise our skin feature extraction method based on cell segmentation to improve the accuracy and efficiency of skin feature analysis. Accurate skin feature extraction is critical for the evaluation of skin conditions. In order to improve the accuracy of analyzing skin features, we use the contrast limited adaptive histogram equalization (CLAHE) method for contrast enhancement. Also, we use the extended-minima transform in order to enhance the depth of wrinkles on the skin. After conducting watershed transform for cell segmentation, we utilize the labeled information of skin cells to extract skin features. We consider two types of skin features that are important for estimating the skin age of users. They are cell features and wrinkle features. To evaluate the performance of our revised method, we collected diverse images using two types of microscopy cameras and estimated the skin age based on their skin features. Through various experiments, we show that our revised method achieves 11% increase in analysis accuracy and 53% decrease in feature extraction time compared to our previous work.**

Keywords- Skin analysis; Feature extraction; Wrinkle feature; Contrast stretching; Microscopy image.

I. INTRODUCTION

Various factors, such as exposure to sunlight or pollution, smoking and excessive drinking are known to accelerate the normal skin aging process and eventually lead to premature skin aging. Usually, the degree of skin aging has been evaluated by dermatologists based on their personal experience or knowledge. This is because there is no standard method for quantitative and objective evaluation. If such method was available, then users would get consistent and quantitative information about their skin condition, and hence perform suitable treatment for their skin more effectively and conveniently.

In our previous work, we proposed a scheme for skin texture aging trend analysis based on diverse skin texture features. To extract such features, we cropped microscopy skin image, carried out histogram equalization, removed noise and then binarized the image using the Otsu threshold. After that, we segmented the skin texture into cells by using the watershed algorithm and calculated their features [1][2].

In this paper, we modify some of the preprocessing steps and segmentation method in the previous work to improve feature extraction accuracy and reduce processing time. Figure 1 shows the overall steps to do that, which consist of preprocessing, cell segmentation and feature extraction. In the preprocessing, the original image is cropped to reduce the effect of vignetting. Then, contrast stretching is applied in order to enhance the intensity between skin and wrinkle. Denoising filters are applied to the image. In the cell segmentation, extended-minima transform and watershed algorithm are used for cell-based segmentation. Each cell cluster is labeled, and the labeled information is utilized for calculating skin features. We extract five features from the skin image to analyze the skin condition. In Figure 1, modified modules are represented by double line rectangles.

The remainder of this paper is organized as follows. In Section 2, we introduce several related works for skin analysis. Detailed techniques for skin segmentation method are described in Section 3 and skin feature extraction method is described in Section 4. We explain our experiment and conclude this paper in Section 5.

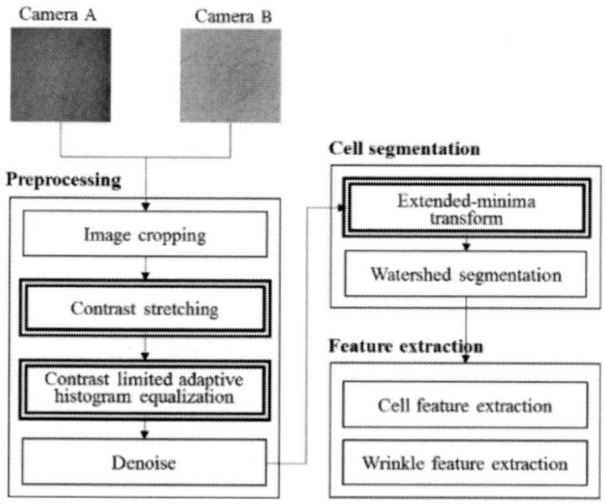

Figure 1. Overall scheme of skin feature extraction

II. RELATED WORKS

So far, medical analysis and diagnosis based on biometric images have been performed in the various domains. Skin analysis is one of the most popular and interesting tasks, since skin is the outermost part of the human body. Various methods have been proposed for evaluating skin condition quantitatively using skin images.

As an effort to detect skin wrinkles, H. Tanaka et al. applied a cross-binarization method to digital skin image to get its binary image, and then, the short straight line matching method to detect wrinkles from the binary image and measure their length [3]. More specifically, for each base line in the cross-binarized image, if more than 70% of its pixels are marked black, then the line is considered a wrinkle. After that, they continue from the end of current base line to create a new base line. This repeats until the end of the wrinkle or the end of the image is reached. J. Ute et al. measured the topography of skin surface using an optical 3D device and showed that there is a significant dependency between skin surface topography and the age [4]. On the other hand, G. O. Cula et al. developed the automatic facial wrinkles detection algorithm based on estimating the orientation and frequency of the elongated spatial feature, captured via digital image filtering [5]. Recently Yow. Ai Ping et al. proposed the ASHIMA system framework and showed how to process HD-OCT (High-Definition Optical Coherence Tomography) skin images automatically to measure the epidermal thickness and skin surface topography [6].

III. Skin Segmentation Method

A. Preprocessing

Direct image processing on microscope image or captured image might face several problems if the image is in RGB (Red-Green-Blue) form. Usually, dealing with RGB image shows less accuracy than dealing with gray image. Other typical factors to decrease the accuracy are vignetting effect and noises. To avoid these problems, original images need to be converted into binary images through preprocessing. In this work, pre-processing consists of three steps. First, the original image is cropped to reduce the effect of vignetting. Second, contrast stretching [7] is applied to make brightness difference between skin and wrinkle bigger. Then, adaptive histogram equalization is applied to the image.

1) Cropping

Due to the limitations of the camera and the interference of the light source, captured images may have noise and vignetting. Vignetting is a phenomenon where the outer edges of the images are dark due to the reduction of light at the periphery of camera lens, and hence causing the captured images to have different color histogram distributions. In order to avoid the problem, we cropped 300 by 300 pixels in the center of the image, which has the concentrated luminous source of the image.

2) Contrast stretching

Correct detection of skin wrinkles is critical in the skin analysis and its accuracy can be improved by clearly separating skin and wrinkle pixels in the image. However, original images often lack sufficient contrast due to diverse variations in the environment such as light source and shooting area. Insufficient contrast could make certain areas in the image have similar contrast even though they must be distinguished. This problem can be moderated by contrast stretching. Contrast stretching expands the dynamic range of the intensity levels so that it spans the color distance between skin and wrinkle. Figure 2 illustrates the effect of contrast stretching.

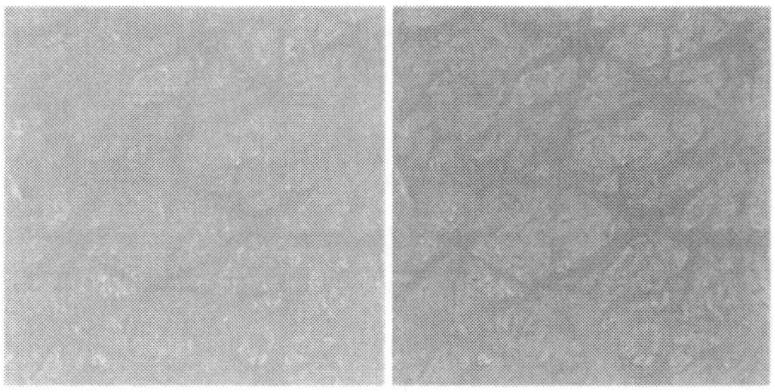

(a) Original image (b) After contrast stretching

Figure 2. Example of contrast stretching

In the figure, we can see that the intensity of the scalp pixels is reduced and the color distinction between skin and winkle becomes more prominent.

3) Contrast limited adaptive histogram equalization

Skin wrinkles can be detected using the watershed algorithm [8]. However, we observed that some of the wrinkles were missing during the detection due to the lack of contrast. Hence, before we use the watershed algorithm to the skin image, we apply the contrast limited adaptive histogram equalization (CLAHE) method to the image to enhance the intensity of winkles [9]. Histogram equalization is a gray scale transformation used for contrast enhancement. The aim is to get an image with uniformly distributed intensity levels over the whole intensity scale. The result of histogram equalization might be worse compared to the original image since the histogram of the resulting image becomes approximately flat. For instance, when high peaks in the histogram are caused by an uninteresting area, histogram equalization results in enhanced visibility of unwanted image area. This means that the local contrast requirement is not satisfied, and as a result, minor contrast differences are entirely ignored when the number of pixels falling in a particular gray range is relatively small.

An adaptive method to avoid this drawback is block-based processing of histogram equalization [10]. In this method, an image is divided into sub-images or blocks, and histogram equalization is performed on each sub-images or blocks. Then, blocking artifacts among neighboring blocks are minimized by filtering or bilinear interpolation.

The CLAHE method uses a clip limit to overcome the noise problem. That is, the amplification is limited by clipping the histogram at a predefined value before computing the Cumulative Distribution Function (CDF). The value at which the histogram is clipped, the so-called clip limit, depends on the normalization of the histogram and thereby on the size of the neighborhood region. The redistribution will push some bins over the clip limit again, resulting in an effective clip limit that is larger than the prescribed limit and the exact value of which depends on the image.

In our work, we need to remove hairs from the gray image. Hairs can be mistaken for wrinkles and hence they are the most critical noise in the wrinkle detection. Skin hairs are easily removed by a simple threshold filter.

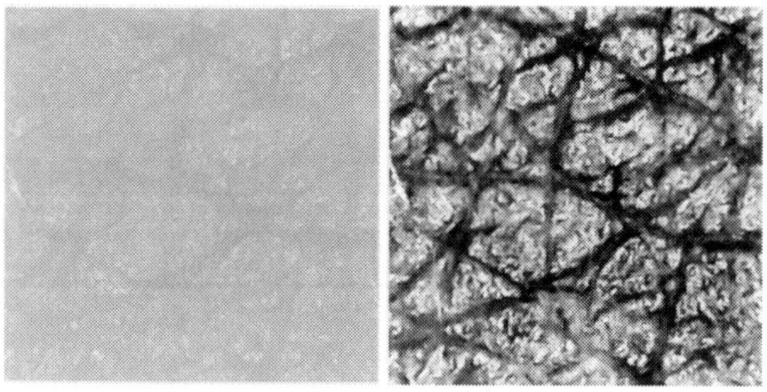

(a) After hair removal (b) After CLAHE

Figure 3. Example of CLAHE

Figures 3 (a) and (b) show images after hair removal and after CLAHE method, respectively.

B. Segmentation processing

In this section, we describe how to segment a skin image into wrinkle cells using the extended-minima transform [11] and watershed transform. Watershed transform is one of the most widely used image segmentation techniques in image processing and we use it for segmentation into wrinkle cells. Especially, we perform the extended-minima transform before the watershed transform in order to increase the accuracy of finding wrinkle cells.

1) Extended-minima transform

Even though watershed transform is widely used for image segmentation, it often suffers from the over-segmentation problem since regional minima or ultimate eroded points are employed for segmenting cells directly. One of the main factors that determines the accuracy of segmenting skin image by wrinkle cells is how much the minima points are extended. In this paper, we revise the extended-minima transform, which is the regional minima of the H-minima transform. Regional minima are connected components of pixels with a constant intensity value, and whose external boundary pixels have higher value.

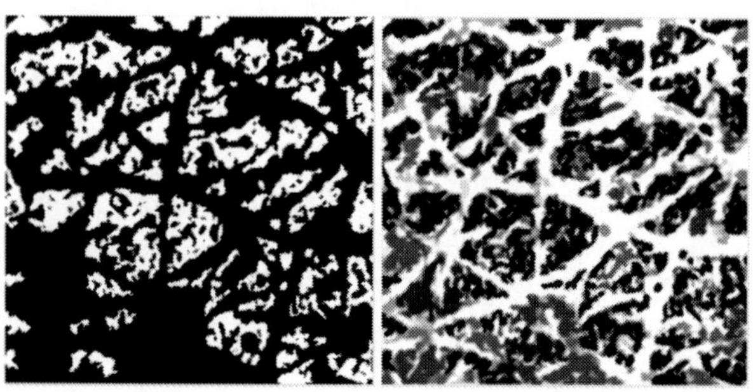

(a) Extended-minima extraction (b) Imposed minima image

Figure 4. Example of extended-minima transform

In other words, the result of h-minimum operator is linked to the depth of the minima. In a skin image, wrinkle cells consist of some minima and maxima. Minima correspond to parts of low depth points and maxima correspond to high depth points. Therefore, using the extended-minima transform, we can increase the depth between wrinkle cell clusters. It can help the watershed transform to cluster the wrinkle cells. Figure 4 shows an example of the extended-minima transform. First, we extract minima from an image and extend the depth of the points. The extended minima are shown in Figure 4 (a). Figure 4 (b) shows the result after imposing the extended minima to original gray scale image.

2) Watershed segmentation

Image segmentation is a computer analysis of image objects to decide which pixel of the image belongs to which object. Basically, this is the process of separating objects from background, as well as from each other. Watershed transform is a powerful and well-known tool for performing image segmentation.

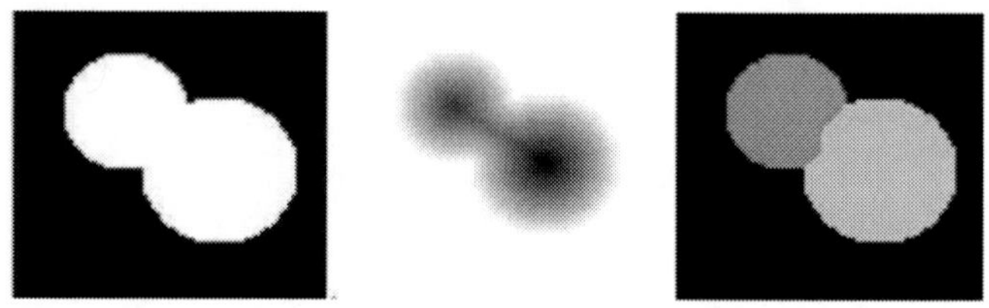

(a) Overlapping objects (b) Distances (c) Separated objects

Figure 5. Segmentation using watershed transform

Figure 5 shows how to segment two overlapping circles using the watershed transform. To segment them, an image distance to the background is computed. The maxima of the distance (i.e., the minima of the opposite of the distance) are chosen as markers, and the flooding of basins from such markers separates the two circles along a watershed line. We adapt these steps to our skin image, so that pixels of each wrinkle cell are clustered.

3) Cell labelling

Wrinkle cell labelling can be easily done by applying the watershed transform to the skin image.

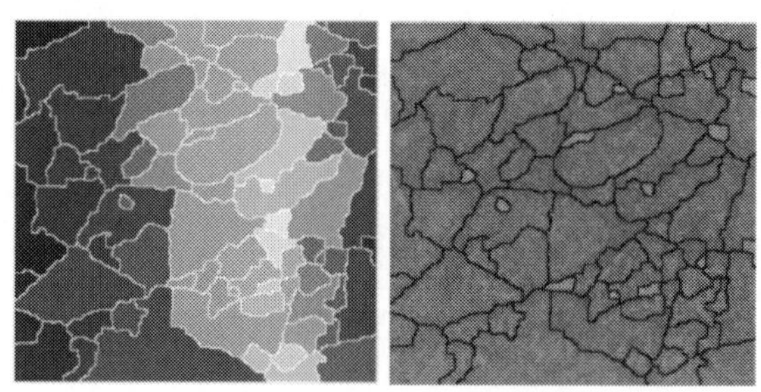

(a) Labeled image (b) Filtered image with valid cells

Figure 6. Labelling process

From the result of watershed transform, we can get a set of wrinkle cells. Each cell contains the positions of pixels in the cell which belong to same cluster. Sometimes, the segmentation result contains unexpected cells with very small size, which are usually noise or moles. Since they are not the regular wrinkle cell, they should be removed. In Figure 6 (a), we can see an example of labelling wrinkle cells. Each cell is labeled using a different color. Figure 6 (b) shows the noise cells that have to be removed. The brown cells need to be removed by merging into a neighboring cell. Currently, we decide the size of noise cells empirically.

IV. Skin Feature Extraction

A. Defining skin features

We have developed algorithms for extracting various features from microscopy images. Our feature extraction method is based on the labeled image described previously. Before defining these features, we made the assumptions presented in Table 1 based on common knowledge of skin [1].

TABLE 1. ASSUMPTIONS BASED ON COMMON KNOWLEDGE OF SKIN

1. Total wrinkle length decreases with age.
2. Wrinkle width increases with age.
3. Wrinkle depth increases with age.
4. Wrinkle cell area increases with age.
5. The number of cells decreases with age.
6. Diameter ratio of inscribed circle and circumscribed circle of a cell decreases with age.
7. Total length of lines connecting cross points of a cell increases with age.

In this paper, we define five features which are critical in the evaluation of aging skin. The five features are cell count, average cell area, average cell gradient, total wrinkle length, and average wrinkle width. Cell count indicates how many cell clusters are in the skin image. Average cell area indicates the average area of cell clusters in the skin image. Every wrinkle cell has its own shape, and the distortion of the shape is relevant to the degree of skin aging. So, it is useful to know how much a skin cell is distorted for skin aging estimation. For this purpose, we consider the slope of principal horizontal axis as distortion of a cell.

The wrinkle itself is also very important clue for estimating the degree of skin aging. We use two wrinkle features in this work; the total wrinkle length and the average wrinkle width.

B. Calculating skin features

In this section, we describe how to calculate those five features. We first estimate the number of cells by counting the number of labeled cells while excluding cells with a size under some threshold.

The average cell area is quite simple to calculate. We can get this feature by just dividing the total number of pixels in the labeled cells by the number of cells which we just described.

Total wrinkle length can be calculated using the line sieving method. This method first counts the pixels on the horizontal and vertical texture lines. It then counts the pixels along the diagonal line, and estimates the actual wrinkle length considering its slope. In the case of single pixel islands on the image, we simply count these islands and add the number to the total length.

We can get wrinkle width using Principal Component Analysis (PCA) analysis [12]. PCA algorithm is a method of calculating Eigen value and Eigen vector by using all data's covariance and average. The result of segmented line (extracted skeleton) is a set of 1×1 points. These pixels have specific direction, thus we can calculate each point's direction. In order to calculate the direction, we used PCA algorithm. When all of points on the skeleton's direction are calculated, we can get a perpendicular line for each point. Figure 7 shows how to calculate average wrinkle thickness. In the figure, each white '×' is skeleton point, and the line passing the skeleton point is a normal line. The red circles indicate the intersection of line and wrinkle contour. The length between these two intersection points is the wrinkle thickness at that point.

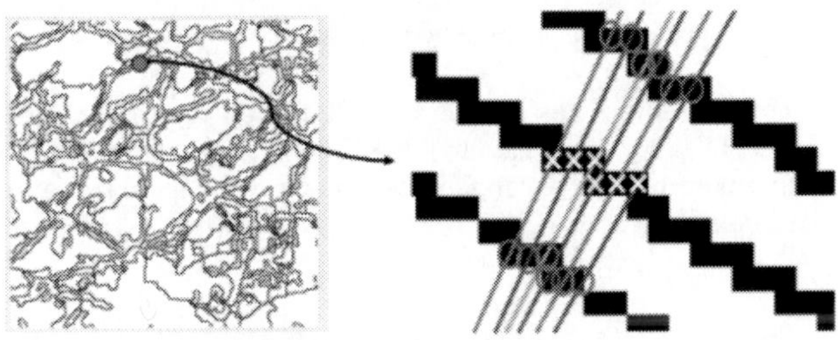

Figure 7. Calculating wrinkle width

Cell gradient is calculated for estimating how irregular a cell is due to skin aging. In order to measure the cell gradient, we used the regionprops function [13] which calculates a set of features for each labeled region. One of the major features in the result of regionprops is a scalar angle value for each labeled region.

Figure 8. Example of calculating angle

It can be obtained by calculating the angle between the x-axis and the major axis of the ellipse that has the same second-moment as the region. Figure 8 illustrates how to calculate the angle.

V. EXPERIMENTS

In order to evaluate the performance of our revised scheme, we performed several experiments based on the Matlab R2016a. The test images were prepared using microscopy cameras compatible with smartphone. We constructed a dataset of skin images using two cameras shown in Figure 9.

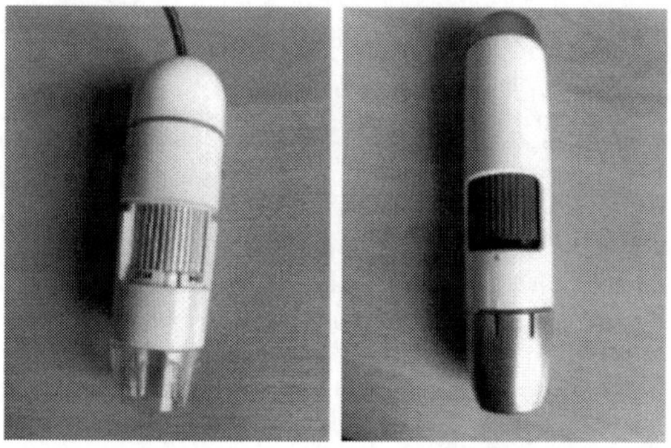

(a) Camera A (b) Camera B

Figure 9. Microscopy cameras compatible with smartphone

One camera has a scale of 50X to 500X, and the other camera has a scale of 25X to 400X. We got approximately 300 skin images from face and 50 skin images from hand using the two cameras.

1) Detection accuracy

Figure 10 depicts the segmentation result after watershed transform. The pixels on the segmented lines are matched to the pixels on the wrinkles in the binarized image. The binarized image can be obtained using the Otsu's method [14]. A skin image is composed of multiple wrinkle cells with different shape and size.

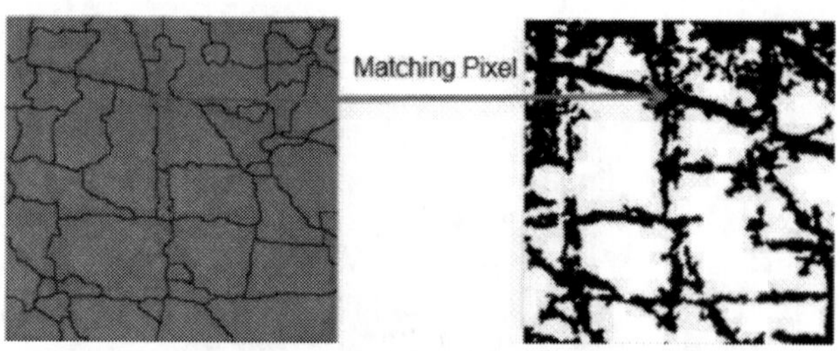

Figure 10. Comparison of cell segmentation and binarized image

We can compute the accuracy of wrinkle cell detection by the matching rate of segmented pixels as shown in Eq. (1). Basically, the equation counts how many matched pixels exist on both images, and then they are divided by the total number of pixels on the cell contour lines in Figure 10.

$$Accuracy = \frac{Cell\_contour\_pixels \cap Wrinkle\_pixels}{Cell\_contour\_pixels} \times 100 \quad (1)$$

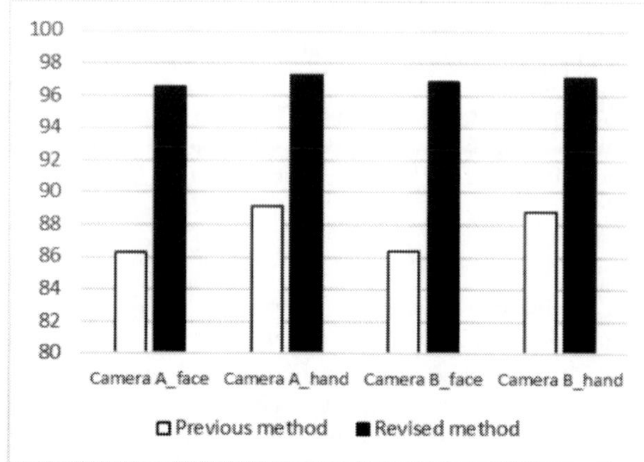

Figure 11. Comparison of detection accuracy

Figure 11 depicts the result. Accuracies of the previous method are under 90 percent. On the other hand, we can see that accuracies of our revised method are over 95 percent. Overall, our revised method achieved about 10 percent improvement over the previous method for each dataset.

B. Execution time

Next, we compared the execution time of our previous method and revised method for cell detection. Here, the execution time includes all the steps for the preprocessing and segmentation. In the case of feature extraction, both methods show little difference.

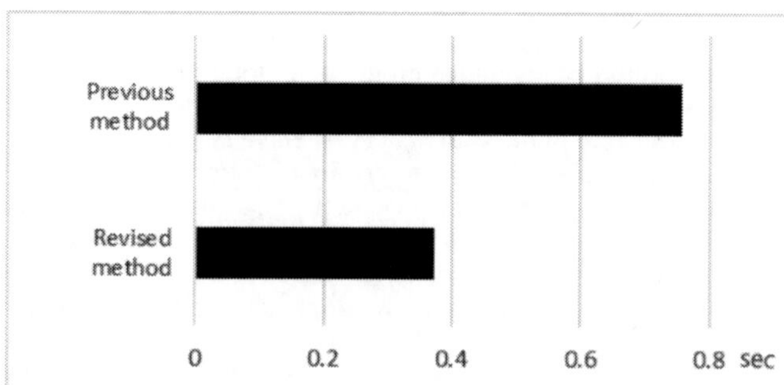

Figure 12. Comparison of excution time

Figure 12 compares the execution time of previous method and revised method taken for analyzing one skin image. As shown in the figure, the execution time of our revised method was about half that of the previous method.

VI. Conclusion

In this paper, we revised our previous scheme for skin feature extraction to improve accuracy and reduce cell detection time. To improve the accuracy of skin cell detection, we used the contrast stretching and CLAHE filter for contrast enhancement, and the extend-minima transform to the skin image for cell segmentation. We performed several experiments to evaluate the accuracy and execution time of our revised method.

Consequently, our revised method improves the accuracy of cell detection by about 10 percent for all the image data set. Also, the total execution time for cell detection was reduced by half compared to our previous work.

Acknowledgement

This work was supported by Institute for Information & communications Technology Promotion (IITP) grant funded by the Korea government (MSIP) (No. R0190-16-2012, High Performance Big Data Analytics Platform Performance Acceleration Technologies Development).

References

[1] Y. H. Choi, D. Kim, E. Hwang, and B. Kim, "Skin texture aging trend analysis using dermoscopy images," Skin Research and Technology, vol. 20, no. 4, pp. 486-497, 2014.

[2] Y.-H. Choi, Y.-S. Tak, S. Rho, and E. Hwang, "Skin feature extraction and processing model for statistical skin age estimation," Multimedia tools and applications, vol. 64, no. 2, pp. 227-247, 2013.

[3] H. Tanaka et al., "Quantitative evaluation of elderly skin based on digital image analysis," Skin research and technology, vol. 14, no. 2, pp. 192-200, 2008.

[4] U. Jacobi et al., "In vivo determination of skin surface topography using an optical 3D device," Skin Research and Technology, vol. 10, no. 4, pp. 207-214, 2004.

[5] G. O. Cula, P. R. Bargo, A. Nkengne, and N. Kollias, "Assessing facial wrinkles: automatic detection and quantification," Skin Research and Technology, vol. 19, no. 1, pp. e243-e251, 2013.

[6] A. P. Yow et al., "Automated in vivo 3D high-definition optical coherence tomography skin analysis system," in Engineering in Medicine and Biology Society (EMBC), 2016 IEEE 38th Annual International Conference of the, pp. 3895-3898, 2016

[7] R. C. Gonzalez and R. E. Woods, "Digital Image Processing," Addison-Wesley, Third edition, 2008.

[8] L. J. Belaid and W. Mourou, "Image segmentation: a watershed transformation algorithm," Image Analysis & Stereology, vol. 28, no. 2, pp. 93-102, 2011.

[9] S. M. Pizer, R. E. Johnston, J. P. Ericksen, B. C. Yankaskas, and K. E. Muller, "Contrast-limited adaptive histogram equalization: speed and effectiveness," in Visualization in Biomedical Computing, 1990., Proceedings of the First Conference on, pp. 337-345, 1990.

[10] Y. C. Hum, K. W. Lai, and M. I. Mohamad Salim, "Multiobjectives bihistogram equalization for image contrast enhancement," Complexity, vol. 20, no. 2, pp. 22-36, 2014.

[11] P. Soille, Morphological image analysis: principles and applications. Springer Science & Business Media, 2013.

[12] S. Wold, K. Esbensen, and P. Geladi, "Principal component analysis," Chemometrics and intelligent laboratory systems, vol. 2, no. 1-3, pp. 37-52, 1987.

[13] A. Othmani, N. Lomenie, A. Piboule, C. Stolz, and L. F. C. L. Y. Voon, "Region-based segmentation on depth images from a 3D reference surface for tree species recognition," pp. 3399-3402, 2013.

[14] N. Otsu, "A threshold selection method from gray-level histograms," Automatica, vol. 11, no. 285-296, pp. 23-27, 1975.

A Data Model for Integrating Data Management and Data Mining in Social Big Data

Hiroshi Ishikawa
Faculty of System Design
Tokyo Metropolitan University
Tokyo, Japan
e-mail: ishikawa-hiroshi@tmu.ac.jp

Richard Chbeir
LIUPPA Lab.
University of Pau and Adour Countries
Anglet, France
e-mail: richard.chbeir@univ-pau.fr

***Abstract*—We propose an abstract data model for integrating data management and data mining necessary for describing social big data applications by using mathematical concepts of families, collections of sets. Our model facilitates reproducibility and accountability required for social big data researches and developments. We have partially validated our proposal by adapting our model to real case studies.**

Keywords- social data; big data; data model; data management; data mining.

I. INTRODUCTION

A. Social Big Data

In the present age, large amounts of data are produced continuously in science, on the internet, and in physical systems. Such phenomena are collectively called data deluge. According to some researches carried by International Data Corporation, or IDC [4][5] for short, the size of data which are generated and reproduced all over the world every year is estimated to be 161 Exa bytes. The total amount of data produced in 2011 exceeded 10 or more times the storage capacity of the storage media available in that year. Experts in scientific and engineering fields produce a large amount of data by observing and analyzing the target phenomena. Even ordinary people voluntarily post a vast amount of data via various social media on the internet. Furthermore, people unconsciously produce data via various actions detected by physical systems, such as sensors and Global Positioning System, or GPS for short, in the real world. It is expected that such data can generate various values. In the above-mentioned research report of IDC, data produced in science, the internet, and in physical systems are collectively called big data. The features of big data can be summarized as follows:

- The quantity (Volume) of data is extraordinary, as the name denotes.
- The kinds (Variety) of data have expanded into unstructured texts, semi-structured data, such as XML, and graphs (i.e., networks).
- As is often the case with Twitter and sensor data streams, the speed (Velocity) at which data are generated is very high.

Therefore, big data is often characterized as V^3 by taking the initial letters of these three terms Volume, Variety, and Velocity. Big data are expected to create not only knowledge in science but also derive values in various commercial ventures. "Volume" and "velocity" require more computing power than ever before. "Variety" implies that big data appear in a wide variety of applications and then data have a wide variety of structures. Further, big data inherently contain "vagueness," such as inconsistency and deficiency. Such vagueness must be resolved in order to obtain quality analysis results. Moreover, a recent survey done in Japan has made it clear that a lot of users have "vague" concerns as to the securities and mechanisms of big data applications [7]. In other words, service providers deploying big data have accountability for explaining to generic users among stake holders how relevant big data are used. The resolution of such concerns is one of the keys to successful diffusion of big data applications. In this sense, V^4 should be used to characterize big data, instead of V^3. Big data typically include IoT data collected by a variety of networked sensors and mobile gadgets, social data posted at social media sites, such as Twitter and Flickr, and open data published for everyone to access.

In big data applications, especially, cases where two or more data sources including at least one social data source are involved, are more interesting from a viewpoint of usefulness to businesses [7]. If more than one data source can be analyzed by relating them to each other, and by paying attention to the interactions between them, it may be possible to understand what cannot be understood, by analysis of only either of them. For example, even if only sales data are deeply analyzed, reasons for a sudden increase in sales, that is, what has made customers purchase more products suddenly, cannot be known. By analysis of only social data, it is impossible to know how much they contributed to sales, if any. However, if both sales data and social data can be analyzed by relating them to each other, it is possible to discover why items have begun to sell suddenly, and to predict how much they will sell in the future, based on the results. In a word, such integrated analysis is expected to produce bigger values than otherwise. We would like to call such an analytic methodology Social Big Data, or SBD for short.

Even if only one social data source, such as Twitter articles and Flickr images is available and if such articles and images have geo-tags (i.e., location information), as well, social big data mining is useful. That is, by collecting those articles and images based on conditions specified with respect to locations and time intervals and counting them for each grid (i.e., unit location), probabilities that users post such data at the locations can be basically computed. By using such probabilities, human activities can be analyzed, such as probabilities of foreigners staying at specific spots or those moving from one spot to another. The results will be applied to tourism and marketing.

Furthermore, a certain level of location can be

represented as a collection of lower levels of locations. Similarly, a time interval can be divided into a collection of shorter time intervals. As such, locations and time have hierarchical structures inherently.

B. Reproducibility

In general, the validity of published results of scientific researches has recently been judged based on not only traditional peer reviews but also reproducibility [15]. Reproducibility means that the same results with reported ones can be obtained by independent researchers. Success of reproduction hinges on detailed descriptions of methods and procedures, as well as data which have led to the published results.

At an extreme end of reproducibility spectrum [1] [10] is repeatability. Repeatability in computer science means that independent researchers can obtain exactly the same results by using the same data and the same codes that the reporters used. However, it is not always possible to use the same data and codes due to several reasons, such as limited space for publishing research results and lack or delayed spread of related standardization. Rex [11] is among ambitious attempts to facilitate repeatability. Rather, reproduction is done in order to make certain the essence of the experiments.

All this is true of SBD researches and developments. Reproducibility in researches and developments of SBD applications requires at least the following requirements.

- Description of SBD applications must be as independent from individual programming languages and frameworks as possible. Generally speaking, it is not always possible for all researchers to access the same data and tools that the authors have used. In other words, by enabling the mapping from description of applications by an abstract *SBD model* proposed in this paper to individual tools available for the other researchers, reproducibility can be realized even if the tools are not the same with the original one. Therefore, application description (i.e., at conceptual level) must be more abstract than codes (i.e., at logical level). It is expected that the amount of description is reduced by this. The descriptions must be even as independent from programing models, such as parallel computing as possible. This *SBD model* approach can lead to increase of accountability of SDB applications to stake holders including generic users.
- Both data management and data mining must be described in an integrated manner. In SBD applications, a lot of time is spent on development and execution of data management including preprocessing and postprocessing in addition to data mining. Further, data management and data mining cannot be always separated in a crisp manner. Rather, most SBD applications require hybrid processes mixed with data management and data mining. Later, such examples will be described in case studies.

This paper, which is rather positional, introduces an integrated data model for describing SBD applications and describes applications using the model as case studies. The reference architecture for SBD is illustrated in Figure 1.

C. Relation with Other Work

To our knowledge, there are no abstract data models that can handle data management and data mining. Indeed, there exist a lot of programming languages and frameworks that can host data management and data mining, such as Spark [17] and MLI [14]. However, such language interfaces have different levels of abstraction from those of our data model proposed in this paper. Rather, those are among candidate targets to which our abstract model can be translated. Section II introduces a data model for SBD and Section III explains case studies for SBD model.

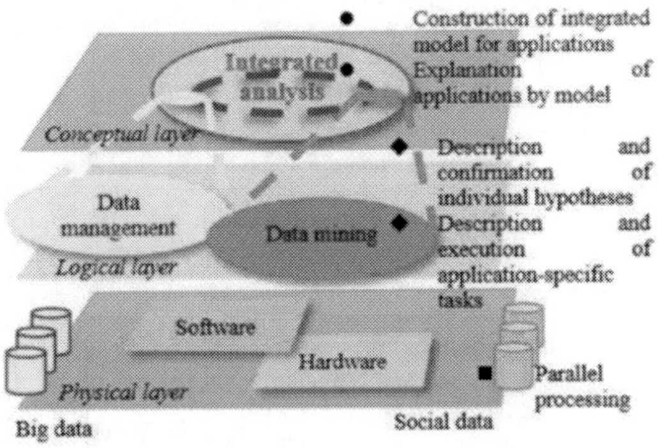

Figure 1. The reference architecture for social big data.

II. DATA MODEL FOR SBD

A. Overview

We propose an abstract data model as an approach to reinforcing both reproducibility and accountability of SBD. Our SBD model aims to satisfy the following requirements:

- Enable to describe data management and data mining in an integrated fashion or seamlessly.
- Be independent enough from existing programming languages and frameworks and easy enough to translate into executable programming languages, as well.

We extend relational model [12] prevalent in data management fields as our approach to SBD model. The Relational model is based on a mathematical concept of a *set*. On the other hand, data mining includes clustering, classification, and association rules [7]. Clustering partitions a given set of data into a collection of sets, each of which has elements similar to each other. Classification divides a given set of data into pre-scribed categories, that is, a collection of sets by using supervised learning. Association rule mining discovers a collection of frequent itemsets collocating in transactional data. Unlike relational models, all these data mining techniques handle a *collection of sets* instead of a set. In other words, we must bridge gaps between data management and data mining with respect to levels of granularity. At the same time, we would like to adopt abstractness comparable to those that relational models [12] and object models [6] have because such abstractness is widely prevalent.

B. Data Structure

Our SBD model uses a mathematical concept of a *family* [13], a collection of sets, as a basis for data structures. Family is an apparatus for bridging the gaps between data management operations and data analysis operations.

Basically, our database is a *Family*. A Family is divided into *Indexed family* and *Non-Indexed family*. A Non-Indexed family is a collection of sets or a collection of Non-Indexed families. In other words, a Non-indexed family can constitute a hierarchy of sets.

- {*Set*} is a Non-Indexed family with *Set* as its element.
- {Set_i} is an Indexed family with Set_i as its *i-th* element. Here *i: Index* is called *indexing set* and *i* is an element of Index. To be more exact, Index is either a set or an Indexed-family. In other words, Index itself can also be nested like Non-Indexed family.
- *Set* is {<*time space object*>}.
- Set_i is {<*time space object*>}$_i$. Here, *object* is an identifier to arbitrary identifiable user-provided data, e.g., record, object, and multimedia data appearing in social big data. *Time* and *space* are universal keys across multiple sources of social big data.

Please note that the following concepts are interchangeably used in this paper.

- Singleton family ⇔ set
- Singleton set ⇔ element

As described later in Section III, we can often observe that SBD applications contain families, as well as sets because such applications involve both data mining and data management. Please note that family is also suitable for representing hierarchical structures inherent in time and locations associated with social big data.

If operations constructing a family out of a collection of sets and those deconstructing a family into a collection of sets are provided in addition to both family-dedicated and set-dedicated operations, SBD applications will be described in an integrated fashion by our proposed model.

C. SBD Operations

SBD model constitutes an algebra with respect to Family as follows.

SBD is consisted of Family data management operations and Family data mining operations. Further, Family data management operations are divided into Intra Family operations and Inter Family operations.

1) *Intra Family Data Management Operations*

a) Intra Indexed Intersect (*i:Index Db p(i)*) returns a singleton family (i.e., set) intersecting sets which satisfy *p(i)*. Database *Db* is a Family, which will not be mentioned hereafter.

b) Intra Indexed Union *(i:Index Db p(i))* returns a singleton family union-ing sets which satisfy *p(i)*.

c) Intra Indexed Difference (*i:Index Db p(i)*) returns a singleton family, that is, the first set satisfying *p(i)* minus all the rest of sets satisfying *p(i)*

d) Indexed Select (*i:Index Db p1(i) p2(i)*) returns an Indexed family with respect to *i* (preserved) where the element sets satisfy *p1(i)* and the elements of the sets satisfy *p2(i)*. As a special case of true as *p1(i)*, this operation returns the whole indexed family. In a special case of a singleton family, Indexed Select is reduced to Select (a Relational operation).

e) Indexed Project (*i:Index Db p(i) a(i)*) returns an Indexed family where the element sets satisfy *p(i)* and the elements of the sets are projected according to *a(i)*, attribute specification.

f) Intra Indexed cross product (*i:Index Db p(i)*) returns a singleton family obtained by product-ing sets which satisfy *p(i)*. This is extension of Cartesian product, one of relational operators.

g) Intra Indexed Join (*i:Index Db p1(i) p2(i)*) returns a singleton family obtained by joining sets which satisfy *p1(i)* based on the join predicate *p2(i)*. This is extension of join, one of relational operators.

h) Sort (*i:Index Db p(i) o()*) returns indexed family where the element sets satisfy *p(i)* and the elements of the sets are ordered according to *compare function o() with respect to two elements.*

i) Indexed Sort (*i:Index Db p(i) o()*) returns an indexed family where the element sets satisfy *p(i)* and the sets are ordered according to *o()*, compare function with respect to two sets.

j) Select-Index (*i:Index Db p(i)*) returns *i:Index* of set_i which satisfy *p(i)*. As a special case of true as *p(i)*, it returns all index.

k) Make-indexed family (*Index Non-Indexed Family*) returns an indexed Family. This operator requires *order-compatibility*, that is , that *i* corresponds to *i-th set of Non-Indexed Family.*

l) Partition (*i:Index Db p(i)*) returns an Indexed family. Partition makes an Indexed family out of a given set (i.e. singleton family either w/ or w/o index) by grouping elements with respect to *p (i:Index)*. This is extension of "groupby" as a relational operator.

m) ApplyFunction (*i:Index Db f(i)*) applies *f(i)* to *i-th* set of DB, where *f(i)* takes a set as a whole and gives another set including a singleton set (i.e., Aggregate function). This returns an indexed family. *f(i)* can be defined by users.

2) *Inter Family Data Operations Index-Compatible*

a) Indexed Intersect (*i:Index Db1 Db2 p(i)*) union-compatible

b) Indexed Union (*i:Index Db1 Db2 p(i)*) union-compatible

c) Indexed Difference (*i:Index Db1 Db2 p(i)*) union-compatible

d) Indexed Join (*i:Index Db1 Db2 p1(i) p2(i)*)

e) Indexed cross product (*i:Index Db1 Db2 p(i)*)

Indexed (*) operation is extension of its corresponding Relational operation. It preserves an Indexed Family. For example, Indexed Intersect returns Indexed family whose element is intersection of corresponding sets of two indexed families *Db1* and *Db2*, which satisfy *p(i)*. At this time, we impose *union-compatibility*. Further, in case both *Db1* and *Db2* are singleton families and *p(i)* is constantly true, Indexed

Intersect is reduced to Intersect, which returns intersection of two sets (a Relational operation). Indexed Union and Indexed Difference are also similar.

3) *Family Data Mining Operations*

a) Cluster (*Family method similarity {par}*) returns a Family as default, where Index is automatically produced. This is an unsupervised learner. In *hierarchical agglomerative clustering* or HAC, as well as similar methods, such as some spatial, temporal, and spatio-temporal clustering, index is merged into new index as clustering progresses. *method* includes k-means, HAC, spatial, temporal, etc. *similarity/distance* includes Euclidean, Cosine measure, etc. *par* (ammeters) depend on *method*.

b) Make-classifier (*i:Index set:Family learnMethod {par}*) returns a classifier (Classify) with its accuracy. This is a supervised learner. In this case *index* denotes classes (i.e., predefined categories). Sample *set* includes both training set and test set. *learnMethod* specifies methods, such as decision tree, SVM, deep learning. *par* (ammeters) depend on *learnMethod*. This operation itself is out of range of our algebra. In other words, it is a *meta*-operation.

c) Classify (*Index/class set*) returns an indexed family with class as its index.

d) Make-frequent itemset (*Db supportMin)* returns an Indexed Family as frequent itemsets, which satisfy *supportMin*.

e) Make-association-rule (*Db confidenceMin*) creates association rules based on frequent itemsets *Db*, which satisfy *confidenceMin*. This is out of range of our algebra, too.

III. CASE STUDY

A. Case One

First, we describe a case study, analysis of behaviors of foreigners (visitors or residents) in Japan [3]

We use the following colors for each category of SBD operations for illustration:

- Relational (set) operation
- Family operation
- Data mining operation

To classify foreign users as *residents* or *visitors*, we will classify the length of the stay in the country of interest as *long* and *short*, respectively. We assume the target country (i.e., the country of interest) uses one language dominantly. We first obtain the tweets that a user posted in Japan. We detect the principal language of the user in order to extract only foreign Twitter users. We define the *principal language* of a user as the language that meets the following two conditions.

- The language must be used in more than half of all the user's tweets. Since the Language-Detection toolkit [8] is over 99% precision according to their claim in detecting the tweet language, we used this toolkit in the experiment.
- The language must be selected by the user in his/her account settings. This means that the user claims that they use that language.

If the resultant principal language for a Twitter user is a language other than the one dominantly used in the target country, we regard the user as a foreign Twitter user and then classify the user as residents or visitors.

First, we sort a user's tweets posted in the target country in chronological order, where t_i denotes i-th tweet. Next, we set parameters *start date* and *stop date*, which specify the start and end date of interest, respectively. We define the oldest tweet between *start date* and *stop date* as T_{old} and define the parameter *travel period* as the maximum length of the stay. We define the newest tweet between T_{old} and T_{old} + *travel period* as T_{new}. Also, we set parameter j, a margin that ensures the foreign user is out of the target country. We identify a foreign user's tweets during a visit, if and only if all his/her tweets satisfy the following conditions:

- The foreign user posts more than T_{min} tweets between T_{old} and T_{new} and the user posts no tweets during the period from j days before to T_{old} to and the period from T_{new} to j days after T_{new}.

Here, T_{min} is the minimum number of tweets to prevent misclassification owing to a small number of tweets. The tweets posted between T_{old} and T_{new} are identified as the tweets during the visit. Since some users repeatedly visit the target country, we repeat the identification of tweets during a visit after T_{new}.

A foreign user is identified as a *visitor* to the target country, if and only if all his/her tweets between *start date* and *stop date* are tweets during visits. Foreign users who are not visitors are identified as *residents*. Here, we excluded foreign users who tweeted equal to or less than T_{min} times between *start date* and *stop date* as *unrecognizable*.

$\text{Classify}_{\text{foreign/domestic}}$ (*{Foreign Domestic}* DB_{tweet}) binarily splits into foreign and domestic sets as *AccountOrigin* (i.e., index class).

This Classifier is based on a heuristic (i.e., manually-coded) rule for deciding foreigner as follows:

if Count *(t:tweet t.AccountId=AccountId & t.DetectedLanguage()=t.AccountLanguage & t.AccountLanguage*<>"Japanese") >=0.5*Count (t:tweet *t.AccountId=id*) then return foreign else domestic

The following fragment of descriptions collects only tweets posted by foreigners ("←" is the assignment operator):

DB_t ← Sort (Select (DB_{tweet} *Time of Interest* & Within "*Japan*") *compare-time*()) ; singleton family (i.e., set).

$DB_{foreign}$ ← Indexed-Select ($\text{Classify}_{\text{foreign/domestic}}$ (*{Foreign Domestic}* DB_t) *AccountOrigin="foreign"*); singleton family.

Next $\text{Classify}_{\text{visitor/resident}}$ (*{Visitor Resident}* DB_{tweet}) binarily splits into visitor and resident sets as *AccountStatus* (i.e., index class).

This is based on a heuristic rule for deciding inbound visitor as follows:

if Count (*t.tweet t.AccountId=AccountId* & T_{old}=<*t.time*=<T_{new})>=C_{min} & *Count (t.tweet t.AccountId=id* & T_{old}-*j*<=*t.time*<T_{old})=0 & Count (*t.tweet t.AccountId=id* & T_{new}<*t.time*<=T_{new}+*j*)=0 then return visitor else resident

The following fragment classifies tweets by foreigners into ones by inbound visitors and ones by foreign residents:

$DB_{foreignVisitorOrResident}$ ← Classify$_{visitor/resident}$ ({*Visitor Resident*} $DB_{foreign}$): This returns an indexed family.

$DB_{visitor}$ ← Indexed-Select ($DB_{foreignerVisitorOrResident}$ *AccountStatus*="*visitor*") ; This returns a singleton family.

$DB_{resident}$ ← Indexed-Select ($DB_{foreignerVisitorOrResident}$ *AccountStatus*="*resident*"); This returns a singleton family.

B. Case Two

Next, we describe another case study, finding candidate access spots for accessible free WIFI in Japan [9].

This section describes our proposed method of detecting attractive tourist areas where users cannot connect to accessible Free Wi-Fi by using posts by foreign travelers on social media.

Our method uses differences in the characteristics of two types of SNSs and we focus on two of these:

Real-time: Immediate posts, e.g., Twitter

Batch-time: Data stored to devices for later posts, e.g., Flickr

Twitter users can only post tweets when they can connect devices to Wi-Fi or wired networks. Therefore, travelers can post tweets in areas with Free Wi-Fi for inbound tourism or when they have mobile communications. In other words, we can obtain only tweets with geo-tags posted by foreign travelers from such places. Therefore, areas where we can obtain huge numbers of tweets posted by foreign travelers are identified as places where they can connect to accessible Free Wi-Fi and /or that are attractive for them to sightsee.

Flickr users, on the other hand, take many photographs by using digital devices regardless of networks, but whether they can upload photographs on-site depends on the conditions of the network. As a result, almost all users can upload photographs after returning to their hotels or home countries. However, geo-tags annotated to photographs can indicate when they were taken. Therefore, although it is difficult to obtain detailed information (activities, destinations, or routes) on foreign travelers from Twitter, Flickr can be used to observe such information. We are based on our hypothesis in this study of "A place that has a lot of Flickr posts but few Twitter posts must have a critical lack of accessible Free Wi-Fi". We extracted areas that were tourist attractions for foreign travelers, but from which they could not connect to accessible Free Wi-Fi by using these characteristics of SNSs. What our method aims to find is places without accessible Free Wi-Fi.

There are two main reasons for areas from where foreign travelers cannot connect to Free Wi-Fi. The first is areas where there are no Wi-Fi spots. The second is areas where users can use Wi-Fi but it is not accessible. We treat them both the same as inaccessible Free Wi-Fi because both areas are unavailable to foreign travelers. Since we conducted experiments focused on foreign travelers, we could detect actual areas without accessible Free Wi-Fi. In addition, our method extracted areas with accessible Free Wi-Fi, and then other locations were regarded as regions without accessible Free Wi-Fi.

This subsection describes a method of extracting foreign travelers using Twitter and Flickr. We obtained and analyzed tweets posted in Japan from Twitter using Twitter's Streaming application programming interface (API) [16]. We used the method introduced in Case study to extract foreign travelers.

We obtained photographs with geo-tags taken in Japan from Flickr using. Flickr's API [2]. We extracted foreign travelers who had taken photographs in Japan. We regard Flickr users who had set their profiles of habitation on Flickr as Japan or associated geographical regions as the users *living* in Japan; otherwise, they are regarded as foreign *visitors*. We used the tweets and photographs that foreign visitors had created in Japan in the analysis that followed. Our method envisaged places that met the following two conditions as candidate access spots for accessible free WIFI:

- Spots where there was no accessible Free Wi-Fi
- Spots that many foreign visitors visited

We use the number of photographs taken at locations to extract tourist spots. Many people might take photographs of subjects, such as landscapes based on their own interests. They might then upload those photographs to Flickr. As these were locations at which many photographs had been taken, these places might also be interesting places for many other people to sightsee or visit. We have defined such places as tourist spots in this paper. We specifically examined the number of photographic locations to identify tourist spots to find locations where photographs had been taken by a lot of people. We mapped photographs that had a photographic location onto a two-dimensional grid based on the location at which a photograph had been taken to achieve this. Here, we created individual cells in a grid that was 30 square meters. Consequently, all cells in the grid that was obtained included photographs taken in a range. We then counted the number of users in each cell. We regarded cells with greater numbers of users than the threshold as tourist spots.

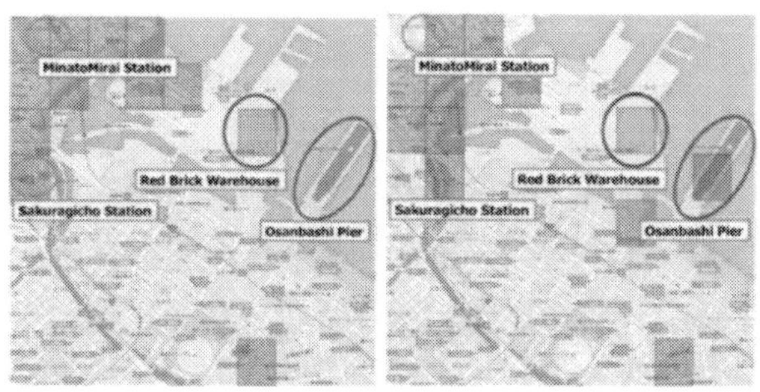

Figure 2. High density areas of tweets (left) and of Flickr photos (right).

The fragment collects attractive tourist spots for foreign visitors but without accessible free WIFI currently (See Figure 2):

$DB_{t/visitor}$ ← Tweet DB of foreign visitors obtained by similar procedures like case one;

$DB_{f/visitor}$ ← Flickr photo DB of foreign visitors obtained by similar procedures like case one;

T ← Partition (*i:Index grid* $DB_{t/visitor}$ *p(i)*); This partitions foreign visitors tweets into grids based on geo-tags; This operation returns a indexed family.

F ← Partition (*j:Index grid* $DB_{f/visitor}$ *p(j)*); This partitions foreign visitors photos into grids based on geo-tags; This operation returns a indexed family.

Index1 ← Select-Index (*i:Index T Density*(*i*) >= *th1*); *th1* is a threshold. This operation returns a singleton family.

Index2 ← Select-Index (*j:Index F Density*(*i*) >= *th2*); *th2* is a threshold.This operation returns a singleton family.

Index3 ← Difference (*Index2 Index1*); This operation returns a singleton family.

For example, grids indexed by *Index3* contain "Osanbashi Pier". Please note that the above description doesn't take unique users into consideration.

IV. CONCLUSION

We have proposed an abstract data model for integrating data management and data mining by using mathematical concepts of families, collections of sets. Our model facilitates reproducibility and accountability required for SBD researches and developments. We have partially validated our proposal by adapting our model to real case studies. However, there still remains to describe mapping from our model to existing programming tools, such as Spark. Further, we must devise some kinds of optimization comparable to query optimization of SQL. We would like to validate our proposed model more thoroughly by adapting it to different kinds of applications and theoretically, stick as well.

ACKNOWLEDGMENT

This work was supported by JSPS KAKENHI Grant Number 16K00157, 16K16158, and Tokyo Metropolitan University Grant-in-Aid for Research on Priority Areas Research on social big data.

REFERENCES

[1] D. G. Feitelson, "From Repeatability to Reproducibility and Corroboration," ACM SIGOPS Operating Systems Review - Special Issue on Repeatability and Sharing of Experimental Artifacts, Volume 49, Issue 1, pp. 3-11, January 2015.

[2] Flickr, *The App Garden*. https://www.flickr.com/services/api/ Accessed 2017.03

[3] M. Hirota, K. Saeki, Y. Ehara, and H. Ishikawa, "Live or Stay?: Classifying Twitter Users into Residents and Visitors," Proceedings of International Conference on Knowledge Engineering and Semantic Web (KESW 2016), 2016.

[4] IDC, *The Diverse and Exploding Digital Universe* (white paper, 2008). http:// www.emc.com/collateral/analyst-reports/diverse-exploding-digital-universe.pdf Accessed 2017.03

[5] IDC, *The Digital Universe In 2020: Big Data, Bigger Digital Shadows, and Biggest Growth in the Far East* (2012). http://www.emc.com/leadership/digital-universe/iview/index.htm accessed 2017.03

[6] H. Ishikawa, Y. Yamane, Y. Izumida, and N. Kawato, "An Object-Oriented Database System Jasmine: Implementation, Application, and Extension," IEEE Trans. on Knowl. and Data Eng. 8, 2, pp. 285-304, April 1996.

[7] H. Ishikawa, Social Big Data Mining, CRC Press, 2015.

[8] GitHub. Language Detection. https://github.com/shuyo/language-detection Accessed 2017.03

[9] K. Mitomi, M. Endo, M. Hirota, S. Yokoyama, Y. Shoji, and H. Ishikawa, "How to Find Accessible Free Wi-Fi at Tourist Spots in Japan," Volume 10046 of Lecture Notes in Computer Science, pp. 389-403, 2016.

[10] R. D. Peng, "Reproducible Research in Computational Science," SCIENCE, VOL 334, 2, December 2011.

[11] S. Perianayagam, G. R. Andrews, and J. H. Hartman, "Rex: A toolset for reproducing software experiments," Proceedings of IEEE International Conference on Bioinformatics and Biomedicine (BIBM) 2010, pp. 613-617, 2010.

[12] R. Ramakrishnan, and J. Gehrke, Database Management Systems, 3rd Edition, McGraw-Hill Professional, 2002.

[13] D. Smith, R. St. Andre, and M. Eggen, A Transition to Advanced Mathematics, Brooks/Cole Pub Co., 2014.

[14] E. R. Sparks, A. Talwalkar, V. Smith, J. Kottalam, X. Pan, J. E. Gonzalez, M. J. Franklin, M. I. Jordan, and T. Kraska, "MLI: An API for distributed machine learning," Proceedings of the IEEE ICDM International Conference on Data Mining (Dallas, TX, Dec. 7–10). IEEE Press, 2013.

[15] T. C. Südhof, "Truth in Science Publishing: A Personal Perspective," PLOS August 26, 2016.

[16] Twitter. Twitter Developer Documentation. https://dev.twitter.com/streaming/overview Accessed 2017.03

[17] M. Zaharia, R. S. Xin, Patrick Wendell, T. Das, M. Armbrust, A. Dave, X. Meng, J. Rosen, S. Venkataraman, M. J. Franklin, A. Ghodsi, J. Gonzalez, S. Shenker, and I. Stoica, "Apache Spark: a unified engine for big data processing," Com. ACM, 59, 11, pp. 56-65, October 2016.

Examination of Best-time Estimation using Interpolation for Geotagged Tweets

Masaki Endo, Shigeyoshi Ohno
Division of Core Manufacturing
Polytechnic University
Tokyo, Japan
e-mail: endou@uitec.ac.jp, ohno@uitec.ac.jp

Masaharu Hirota
Department of Information Engineering
National Institute of Technology, Oita College
Oita, Japan
e-mail: m-hirota@oita-ct.ac.jp

Yoshiyuki Shoji, Hiroshi Ishikawa
Graduate School of System Design
Tokyo Metropolitan University
Tokyo, Japan
e-mail: y_shoji@tmu.ac.jp, ishikawa-hiroshi@tmu.ac.jp

***Abstract*—Various studies have been conducted to analyze social media data in real time and to extract events in the real world. A benefit of analysis using data with position information is that it can accurately extract the event from a target area to be analyzed. However, because the proportion of data with position information in social media data is small, the amount to analyze is insufficient in almost areas. In other words, the problem indicates that we cannot fully extract most events. Therefore, efficient analytical methods are necessary for accurate extraction of events with position information, even in areas with few data. For this research, we conducted an experiment using information interpolation to estimate the times for biological season observation using tweets with Twitter location information. Then we evaluated its effectiveness. Herein, we explain results obtained using interpolated information and analysis of cherry blossoms in Japan in 2016.**

Keywords–trend estimation; phenological observation; Twitter.

I. INTRODUCTION

In recent years, because of wide dissemination and rapid performance improvement of various devices such as smart phones and tablets, diverse and vast data are generated on the web. Particularly, social networking services (SNSs) have become popular because users can post data and various messages easily. Twitter [1], an SNS that provides a micro-blogging service, is used as a real-time communication tool. Numerous tweets have been posted daily by vast numbers of users. Twitter is therefore a useful medium to obtain, from a large amount of information posted by many users, real-time information corresponding to the real world.

Here, we describe the provision of information to tourists using the web. Such information is useful for tourists, but providing timely and topical travel information entails high costs for information providers because they must update the information continually. Today, providing reliable information related to local travel is not only strongly demanded by tourists, but also by local governments, tourism organizations, and travel companies, which bear high costs of providing such information.

Therefore, providing current, useful, real-world information for travelers by ascertaining the change of information in accordance with the season and time zone of the tourism region is important for the travel industry. As described herein, we define "now" information as information that travelers require for tourism and disaster prevention, such as best flower-viewing times, festivals, and local heavy rains. As one might expect, the period estimated for disaster prevention information would be an estimate of the “worst” time instead of the best time.

We propose a method to estimate best-time viewing for phenological observations for tourists, such as cherry blossoms and autumn leaves, in each region by particularly addressing phenology observations that must be made “now” in the real world. Tourist information for the best time requires a peak period: the best time is not a period after or before the falling of flowers, but a period when one can view blooming flowers. Furthermore, such best times differ among regions and locations. Therefore, it is necessary to estimate a best time of phenological observation for each region and location. To estimate best-time viewing, one must collect large amounts of information with real-time properties. For this study, we use Twitter data obtained from many users throughout Japan.

However, to analyze the information of each region from Twitter data, it is necessary to specify the location from tweet information. Because geotagged tweets can identify places, they are effective for analysis, but because the proportion of geo-tagged tweets accounts for a very small proportion of the total information content of tweets, it is not possible to analyze all regions. Therefore, we propose an information interpolation method using geo-tagged tweets. We conducted experiments to estimate the position around areas not identified by location information.

The remainder of the paper is organized as follows. Section II presents earlier research related to this topic. In Section III, we propose a method for estimating the best time for phenotypic observations using information interpolation.

Section IV describes experimentally obtained results for our proposed method and a discussion of the results. Section V presents a summary of the contributions and future work.

II. RELATED WORK

The amounts of digital data are expected to increase greatly in the future because of the spread of SNSs. Reports describing studies of the effective use of these large amounts of digital data are numerous. Some studies use microblogs to conduct real-world understanding and prediction by analyzing information transmitted from microblogs. Kleinberg [2] detected a "burst" of keywords signaling a rapid increase in time-series data. Sakaki et al. [3] proposed a method to detect events such as earthquakes and typhoons based on a study estimating real-time events from Twitter. Kaneko et al. [4] proposed a method of detecting an event using geotagged non-photo tweets and non-geotagged photo tweets, as well as geotagged photo tweets. Yamagata et al. [5] proposed a real-time urban climate monitoring method using geographically tagged tweets, demonstrating the effectiveness of tweets for urban risk management. Consequently, various methods for extracting event and location information are discussed. However, event detection has been done in earlier studies, but discussion of the validity period of the event has not been reported. As described in this paper, we propose a method for extracting such information. Then we estimate "now" in relation to tourism information, such as the full bloom period of phonological observations. Additionally, we treat a crucially important difficulty related to analysis of geotagged contents: what amount of data is effective for an analyzed area.

III. OUR PROPOSED METHOD

This section presents a description of an analytical method for target data collection and presents our best-time estimation to obtain a guide for phenological change from Twitter in Japan. Our proposal is portrayed in Figure 1.

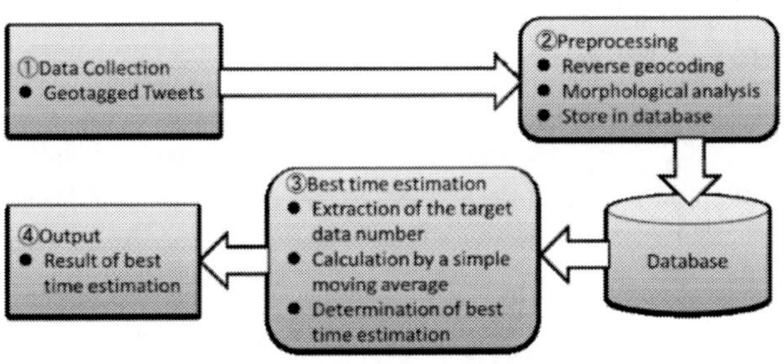

Figure 1. Our proposal.

A. Data collection

This section presents a description of the Method of (1) data collection presented in Figure 1. Geotagged tweets sent from Twitter are a collection target. The range of geo-tagged tweets includes the Japanese archipelago (120.0°E ≤ longitude ≤ 154.0°E and 20.0°N ≤ latitude ≤ 47.0°N) as the collection target. Collection of these data was done using a streaming API [6] provided by Twitter Inc.

Next, we describe the number of collected data. According to a report described by Hashimoto et al. [7], among all tweets originating in Japan, about 0.18% are geotagged tweets: they are rare among all data. However, the collected geo-tagged tweets, shown as an example in Table I, number about 70,000, even on weekdays. On some days during weekends, more than 100,000 such messages are posted. We use about 30 million geo-tagged tweets from 2015/2/17 through 2016/4/30. For each day of collection, the number during the period covered was about 72,000. We calculated the best time for flower viewing, as estimated by processing the following sections using these data.

TABLE I. TRANSITION OF GEOTAGGED TWEETS (2015/5/9 – 6/3)

Date (Day of the week)	Volume [tweet]	Date (Day of the week)	Volume [tweet]
5/9 (Sat)	117,253	5/22 (Fri)	92,237
5/10 (Sun)	128,654	5/23 (Sat)	55,590
5/11 (Mon)	91,795	5/24 (Sun)	72,243
5/12 (Tue)	87,354	5/25 (Mon)	82,375
5/13 (Wed)	67,016	5/26 (Tue)	83,851
5/14 (Thu)	88,994	5/27 (Wed)	83,825
5/15 (Fri)	89,210	5/28 (Thu)	85,024
5/16 (Sat)	116,600	5/29 (Fri)	121,582
5/17 (Sun)	126,705	5/30 (Sat)	119,387
5/18 (Mon)	89,342	5/31 (Sun)	81,431
5/19 (Tue)	83,695	6/1 (Mon)	76,364
5/20 (Wed)	87,927	6/2 (Tue)	76,699
5/21 (Thu)	86,164	6/3 (Wed)	78,329

B. Preprocessing

This section presents a description of the method of (2) preprocessing presented in Figure 1. Preprocessing includes reverse geocoding and morphological analysis, with database storage for data collected using the process explained in Section III.A.

Reverse geocoding identified prefectures and municipalities by town name using latitude and longitude information from the individually collected tweets. We use a simple reverse geocoding service [8] available from the National Agriculture and Food Research Organization in this process: e.g., (latitude, longitude) = (35.7384446N, 139.460910W) by reverse geocoding becomes (Tokyo, Kodaira City, Ogawanishi-cho 2-chome). Furthermore, based on latitude and longitude information of collected tweets, data are accumulated for each division of land using tertiary mesh data provided by the Land Numerical Information download service of the Ministry of Land, Infrastructure, and Transport [9]. The tertiary mesh is a section of about 1 km square.

Morphological analysis divides the collected geo-tagged tweet morphemes. We use the "Mecab" morphological analyzer [10]. As an example, "桜は美しいです" ("Cherry blossoms are beautiful." in English) is divisible into "(桜 / noun), (は / particle), (美しい / adjective), (です / auxiliary verb), (。 / symbol)".

Preprocessing performs the necessary data storage for the best-time viewing, as estimated based on results of the processing of data collection, reverse geocoding, and morphological analysis. Data used for this study were the tweet ID, tweet post time, tweet text, morphological analysis result, latitude, and longitude.

C. Estimating the best-time viewing

This section explains the method of (3) best-time estimation presented in Figure 1. In our method of estimating best-time viewing, we first process the target number of extracted data and then calculate a simple moving average, yielding an inference of the best flower-viewing time. The method defines a word related to best-time viewing, estimated as the target word. The target word includes Chinese characters, hiragana, and katakana, which represents an organism name and seasonal change, as shown in Table II.

TABLE II. TARGET WORD EXAMPLES

Items	Target Words	In English
さくら	桜, さくら, サクラ	Cherry blossoms
かえで	楓, かえで, カエデ	Maple
いちょう	銀杏, いちょう, イチョウ	Ginkgo
こうよう	紅葉, 黄葉, こうよう, もみじ, コウヨウ, モミジ	Autumn leaves

Next, the granularity for estimation is shown. For an estimate for Japan as a whole, prefecture units are assumed and acquired by reverse geocoding. However, when conducting more detailed analyses, a difficulty arises: it is impossible to estimate the number of geotagged tweets for each city or town or village or tourist spot. Therefore, we attempted estimation through information interpolation using data aggregated for each section of tertiary mesh data. For interpolation, we used Kriging [11], an estimation method used for estimating values for points where information was not acquired, to ascertain the distribution of the information in the whole space in geostatistics. The estimated value of the target data at a certain point S_0 is represented in formula (1) as a weighted average of the measured values $Z(S_i)$ (i = 1, 2..., N) at N points S_i existing around point S_0. As described in this paper, we experimentally assigned a +1 weight for 'full bloom' and 'beautiful', and assigned -1 on 'still' or 'falling'. Then we assigned value Z to tweets including the target word and Z. N denotes the 30 nearby targeted tweets. λ has adopted a spherical model that decreases the influence as the distance increases.

$$\hat{z}(S_0) = \sum_{i=1}^{N} \lambda_i Z(S_i) \quad (1)$$

$Z(S_i)$: Measurement value at i-th position
λ_i: Unknown weighting of measured value at i-th position
S_0 : Predicted position
N : Number of measurements

Next, we describe the simple moving average calculation, which uses a moving average of the standard of the best-time viewing judgment. It calculates a simple moving average using aggregate data on a daily basis by the target number of data extraction described above. Figure 2 shows an overview of the simple moving average of the number of days.

We calculate the simple moving average in formula (2) using the number of data going back to the past from the day before the estimated date of the best-time viewing.

Standard lengths of time we used for the simple moving averages were seven days and one year. A 7-day moving

$$X(Y) = \frac{P_1 + P_2 + \cdots + P_Y}{Y} \quad (2)$$

$X(Y)$:Y day moving average
P_n:Number of data of n days ago
Y: Calculation target period

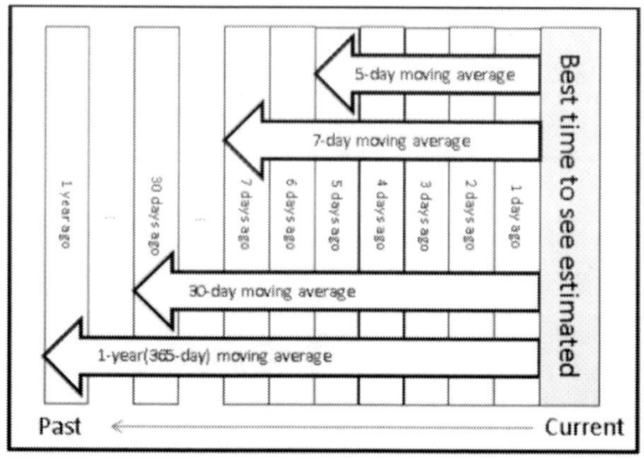

Figure 2. Number of days simple moving average.

average has one week as the criterion of the estimated period of full bloom because, as shown in Table I, a tendency exists for a transition of geotagged tweets of the increases on weekends compared to weekdays. In addition, phenological observations are based on the moving average of best-time viewing estimated in prior years because many such "viewing" events occur every year: cherry blossom viewing, autumn leaf viewing, and even moon viewing.

A simple moving average of the number of days is described for each type of event to compare the 7-day moving average and the one-year moving average. In this study, the period of the best-time viewing depends on the specified type of event, the individual event, and the number of days during the biological period related to the event.

As an example, we describe cherry blossoms. The Japan Meteorological Agency [12] carries out phenological observations of "Sakura," which yields two output items of the flowering date and the full bloom date observation target. "Sakura flowering date" [13] is the first day of blooming 5–6 or more wheels of flowers of a specimen tree. "Sakura in full bloom date" is the first day of a state in which about 80% or more of the buds are open in the specimen tree. In addition, "Sakura" is the number of days from general flowering until full bloom: about 5 days. Therefore, "Sakura" in this study uses a standard 5-day moving average.

Next, we describe an estimated judgment of best-time viewing, which was calculated using the simple moving average (7-day moving average, 1-year moving average, and another biological moving average). It specifies the two conditions as a condition of an estimated decision for best-time viewing. Condition 1 is the number of data one day before expression. Formula 3 is a simple moving average greater than that of the estimated best-time viewing date.

Condition 2 is a case that follows formulas 4 ((A) / (2)) or more.

$$P_1 \geqq X(365) \quad (3)$$
$$X(A) \geqq X(B) \quad (4)$$

Finally, an estimate is produced using conditions 1 and 2. By the proposed method, a day that satisfies both condition 1 and condition 2 is estimated as best-time viewing.

D. Output

This section presents a description of the method of (4) output presented in Figure 1. Output can be visualized using a best-time viewing result, as estimated by processing explained in the previous section. A time-series graph presents the results inferred for best-time viewing. The graph presents the number of data and the date, respectively, on the vertical axis to the horizontal axis. We are striving to develop useful visualization techniques for travelers.

IV. EXPERIMENTS

In this section, we describe an estimation experiment of best-time viewing for cherry blossoms using the method proposed in Section III.

A. Dataset

Datasets used for this experiment were collected using streaming API, as described for data collection in Section 3.1. Data are geo-tagged tweets from Japan during 2015/2/17 – 2016/4/30. The data include about 27 million items. We are using these datasets for experiments to infer the best time for cherry blossom viewing in 2016.

B. Estimation experiment for best-time viewing of cherry blossoms

The estimation experiment to ascertain the best-time viewing of cherry blossoms uses the target word in Table II: "Sakura". The target word is "cherry blossom," which is "桜" and "さくら" and "サクラ" in Japanese. The subject of the experiment was set as tourist spots in Tokyo. In this report, we describe "Takao mountain," "Showa Memorial Park," "Shinjuku gyoen," and "Rikugien."

Figure 3 presents the target area location. A, B, C and D in the figure respectively denote "Takao mountain," "Showa Memorial Park," "Rikugien," and "Shinjuku Gyoen." A and B are separated by about 16 km straight line distance. B and C are about 32 km apart. C and D are about 6 km apart.

The following two experiments were conducted. The first is an experiment using the number of tweets including the target word and the sightseeing spot name without information interpolation. This is Experiment 1 described in this paper. The second is an experiment using information interpolation for tertiary mesh including sightseeing spots. In the second experiment, the numerical value obtained by summing the result of the information interpolation and the first experiment result was used for observation estimation. This is Experiment 2 in this paper.

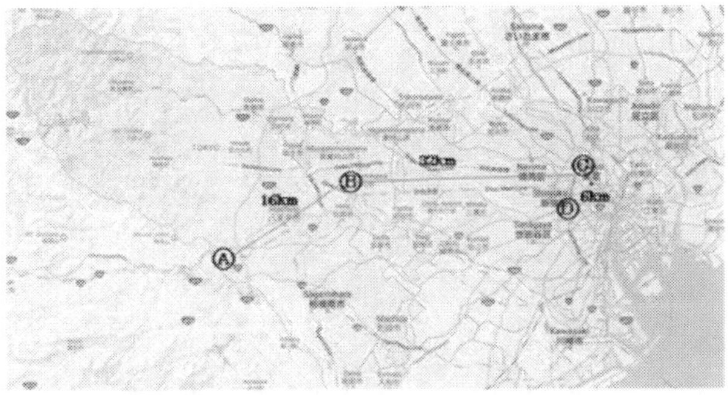

Figure 3. Position of target area.

C. Experimental result

We can present experimentally obtained results from tweets including a target word and a tourist spot name. Figure 4 shows those results for the estimated best-time viewing in 2016 using the target word 'cherry blossoms' in the target tourist spots of Figure 3. The dark gray bar in the figure represents the number of tweets. The light gray part represents best-time viewing as determined using the proposed method. In addition, the solid line shows a 5-day moving average. The dashed line shows a 7-day moving average. The dotted line shows a 1-year moving average.

At tourist spots targeted for the experiment in 2016, as portrayed in Figure 4, much data was obtained in C and D. The maximum number of tweets per day was about 30. For this reason, it was confirmed that some estimation can be done by near-sight estimation method without interpolation. However, best-time viewing cannot be done in A and B because of the very small number of tweets.

Next, Figure 5 portrays an experimentally obtained result from interpolation results for a tertiary mesh including tourist spots we examined. The notation is the same as that in Figure 4.

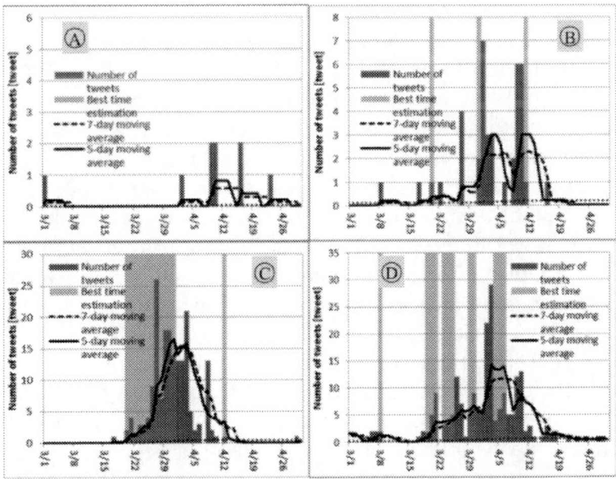

Figure 4. Experimental results obtained using tweets including the target word and the tourist spot name.

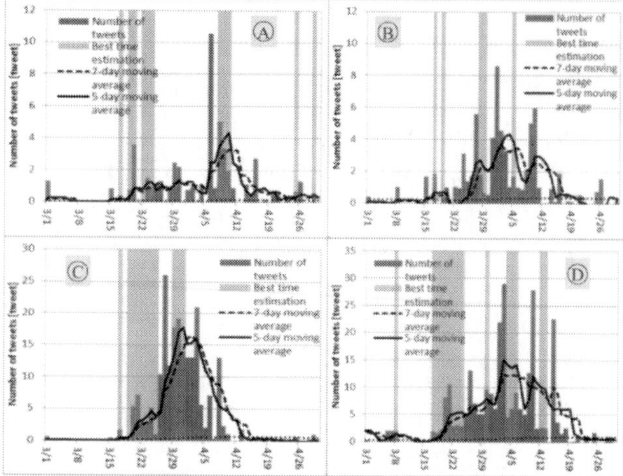

Figure 5. Experimental results obtained using interpolation.

Apparently, A and B were able to produce an estimate using the proposed method by increasing the number of tweets using information interpolation with surrounding tweets. In C and D, there are days when it can be determined more accurately by interpolating the number of tweets. However, because there were tweets of negative judgments such as "still" or "scattered" among surrounding tweets, in some cases, interpolation excluded the day determined as the best time in Experiment 1. Therefore, the judgment condition of the tweet is subject to further study.

These results confirmed the possibility of estimating the peak period, even in an area without tweets, using data interpolation and overall tweet number interpolation.

Table III presents results of the optimal time for viewing in 2016, as estimated using the proposed method. Experiment 1 used co-occurring words in tweets including the sightseeing spot name coexisting with the target word "Sakura." Experiment 2 used information interpolation on a tertiary mesh including sightseeing spots. The numerical values in the table are the numbers of tweets including the target word and co-occurrence word in Experiment 1. Experiment 2 uses the sum of the number of tweets in Experiment 1 plus numerical values by interpolation. The light gray area indicates the date when the fullness prediction was made using the proposed method.

Confirming the flowering day and full bloom period of each sightseeing spot using JMA data is difficult, but this experiment to evaluate SNS data for flowering is valid also for weather forecasting companies [14] and public service organizations [15] to evaluate optimum times for viewing based on services and blogs that are used. Arrows indicating the flowering time can be checked manually at tourist sites.

Experimental results confirmed the tendency by which the relevance ratio and the recall rate become higher for tourist spots with few tweets. Therefore, we presented the possibility of estimating sightseeing sites with few tweets using information interpolation. However, because the interpolation information amount is insufficient in the current method, it is necessary to improve the information interpolation method further. In addition, sightseeing spots with many tweets are affected by tweets of minus judgments in the surroundings, so accuracy is lower than in Experiment 1. However, one might be able to estimate more details, such as the start time, using interpolation.

TABLE III. ESTIMATION RESULTS AT RESPECTIVE SIGHTSEEING SPOTS

	Takao mountain		Showa Memorial park		Rikugien		Shinjuku gyoen	
	Exp.1	Exp.2	Exp.1	Exp.2	Exp.1	Exp.2	Exp.1	Exp.2
3/1	1	1.27	0	0.40	0	0.58	0	0.28
3/2	0	0.00	0	0.00	0	0.00	0	0.00
3/3	0	0.00	0	0.00	0	0.00	0	0.00
3/4	0	0.00	0	0.00	0	0.00	1	1.00
3/5	0	0.00	0	0.00	0	0.00	0	0.00
3/6	0	0.00	0	0.00	0	0.00	2	2.00
3/7	0	0.00	0	0.00	0	0.00	2	2.00
3/8	0	0.00	1	1.00	0	0.00	2	2
3/9	0	0.00	0	0.00	0	0.00	0	0.00
3/10	0	0.00	0	0.00	0	0.00	0	0.00
3/11	0	0.00	0	0.00	0	0.00	0	0.00
3/12	0	0.00	0	0.00	0	0.00	0	0.00
3/13	0	0.00	0	0.00	0	0.00	0	0.00
3/14	0	0.00	0	0.00	0	0.00	0	0.00
3/15	0	0.84	0	1.68	0	0.41	0	0.24
3/16	0	0.00	0	0.00	0	0.00	0	0.00
3/17	0	0.40	1	1.85	1	1.67	1	1.85
3/18	0	-0.51	0	-0.43	0	0.02	2	1.64
3/19	0	0.78	0	0.49	0	0.22	2	2.30
3/20	0	3.61	1	1.00	2	5.42	5	8.18
3/21	0	0.00	0	-4.81	4	7.16	9	10.49
3/22	0	0.14	1	1.06	1	2.93	0	2.97
3/23	0	1.51	0	0.93	3	2.70	3	3.06
3/24	0	0.84	0	3.13	3	5.11	3	3.00
3/25	0	1.06	0	1.40	4	1.00	5	5.00
3/26	0	1.27	0	1.67	9	10.41	12	13.14
3/27	0	-0.08	4	5.57	26	26.00	7	7.00
3/28	0	0.94	0	1.85	7	11.74	1	5.19
3/29	0	2.50	0	0.66	18	17.83	5	5.00
3/30	0	2.21	0	0.52	18	19.18	9	9.62
3/31	0	0.00	2	4.13	14	14.00	6	8.82
4/1	0	0.74	7	8.60	13	13.00	6	6.00
4/2	1	0.91	3	4.56	13	13.00	22	22.00
4/3	0	0.00	3	3.30	21	21.00	29	29.00
4/4	0	1.12	0	1.05	5	5.62	4	4.55
4/5	0	0.00	0	1.73	2	2.00	6	6.00
4/6	0	10.52	1	1.00	3	7.05	9	9.00
4/7	0	0.89	0	0.88	0	0.33	5	6.06
4/8	0	5.05	2	2.00	13	13.00	5	5.00
4/9	2	3.37	6	5.05	2	2.29	12	12.62
4/10	2	2.00	6	6.00	1	1.00	13	27.88
4/11	0	0.88	1	1.00	0	0.00	2	2.47
4/12	0	0.00	0	0.00	1	-0.24	3	2.61
4/13	0	-0.50	0	0.02	0	1.79	1	2.55
4/14	0	1.11	0	0.95	0	-0.67	0	-0.37
4/15	0	0.51	0	0.12	0	0.00	1	22.54
4/16	2	2.75	1	1.91	0	0.60	3	3.63
4/17	0	0.00	0	0.00	0	0.42	1	1.54
4/18	0	0.14	0	0.17	0	0.36	2	2.51
4/19	0	-0.34	0	0.13	0	0.30	0	0.07
4/20	0	0.66	0	-0.43	0	-0.20	0	0.21
4/21	0	0.58	0	0.58	0	0.00	1	1.00
4/22	0	0.00	0	0.00	0	0.00	0	0.00
4/23	1	0.43	0	-4.08	0	0.00	1	1.19
4/24	0	0.00	0	0.00	0	0.00	0	0.00
4/25	0	0.68	0	0.76	0	0.64	1	1.75
4/26	0	1.33	0	1.61	0	-1.03	0	-0.26
4/27	0	0.00	0	0.00	0	0.00	0	0.00
4/28	0	-0.25	0	-0.34	0	0.19	1	1.11
4/29	0	0.60	0	0.00	1	1.00	1	1.00
4/30	0	0.00	0	0.09	0	0.00	0	0.00
Precision	0.26	0.38	0.72	0.75	0.89	0.89	0.84	0.75
Recall	0.00	0.20	0.11	0.22	0.67	0.61	0.56	0.50

V. CONCLUSION

As described herein, to improve best-time estimation accuracy and thereby enhance tourist information related to phenologic observation, we proposed an information interpolation method. For the proposed method, information was interpolated using neighbor-weighted tweets on a tertiary mesh including sightseeing spots, thereby indicating the optimum time to view flowers at sightseeing spots.

The results of cherry blossom experiments at sightseeing spots in Tokyo in 2016 confirm the tendency for improvement of accuracy of estimation by information interpolation. The proposed method using information interpolation for tweets related to organism names might improve the accuracy of estimating the best time in the real world. We confirmed the possibility of applying this proposed method to estimation of the viewpoint and line of sight in areas and sightseeing spots with few tweets and little location information. However, because the experimental case was related only to cherry blossoms, it is necessary to verify other cases as well.

Future research with manual experimental weighting and geotagged tweets will facilitate further improvements to overcome insufficiencies in measured values used for interpolation. Additionally, we expect to reconsider the viewing angle estimation conditions. Eventually, this system might be extended to a system by which travelers can obtain travel-destination-related event information and disaster information in real time.

ACKNOWLEDGMENTS

This work was supported by JSPS KAKENHI Grant Nos. 16K00157 and 16K16158, and by a Tokyo Metropolitan University Grant-in-Aid for Research on Priority Areas "Research on Social Big Data."

REFERENCES

[1] Twitter. *It's what's happening.* [Online]. Available from: https://Twitter.com/ [retrieved: 2, 2015]

[2] J. Kleinberg, "Bursty and hierarchical structure in stream," In Proc. of the Eighth ACM SIGKDD International Conference on Knowledge Discovery and Data Mining, pp.1–25, 2002.

[3] T. Sakaki, M. Okazaki, and Y. Matsuo, "Earthquake shakes Twitter users: real-time event detection by social sensors," WW W 2010, pp.851–860, 2010.

[4] T. Kaneko and K. Yanai, "Visual Event Mining from the Twitter Stream," WWW '16 Companion Proceedings of the 25th International Conference Companion on World Wide Web, pp.51–52, 2016.

[5] Y. Yamagata, D. Murakami, G. W. Peters, and T. Matsui, "A spatiotemporal analysis of participatory sensing data "tweets" and extreme climate events toward real-time urban risk management," arXiv preprint arXiv:1505.06188, pp.1–34, 2015.

[6] Twitter Developers. *Twitter Developer official site.* [Online] Available from: https://dev.twitter.com/ [retrieved: 2, 2015]

[7] Y. Hashimoto and M. Oka, "Statistics of Geo-Tagged Tweets in Urban Areas (<Special Issue>Synthesis and Analysis of Massive Data Flow)," JSAI, vol. 27, No. 4, pp.424–431, 2012 (in Japanese).

[8] National Agriculture and Food Research Organization. *Simple reverse geocoding service.* [Online]. Available from: http://www.finds.jp/wsdocs/rgeocode/index.html.ja [retrieved: 4, 2015]

[9] Ministry of Land, Infrastructure and Transport. *Land Numerical Information download service.* [Online]. Available from: http://nlftp.mlit.go.jp/ksj-e/index.html [retrieved: 4, 2015]

[10] MeCab. *Yet Another Part-of-Speech and Morphological Analyzer.* [Online]. Available from: http://mecab.googlecode.com/svn/trunk/mecab/doc/index.htm l [retrieved: 4, 2015]

[11] M. A. Oliver, "Kriging: A Method of Interpolation for Geographical Information Systems.," International Journal of Geographic Information Systems 4, pp.313–332, 1990.

[12] Japan Meteorological Agency. *Disaster prevention information XML format providing information page.* [Online]. Available from: http://xml.kishou.go.jp/ [retrieved: 4, 2015]

[13] Japan Meteorological Agency. *Observation of Sakura.* [Online]. Available from: http://www.data.jma.go.jp/sakura/data/sakura2012.pdf [retrieved: 4, 2015]

[14] Weathernews Inc. *Sakura information.* [Online]. Available from: http://weathernews.jp/sakura [retrieved: 4, 2015]

[15] Japan Travel and Tourism Association. *Whole country cherry trees.* [Online]. Available from: http://sakura.nihon-kankou.or.jp [retrieved: 4, 2015]

Classification of Unlabeled Deep Moonquakes Using Machine Learning

Shiori Kikuchi *, Ryuhei Yamada†, Yukio Yamamoto‡, Masaharu Hirota§, Shohei Yokoyama¶ and Hiroshi Ishikawa||
* Faculty of System Design, Tokyo Metropolitan University, 6-6 Asahigaoka, Hino-shi, Tokyo, Japan
Email: kikuchi-shiori@ed.tmu.ac.jp
† National Astronomical Observatory of Japan, RISE project, 2-12 Hoshigaoka-cho, Mizusawa-ku, Oshu-shi, Iwate, Japan
Email: r.yamada@nao.ac.jp
‡ Japan Aerospace Exploration Agency, 3-1-1, Yoshinodai, Chuo-ku, Sagamihara-shi, Kanagawa, Japan
Email: yamamoto.yukio@jaxa.jp
§ Department of Information Engineering National Institute of Technology, Oita College 1666 Maki Oita-shi, Oita, Japan
Email: m-hirota@oita-ct.ac.jp
¶ Faculty of Informatics, Shizuoka University, 3-5-1 Joho-ku, Hamamatsu-shi, Shizuoka, Japan
Email: yokoyama@inf.shizuoka.ac.jp
|| Faculty of System Design, Tokyo Metropolitan University, 6-6 Asahigaoka, Hino-shi, Tokyo, Japan
Email: ishikawa-hiroshi@tmu.ac.jp

***Abstract*—This paper investigates classification of deep moonquakes. Because some waveforms in deep moonquake contain much noise and small amplitude, estimating the source using conventional means is difficult. Therefore, we use machine learning based on waveform similarity to estimate the seismic sources of moonquakes. However, when the source of moonquake is unknown, the arrival time to the observation points is not determined. Therefore, cutting the S wave of a moonquake based on the arrival time is difficult. To classify waveforms for which the arrival time is not determined, we use long waveform from the start time of event, which might contain the arrival time. Moreover, we classify 43 unlabeled moonquakes observed by Apollo 12. As a result, labels were given with high classification probability for many moonquakes.**

Keywords–Waveform analysis; Neural Network.

I. Introduction

With the NASA Apollo mission, observation devices called the Apollo Lunar Surface Experiments Package (ALSEP) were installed. The Passive Seismic Experiment (PSE), one experiment using ALSEP, is an experiment of observing moonquakes on the lunar surface using five seismometers. Each of them includes three long-period instruments (one vertical and two horizontal components) and one short-period instrument (vertical component). Among them, using 1-4 seismometers (Apollo 12, 14, 15, 16), records of moonquakes were kept for about seven and a half years.

The moonquake data observed by PSE are still being analyzed. Much knowledge has been gained for the prediction of the cause of occurrence, the degree of activity, and the internal structure of the Moon [1] [2]. Based on the depth and factors, moonquakes have four types: artificial impacts, natural impacts, shallow moonquakes, and deep moonquakes. Deep moonquakes are the most numerous types of events [3] recorded by the PSE. Moreover, deep moonquakes are known to occur periodically from the same source. Waveforms [4] of moonquakes of the same source are similar [5] [6].

To analyze the substances constituting the Moon and the Moon ' s internal structure, some researches try to estimate the source of the deep moonquakes. As a result, labels representing the source are assigned to a part of the observed deep moonquake. The labeled deep moonquake is published in a moonquake event catalog [7]–[9].

Although waveforms observed at three observation points are used generally to estimate sources, the number of such waveforms is few. Previous researches estimate sources by visual inspection and similarity of waveforms. The most current event catalog still lists events selected from the data in this manner. A combination of waveform cross correlation and single-link cluster analysis performed on this catalog [10]. However, many events are difficult to classify into existing sources because of the noise and other hindrances. In fact, the catalog has more than 300 undefined deep moonquake tremors that have not been identified, and more than 3,300 unknown types of moonquakes. To solve this problem, it is necessary to discover applicable features to classify the waveforms into the sources. Therefore, in this study, we specifically examine machine learning as a new classification method for deep moonquake sources. In addition, if we manually label large amounts of data that are not labeled, then analytical processing takes enormous amount of time. However, it is assumed that it can be automated using machine learning.

In this study, the source estimation of deep moonquakes is regarded as a multi-class classification problem. Labeled events are regarded as learning data. We have studied a method to classify sources of deep moonquake automatically and assign labels to deep moonquakes.

Because Kikuchi et al. [11] indicated that Neural [12] has the highest classification performance of deep moonquakes, we used Neural Network to classify the moonquakes. Neural Network outputs the output class with a probability. Therefore, in this study, we labeled the probabilities of deep moonquakes.

Because the source is unknown and S / N is low, it is unclear when the wave arrives. Therefore, we apply some estimation method of arrival time of the moonquakes, and evaluate the classification of these based on the estimated time.

The structure of this paper is the following. Section 2 presents a description of related studies. Section 3 presents a description of the method, results, and discussion of determining the waveform classification method for unclassified events.

Section 4 presents a description of the method, results, and discussion of classification of unclassified events. Section 5 presents a description of the summary and future tasks of this paper.

II. RELEVANT STUDIES

A. Studies of moonquake classification

Some studies have been conducted to estimate sources of deep moonquakes. Nakamura [13] used a combination of waveform cross-correlation and single-link cluster analysis for deep moonquake events and estimated the source manually based on the results. In addition, Bulow [14] devised pre-processing methods and discovered new events. First, noise included in the waveform was removed using a band pass filter in a process known as despiking. Next, they performed clustering with cross-correlation as similarity. Consequently, many deep moonquakes were newly discovered and labeled. Actually, A1 found many deep moonquakes. Particularly, it has been found that many deep moonquakes of A1 have remarkable features. The estimation results of these two studies are reflected in the lunar event catalog. Endrun [15] uses Hidden Markov Model to classify more than 50% of the unclassified deep moonquakes of Apollo 16 and proposes those labels. Moreover, in that study, more than 200 new deep moonquake events were discovered. In this study, we attempt to classify the sources of deep moonquakes using Neural Networks, which have attracted much attention in recent years.

Some studies convert conversion of moonquake data to a power spectral density (PSD). The PSD is the amplitude intensity calculated for each frequency component. Goto [16] et al. compare the classification performance using four features: PSD, its envelope, the envelope of the waveform, and conversion to PSD. Among them, a feature quantity with high classification performance is the conversion of the waveform to PSD. Therefore, in this paper, we use PSD as a feature of the classification. Research by Kato [17] et al. is a study that converts waveforms into PSD and performs clustering. In the research, the cutout time from the P wave arrival time is changed. Classification is performed using the PSD. As a result, the classification performance was highest immediately after the P wave arrival time. In this study, PSD from P wave arrival time is used as training data.

III. DETERMINATION OF WAVEFORM CLASSIFICATION METHODS FOR UNCLASSIFIED EVENTS

In this section, we describe a method to classify waveforms of unclassified event. As described before, the arrival time of the unclassified event is unknown. Therefore, we propose the classification procedure of the event even if the arrival time of the unclassified event is unknown.

A. Experiment method

In this section, we describe datasets, feature quantity, evaluation index, and classification methods of waveforms of unclassified events. In this research, from a study by Kikuchi et al. [11], we use Neural Network, which has the highest classification performance of moonquakes, to classify the lunar earthquake. Neural Network is a machine-learning algorithm produced by various researchers [12]. In image contest [18] in 2012, since Hinton et al. first used this method, attention has been devoted to its effectiveness. Neural Network changes the value of input data in each neuron using weights and activation functions. Moreover, the output of the output layer is compared with the correct solution data to calculate an error. The weight is updated by back-propagating the error. Consequently, Neural Network learns. For this research, we use multilayer perceptron, which is a kind of Neural Network. The multilayer perceptron performs linear classification only in two layers: the input layer and the output layer. Adding an intermediate layer makes it possible to perform nonlinear classification. In this study, to perform multi-class classification, cross entropy was used for the error function of the output layer. A soft-max function was used as the activation function. The soft max function is a function for making classes of classification into a probability distribution by setting the sum of output values to 1. The number of neurons in the output layer was set to 9, which is the number of classes of classification to be done in this study.

1) Dataset: In this paper, we only use the deep moonquakes, for which there are a particularly large number of events [19]. Moonquake data are recorded as components in three directions of the X axis, Y axis, and Z axis. In this research, because the data of the long-period seismograph are used, the three components of X axis, Y axis, and Z axis are expressed respectively as LPX, LPY, and LPZ. In addition, because the waveform of the moonquakes includes much noise, the seismic source in this study is classified using the waveform to which preprocessing is applied. As preprocessing, average subtraction, trend subtraction, band pass filter of 0.3–1.5 Hz, and spike removal processing were performed. An example of the lunar wave waveform after preprocessing is shown in Figure 1 for each of the three components. In Figure 1, the horizontal axis shows time. The vertical axis shows amplitude. From Figure 1, it is apparent that the waveform differs depending on the difference in components in one event. According to an earlier study [11] conducted by the authors, we use LPZ data also in this research because the classification performance in case of using LPZ was high.

For this research, we use only the moonquake data observed by Apollo 12, for which the observation period was long and the number of events was large. Our dataset consists of 9 sources with 50 and more events labeled. The label assigned by the conventional method cited the catalog. Seismometers of two types, peak mode and flat mode, differ depending on the period of the moonquake observation. These two modes have different frequency characteristics. In this study, we used only events observed in peak mode, where the observation period was long. The number of events for each epicenter is shown in Table I. From Table I, the number of events is shown to differ depending on the source. However, as shown in our earlier study [11], classification performance was high even when the number of events was not balanced. Therefore, we do not do preprocessing such as balancing events.

In this study, the continuing length of the event used for classification was set to 15 min because the classification performance was high in a preliminary experiment and the amount of data was reduced in our earlier research [11]. The sampling frequency of the moonquake is 6.62514 Hz. One point represents about 0.151 s. As a result the data of 15 min constitute 5,962 points.

2) Evaluation criteria: In this study, we use three criterions F-score, precision, and recall. F-score is calculated by the

TABLE I. NUMBER OF MOONQUAKE EVENTS USED FOR THE EXPERIMENT (FOR EACH SOURCE.)

Source	A1	A6	A8	A9	A10	A14	A18	A20	A23
Number of events	262	85	93	94	108	87	106	106	54

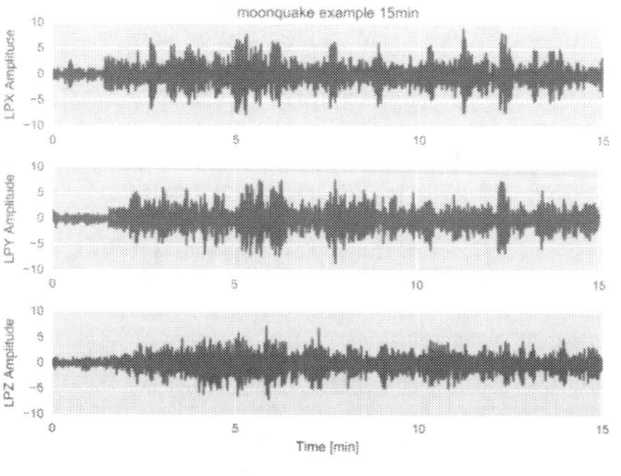

Figure 1. Moonquake waveform example.

harmonic mean of the precision and recall score. The precision score is the ratio of how many correct answers are included in the classification result. The recall score is the ratio of what was actually classified correctly among those that should come out as a result of classification. As an example, the precision score, recall score, and F-score of A1 when classifying events are shown in the following equations.

$$\text{Precision score} = \frac{\text{Number correctly predicted as A1}}{\text{Number predicted as A1}}$$

$$\text{Recall score} = \frac{\text{Number correctly predicted as A1}}{\text{Total number of A1}}$$

$$\text{F-score} = \frac{2 * \text{Precision score} * \text{Recall score}}{\text{Precision score} + \text{Recall score}}$$

We use the equations above to calculate the F-score for other sources also.

3) Feature value: In this study, we use PSD using the waveform of the moonquake. PSD is a calculation of the amplitude intensity for each frequency component and is used for time correlation analysis of time series data. In this study, PSD is calculated using the Welch method. In our previous study [11], we compared the classification performance of the sampling number from 256 points to 2,048 points: the higher the sampling number was, the higher the achieved classification performance. Therefore, as a preliminary experiment, the classification performances of 2,048 points, 4,096 points, and 8,192 points of sampling numbers were compared. The classification performance of 4,096 points was high, so PSD of 4,096 sampling points was also used in this experiment.

4) Waveform classification method of unclassified events: In this section, we describe the approach for classifying the waveforms for which the arrival time is unknown. Since arrival time is not able to be used for the classification, we use segments, which might contain correct arrival time, extracted from the waveform of event. The segments consist of divided waveforms by 15 minutes. We divide waveforms segments by 15 minutes in accordance with previous research [11]. As a result, the evaluation data contains 30,000 points from the start time of the event. We compare five approaches for the classification as presented below.

Method 1
: We classify the waveforms based on center of the time at which the amplitude is the largest.
In this method, we set waveform of 15 min from 7 min and 30 s before the maximum amplitude.

Method 2
: We divide the waveform into segments, and classify them all into a source. We regard the largest number of label as the label of waveform.
Figure 2 is an image diagram when one waveform is divided into segments. Figure 3 shows an image for which waveforms divided into segments as shown in Figure 2 are labeled by Methods 2, 3, and 4. In Figure 3, a classification probability and a label based on that were assigned to each segment.

Method 3
: We divide the waveform into segments, and classify them all into a source. We regard the highest classification probability as the label of waveform.

Method 4
: We divide the waveform into segments, and classify them all into a source. We regard the highest value in the average of classification probability as the label of waveform.

Method 5
: We classify the waveform using the waveform after the arrival time specified by preliminary experiments.
For determination of a specific segment of method 5, waveforms to be used as evaluation data are divided into segments and are classified using segments of the same time. Moreover, classification is performed using the segment of the time with the largest F-score.

The segment was shifted by 10 points; the 15-minute waveform was regarded as one segment. Methods 2, 3, and 4 differ in their methods of classifying the results of all segments into classification results of one waveform. To ascertain the method of classifying waveforms of unclassified events, we conducted five cross validations using events with a known source.

Unclassified events are classified using the method with the highest F-score among these five methods.

B. Results and discussion

In this section, we use each method described in Section III-A4 to classify the moonquakes and to evaluate their classification performance.

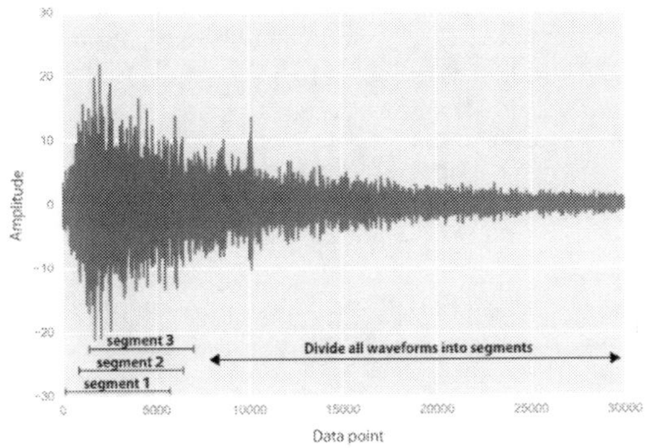

Figure 2. The waveform image divided into segments.

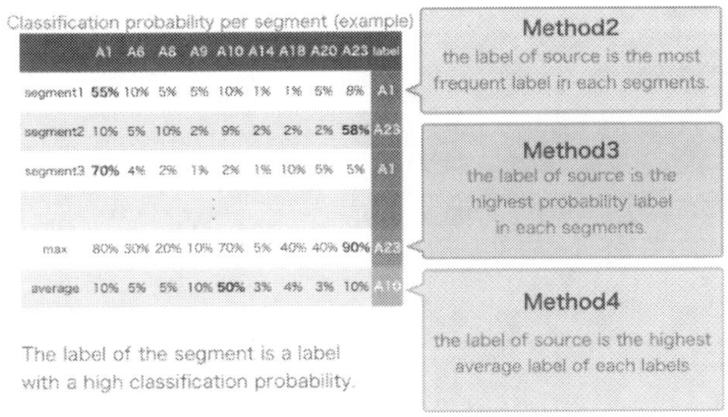

Figure 3. Images of Method 2, Method 3, Method 4 in Section III-A4I.

TABLE II. HYPERPARAMETERS OF THE NEURAL NETWORK.

Number of neurons				Activation function	Optimization function	Dropout
first layer	second layer	third layer	fourth layer			
1,500	1,000	500	250	tanh	Adam	Yes

1) Determination of hyperparameters: The Neural Network used for the classification of the lunar earthquake in this study has an arbitrarily determinable value called a hyperparameter. To improve the classification performance, it is necessary to adjust the hyperparameter and to construct a classifier that is optimal for the dataset.

Preliminary experiments determine hyperparameters such as the number of neurons of the middle layers, number of layers, activation function, optimization function, presence or absence of dropout. In this study, we change the parameters of numbers of neurons in the middle layer, numbers of layers, activation function, optimization function, presence or absence of dropout, and compare performance of the classfication result. An appropriate hyperparameter is determined by finding the highest F-score for each classification result. First, the number of neurons in the first middle layer is determined. The number of neurons used for this study is the number of neurons at the time when fluctuation of the F-score of the classification result disappears because of the increase in the number of neurons.

Second, the number of middle layers and the number of neurons in the added middle layer are determined. We increase the number of layers in the middle layer and increase the number of layers if the F-score of the classification result rises. At this time, for the newly added layer, the number of neurons is determined in the same way as in the case of the first layer. These are repeated until there is no increase in the F-score of the classification result.

Third, we determine various functions to be applied to each layer. Classification is performed using one of the activation functions such as sigmoid, tanh, and ReLU, and a function with the highest F-score is applied to each layer.

With Neural Network, there is a technique called Dropout that stops the operation of some neurons randomly selected during learning. Using this, it is robustly learned and its effectiveness is improved. Dropout was applied to the middle layer of Neural Network because it was observed that overlearning was occurring as a result of classification without Dropout.

TABLE III. F-SCORE OF CLASSIFICATION RESULT OF EACH METHOD.

Method name	F-score
Method 1	0.31
Method 2	0.21
Method 3	0.30
Method 4	0.19
Method 5	**0.68**

Finally, the optimization function is determined. Classification was performed using each of Adam [20], AdaGrad [21], AdaDelta [22], and SGD as optimization functions. The optimization function with the highest F-score of its classification result was used for this study. Table II shows parameters applied to Neural Network, as determined by tuning.

Implementation of Neural Network used Chainer [23], which is a module of Python.

2) Classification results of respective methods and discussion: After the tuning of Section III-B1, the dataset of the moonquake was classified using the five methods of Section III-A4. Then, we compare their classification performances. Table III shows the F-score obtained as a result of the classification. The values in the table are averages of those calculated for each source. From Table III, when classification was done using method 5, the F-score was the highest result. Method 5 is a method of determining the segment with the highest F-score and classifying it using the waveform from that time. As in Method 2, Method 3, and Method 4, because all segments are not considered in classification, Method 5 does not affect the segment of noise. Therefore, the F-value of Method 5 is regarded as being higher than these methods.

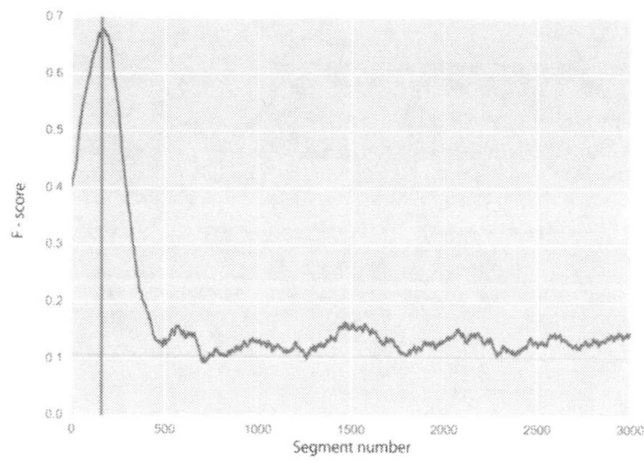

Figure 4. F-score of classification in the same time segment between events.

Figure 4 shows visualization of F-score using method 5 for each segment. The horizontal axis of Figure 4 represents the segment number. Because the segments that shifted by 10 points are made, the waveform of 30,000 points is 3,000 segments. Because the segment is made from the event start time, the origin is the segment immediately after the event is started. Figure 4 shows that the F-score near the 160th segment was high and the 167th segment was the highest F-score. In other words, the classification performance of the segment after 1,670 points (252.07 s) from the event start time was the highest. For each source used for classification this time, the median value of the P wave arrival time from the event start time is 1,583 points (238.94 s). The minimum is 1,523 points (229.88 s). This time 1,670 points (252.07 s) are close to the two values. It seems reasonable to observe the highest F-value near 1,670 points (252.07 s) by these factors.

Table III shows that Method 1 for classifying waveforms using the waveform centered at the largest amplitude caused a low F-score. The classification performance is low, because the part with the largest amplitude of the waveform is hidden by noise.

Method 2, Method 3, and Method 4, for which waveforms are divided into segments and classification is performed considering all the segments, also produced a low F-score in Table III. Method 2 is a method of using the label which is the largest in the classification result of each segment as the label of the waveform. Using this method, it seems that since the waveform contains many noise segments, the label of the segment of noise is better than the label of less S wave by majority decision. Therefore, the classification performance of Method 2 was low.

Method 3 is a method of using the label with the largest classification probability of all segments as the label of the waveform. Similarly to Method 2, it seems that there is a noisy segment that has a high classification probability, and that the label influenced the classification result. However, we assume Method 3 is attributable to one segment. Compared to Method 2 and Method 4, because it was not influenced by noise, it is considered that the F-value was higher than Method 2 and Method 4. Method 4 is a method by which the label having the largest average classification probability of each segment is used as the waveform label. Similarly to Method 2, it seems that since there were many segments of noise in the waveform, when calculating the average, the influence of noise was much received. Therefore, the classification performance of Method 4 was low. In other words, Method 2, Method 3, and Method 4, which are methods using all segments, are regarded as having lowered classification performance because there were many segments for which noise dominates the waveform used for classification.

TABLE IV. CLASSIFICATION RESULT OF UNCLASSIFIED EVENTS (RANKING TOP 5).

Event	Source	Classification probability
1974-06-28-13:49	A1	0.99993
1972-12-09-01:39	A10	0.99992
1972-05-10-07:43	A1	0.99985
1972-05-15-18:06	A20	0.99982
1977-04-27-15:41	A10	0.99944

TABLE V. NUMBER OF UNCLASSIFIED EVENTS CLASSIFIED IN EACH SOURCE.

Source	Number of events
A1	7
A6	3
A8	12
A9	1
A10	11
A14	2
A18	4
A20	3
A23	0

IV. CLASSIFICATION OF UNCLASSIFIED EVENTS

In this section, we classify unclassified deep moonquakes using the method with the highest classification performance determined in Section III.

A. Experiment procedure

The same data as those in Section III were used as training data in this experiment. Unclassified events are 43 events observed in Peak mode at Apollo 12 point, known as a deep moonquake. Then, the same preprocessing as that used in Section III-A1 was applied; LPZ data were used. Moreover, as explained in Section III, the 15-minute waveform after 1670 points from the event start time was used. These are converted to PSD and are classified by a neural network.

B. Results and discussion

Table IV presents the ranking in descending order of event classification probability as a result of classification of unclassified moonquakes using neural networks. The event with the highest classification probability is the event of 1974-06-28-13: 49. It was classified into A1 with the probability of about 1.00. Figure 5 shows this event of 1974-06-28-13: 49. Figure 6 presents an example of the event of A1 in which the event of 1974-06-28-13: 49 is classified. The red lines in Figure 5 and Figure 6 refer to 1670 points of waveform arrival time determined in Section III. Even comparing Figure 5 and Figure

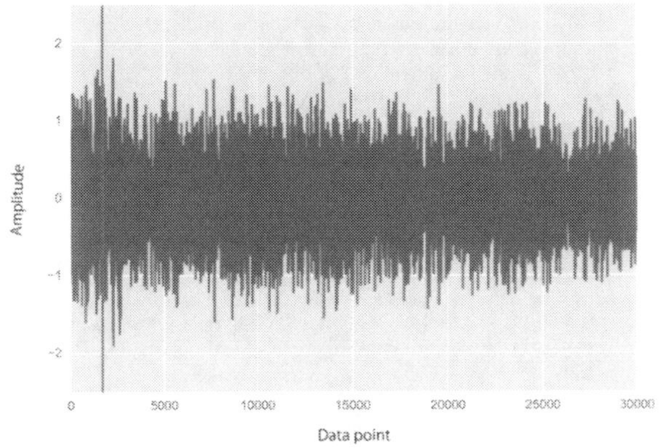

Figure 5. Event with the highest classification probability (1974-06-28-13:49).

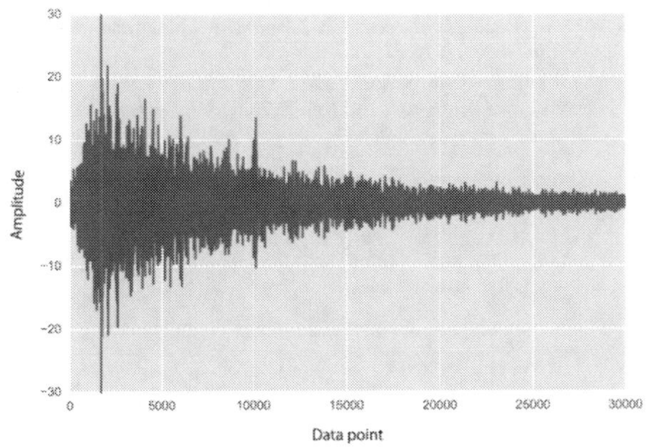

Figure 6. Example of waveform of A1 (1975-04-23-12:05).

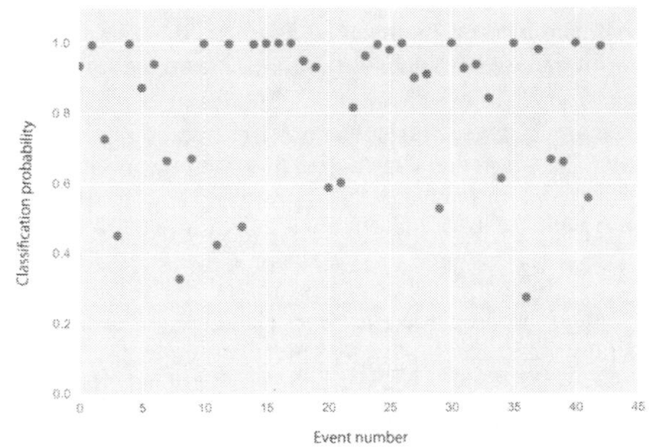

Figure 7. Classification probability of each event.

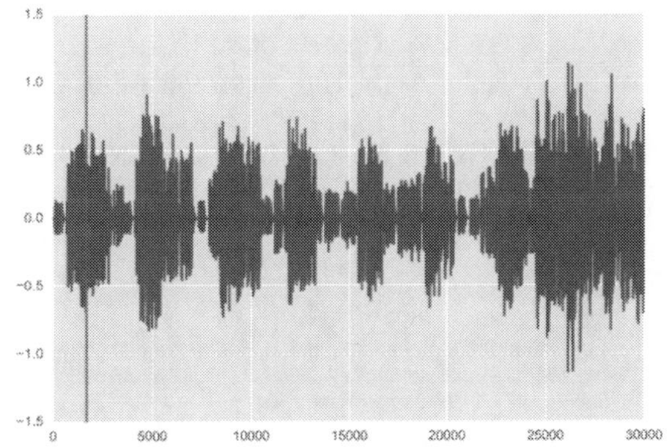

Figure 8. Example of event used for classification (1972-05-20-08:45).

6, it is difficult to classify the unclassified waveform by the naked eye. However, as presented in this report, classification by machine learning is considered to be a new proposal of classification. The associated human cost can be reduced.

Figure 7 presents the classification probability of each event. The horizontal axis is the event number. It is in the order in which the event occurred. The vertical axis is the classification probability. Figure 7 shows that the classification probability is high overall. Moreover, Table V shows the number of each label in this classification. Among the sources, A8 has the largest number of events classified; A23 has none of the events classified.

However, some problems exist with the results of the classification. This is caused by the following limitations in our experiments. Some of unlabeled event might happen from undiscovered sources. Also, we use a part of sources as dataset in those experiments, since the small number of events is difficult to train in neural networks. Therefore, the correct source of some events does not exist in our dataset.

There are also preprocessing problems. Figure 8 presents an example of the event used for classification this time. Figure 8 shows that the amplitude of the waveform fluctuates greatly at regular time intervals. Parts with large amplitude and small parts are regarded as formed because despiking of preprocessing deletes a large value for a certain period of time and linearly interpolates. In other words, a waveform exists with an error in the waveform information at the stage of preprocessing. More accurate classification might be achieved by reviewing pretreatment methods or using a waveform to which preprocessing is not applied.

V. CONCLUSION

As described in this paper, moonquake sources were classified using neural networks. To examine the classification method of the event where the arrival time of the moonquake is unknown, the classification performance of several methods was compared. Results show that the method with the highest classification performance was to divide the waveform into segments and to classify them using specific segments. That particular segment was the segment with the highest classification performance, as a result of classification of segments by simultaneity. Moreover, the start time of the segment is the arrival time of the waveform. Additionally, we classified unclassified events using this method. We proposed a new classification result by machine learning of unclassified events for which classification is difficult to accomplish by the naked eye.

Future tasks include expansion of the source to be classified. The classifiers used for this study can only classify sources used for teaching data. However, because sources other than teaching data of this study include few events, it is difficult to regard each source as one class. It is necessary to devise a means by which all sources except the teaching data of this study are regarded as one class. As a result, a more accurate classification is possible. Throughout this study, if the location of the source of the event which has not been classified to date is decided, then the number of events of each source will increase. Results show that the occurrence cycle of deep moonquake is reviewed. Further constraints are imposed on the mechanism of occurrence of the moonquake. Moreover, depending on the source, by increasing the number of observation points, the source position can be ascertained accurately from the runtime data.

Acknowledgment

We are grateful to Dr. Hiroyuki Shoji for helpful discussions.

This work was supported by JSPS KAKENHI Grant Numbers 16K00157, 16K16158, and Tokyo Metropolitan University Grant-in-Aid for Research on Priority Areas "Research on social big data."

References

[1] Y. Nakamura, G. V. Latham, and H. J. Dorman, "Apollo lunar seismic experiment—final summary," *Journal of Geophysical Research: Solid Earth (1978–2012)*, vol. 87, no. S01, pp. A117–A123, 1982.

[2] P. Lognonné, J. Gagnepain-Beyneix, and H. Chenet, "A new seismic model of the moon: implications for structure, thermal evolution and formation of the moon," *Earth and Planetary Science Letters*, vol. 211, no. 1, pp. 27–44, 2003.

[3] This paper, we define a moonquake which is observed by pse as a event.

[4] Hereinafter, the waveform represents the waveform of moonquake, unless otherwise specified.

[5] D. R. Lammlein, "Lunar seismicity and tectonics," *Physics of the Earth and Planetary Interiors*, vol. 14, no. 3, pp. 224–273, 1977.

[6] R. C. Bulow, C. L. Johnson, B. G. Bills, and P. M. Shearer, "Temporal and spatial properties of some deep moonquake clusters," *Journal of Geophysical Research: Planets (1991–2012)*, vol. 112, no. E9, 2007.

[7] R. Yamada, Y. Yamamoto, J. Kuwamura, and Y. Nakamura, "Development of an online retrieval system of apollo lunar seismic data," *Journal of Space Science Informatics Japan*, vol. 1, pp. 121–131, 2012.

[8] Hereinafter, this is called a catalog.

[9] (2017, 3) Darts as isas/jaxa. [Online]. Available: http://www.darts.isas.jaxa.jp

[10] Y. Nakamura, G. Latham, J. Dorman, and J. Harris, "Passive seismic experiment long-period event catalog," *Galveston Geophysics Laboratory Contribution*, vol. 491, p. 314, 1981.

[11] S. Kikuchi, R. Yamada, Y. Yamamoto, S. Yokoyama, and H. Ishikawa, "Gesshinbunrui ni tekishita kikaigakusyu no kentou (study on machine learning method suitable for moonquake classification)," *8th Forum on data engineering and information management, E4-1*, 2016.

[12] S. Haykin and N. Network, "A comprehensive foundation," *Neural Networks*, vol. 2, no. 2004, 2004.

[13] Y. Nakamura, "New identification of deep moonquakes in the apollo lunar seismic data," *Physics of the Earth and Planetary Interiors*, vol. 139, no. 3, pp. 197–205, 2003.

[14] R. C. Bulow, C. L. Johnson, and P. M. Shearer, "New events discovered in the apollo lunar seismic data," *Journal of Geophysical Research: Planets (1991–2012)*, vol. 110, no. E10, 2005.

[15] B. Knapmeyer-Endrun and C. Hammer, "Identification of new events in apollo 16 lunar seismic data by hidden markov model-based event detection and classification," *Journal of Geophysical Research: Planets*, vol. 120, no. 10, pp. 1620–1645, 2015.

[16] Y. Goto, R. Yamada, Y. Yamamoto, S. Yokoyama, and H. Ishikawa, "A system for visualizing large-scale moonquake data considering waveform similarity using som," *JAXA Research and development report: Journal of Space Science Informatics Japan*, vol. 3, pp. 137–146, 2014.

[17] K. Kato, R. Yamada, Y. Yamamoto, S. Yokoyama, and H. Ishikawa, "Kizongesshinbunnrui no kikaigakusyu wo motiita datousei no kensyou (validation of existing moonquakes classification using machine learning)," *8th Forum on data engineering and information management, E4-1*, 2016.

[18] (2017, 3) Imagenet large scale visual recognition challenge. [Online]. Available: http://image-net.org/challenges/LSVRC/2012/index

[19] Hereinafter, when not explicitly stated, the deep moonquakes are called simply moonquakes.

[20] D. Kingma and J. Ba, "Adam: A method for stochastic optimization," *arXiv preprint arXiv:1412.6980*, 2014.

[21] J. Duchi, E. Hazan, and Y. Singer, "Adaptive subgradient methods for online learning and stochastic optimization," *Journal of Machine Learning Research*, vol. 12, no. Jul, pp. 2121–2159, 2011.

[22] M. D. Zeiler, "Adadelta: an adaptive learning rate method," *arXiv preprint arXiv:1212.5701*, 2012.

[23] S. Tokui, K. Oono, S. Hido, and J. Clayton, "Chainer: a next-generation open source framework for deep learning," in *LearningSys Workshop on Machine Learning Systems at Neural Information Processing Systems (NIPS)*, 2015.

Analysis of Spatial and Temporal Features to Classify the Deep Moonquake Sources Using Balanced Random Forest

Kodai Kato *, Ryuhei Yamada†, Yukio Yamamoto‡,
Masaharu Hirota§, Shohei Yokoyama¶ and Hiroshi Ishikawa‖
* Faculty of System Design, Tokyo Metropolitan University, 6-6 Asahigaoka, Hino-shi, Tokyo, Japan
Email: kato-kodai@ed.tmu.ac.jp
† National Astronomical Observatory of Japan, RISE project, 2-12 Hoshigaoka-cho, Mizusawa-ku, Oshu, Iwate, Japan
Email: r.yamada@nao.ac.jp
‡ Japan Aerospace Exploration Agency, 3-1-1, Yoshinodai, Chuo-ku, Sagamihara-shi, Kanagawa, Japan
Email: yamamoto.yukio@jaxa.jp
§ Department of Information Engineering National Institute of Technology, Oita College 1666 Maki Oita-shi, Oita, Japan
Email: m-hirota@oita-ct.ac.jp
¶ Faculty of Informatics, Shizuoka University, 3-5-1 Joho-ku, Hamamatsu-shi, Shizuoka, Japan
Email: yokoyama@inf.shizuoka.ac.jp
‖ Faculty of System Design, Tokyo Metropolitan University, 6-6 Asahigaoka, Hino-shi, Tokyo, Japan
Email: ishikawa-hiroshi@tmu.ac.jp

***Abstract*—In this paper, we evaluate other features different from the waveforms to classify seismic sources. Classification of sources of the deep moonquakes is an important issue for analyzing the focal mechanisms and the lunar deep structures. It was found that deep moonquakes that occur from the same source have similar waveforms. Some studies have been conducted to identify the deep moonquake sources using the waveform similarities. However, classifying some deep moonquakes using only the waveforms is difficult due to large noise and the small amplitude. If we could show that other features different from the waveforms are effective for classification of deep moonquakes, we can increase the number of classifiable moonquakes even if moonquakes include noise and small amplitude of the waveforms. Therefore, we use other features to classify deep moonquakes (position and velocity relative to the Earth, Sun, Jupiter, and Venus, as seen from the Moon). We apply these features to classify deep moonquakes that are not classified based on only waveforms, and it is useful to analyze the deep moonquake occurrence mechanisms. Our experiments showed that the position and velocity relation between the Moon and the Earth or Jupiter are effective for classification.**

Keywords–Planetary Science; Machine learning; Geophysical

I. INTRODUCTION

The Apollo Lunar Surface Experiments Package (ALSEP) was deployed on the Moon to investigate the lunar surface, internal structure and surrounding environment through NASA's Apollo missions. The Passive Seismic Experiment (PSE) in the ALSEP has been performed to observe the lunar seismicity. The observations revealed that seismic events called moonquakes occur on the Moon. All observed data are acquired and viewed on the Web [1] [2]. The moonquake data are very important to analyze the lunar internal structure and the focal mechanisms of moonquakes, even after 40 years since PSE finished [3] [4].

Earlier studies have revealed that moonquake characteristics differ widely from those of earthquakes. For instance, contrary to earthquakes, moonquakes do not occur due to plate tectonics. Additionally, moonquakes have several types: 'Deep Moonquakes', 'Shallow Moonquakes', 'Thermal', and 'Meteoroid Impact', which are classified based on the occurrence factor or depth of seismic sources. About 13,000 events have been found to date including about 7,300 deep moonquakes, about 30 shallow moonquakes, and about 1,700 meteoroid impacts. Deep moonquakes account for over half of all moonquakes.

Deep moonquakes that occurred from the same source are similar waveforms [5] [6]. Earlier studies have classified deep moonquakes based on the similarities [7] (sources of deep moonquakes are labeled as Axx e.g., A1, A6, A200.). The purpose of this study is the classification of unclassified deep moonquakes to elucidate the deep moonquake focal mechanisms. Goto et al. [8] classified deep moonquakes, specifically examining frequency spectra of deep moonquakes using machine learning. Machine learning has advantages to classify deep moonquakes such as automation of analyses and the great reduction of human cost.

Although the waveforms are effective features to infer moonquake sources, determination of sources of some moonquakes is difficult due to large noise and the small amplitude. Previous studies have not applied any features other than the waveforms. Therefore, we specifically examine features other than the waveforms. If we show that feature such as velocity is effective for classification of deep moonquake, classification using a combination of the feature and waveforms may increase the number of classifiable moonquakes even if moonquakes include noise and small amplitude of the waveforms. Deep moonquakes occur periodically from the same source related with the tidal stresses [9]–[11]. As described herein, we extract features from the occurrence time of deep moonquakes. Then, using machine learning, we verify the effective features to classify sources of deep moonquakes. A principal benefit of our approach is that we can infer sources of deep moonquakes, irrespective of noise and amplitude of the waveforms.

This paper is organized as follows. Section II presents a review of related works including moonquake analyses.

Section III presents a method of feature evaluation. Section IV presents both experimental and analytical results. Finally, concluding remarks are presented in the last section.

II. Related Works

Generally, time differences among arrival times of the seismic phases observed at several seismic stations are available to determine the moonquake sources. If we cannot use the time differences to estimate sources due to the noise and small amplitudes in the waveforms, then similarities of waveforms are useful to classify sources. In 1970, the moonquakes were classified manually by visual observation [12].

With the evolution of computers, Nakamura et al. [7] classified deep moonquakes using hierarchical clustering based on cross correlation of waveforms. This classified result of deep moonquakes is cataloged as a standard criterion for classification in this study. The improvement of the preprocessing methods, which use cross-correlation analyses, enables us to discover new events and to classify the unclassified deep moonquakes [13]. Furthermore, the paper written by Endrun et al. [14] proposed a method for event detection and classification using a Hidden Markov Model. Goto et al. [8] developed a web system for visualizing moonquakes considering waveform similarity using Self-Organizing Map (SOM) to advance the study of moonquake classification. This study showed that noise and small amplitudes of the waveforms affect classification criteria. Therefore, we propose an approach to classify deep moonquakes, not using the waveforms.

III. Methods

To verify the features for classification of deep moonquakes, we apply Balanced Random Forest [15] extended from Random Forest [16], which is a representative supervised learning method. We verify whether seismic sources can be reproduced or not using Balanced Random Forest.

A. Features

We extract the position (x, y, z), velocity (vx, vy, vz), distance $(\sqrt{x^2 + y^2 + z^2})$, and the magnitude of the velocity $(\sqrt{vx^2 + vy^2 + vz^2})$ of each planet (the Earth, Sun, Jupiter and Venus) relative to the Moon in the IAU_MOON coordinate system, calculated using SPICE [17] at the deep moonquake occurrence time. We apply the orbit parameters as the features. The IAU_MOON coordinate system is the Moon fixed coordinate system. The z-axis is the North Pole direction of the Moon. The x-axis is the meridian direction of the Moon. The y-axis is to the right of the x-z plane.

B. Balanced Random Forest

Random Forest [16] is a classification algorithm that fits a number of decision tree classifiers on various sub-samples of the dataset. This algorithm can compute feature importance. However, Random Forest has a serious problem: the classifier might overfit with imbalanced data. Generally, when we apply Random Forest, we assign weights based on class, with the minority class assigned a larger weight to make the classifier more suitable for the imbalanced data. However, this approach can cause over-learning of minority data if the data are extremely imbalanced. We must apply a method for the imbalanced data to analyze of deep moonquakes because a different number of events occurs at each seismic source.

As described herein, we apply Balanced Random Forest [15], which equalizes the number of samples per class for each iteration in random forest. The decision tree of Balanced Random Forest uses a Gini coefficient to find splits. We then compute the feature importance by calculating the average reduction ratio of the Gini coefficient in the tree split for each feature.

TABLE I. NUMBER OF EVENTS AT EACH SEISMIC SOURCE.

Source	Number of events
A1	441
A5	76
A6	178
A7	85
A8	327
A9	145
A10	230
A14	165
A18	214
A20	153
A23	79
A25	72
A35	70
A44	86
A204	85
A218	74

IV. Results and Discussion

In this section, we present the results obtained from application of our method to the dataset. The procedures used for our proposed method are presented below.

- We extract the orbit parameters as the features at the occurrence time of deep moonquake event.
- We create a Balanced Random Forest classifier for every pair of seismic sources.
- We verify the relation of seismic sources and the features based on the classification performance and feature importance of each classifier.

In these experiments, we applied one-vs.-one, which creates a classifier for each pair of seismic sources.

As described in this paper, the number of iterations in Balanced Random Forest is 1,000. Each iteration randomly selects 30 samples for each class using bootstrap method and 3 features from 8 features. Each iteration tree is implemented using the scikit-learn [18].

A. Dataset

The number of events in each source is given in Table I. We chose the seismic sources with more than 70 events in the lunar event catalog. The used dataset has 16 sources and 2,480 events.

B. Criterion

We used the classification performance and the feature importance to evaluate the features. We performed 10-fold cross validation, and used the minimum f-measure in each class for the classification performance. Due to different number of seismic events at each source, the minimum score was applied because the scores depend on the amount of data in each class. We calculated feature extraction from all classifier-learned data of the target class without cross validation and the classification performance and the feature importance among each planet.

C. Classification performance

The average of classification performance for each seismic source and planet is shown in Table II. "avg./total", which is in the last row, shows the average of all classifiers. The averages

TABLE II. AVERAGE CLASSIFICATION PERFORMANCE.

Source	Earth	Sun	Jupiter	Venus
A1	0.67	0.46	0.55	0.35
A5	0.85	0.6	0.74	0.48
A6	0.78	0.59	0.69	0.5
A7	0.82	0.53	0.7	0.41
A8	0.72	0.48	0.64	0.41
A9	0.87	0.65	0.72	0.46
A10	0.77	0.54	0.67	0.45
A14	0.81	0.57	0.73	0.52
A18	0.8	0.58	0.74	0.48
A20	0.78	0.53	0.69	0.46
A23	0.88	0.65	0.73	0.45
A25	0.83	0.54	0.75	0.45
A35	0.76	0.52	0.68	0.46
A44	0.79	0.59	0.74	0.54
A204	0.8	0.52	0.72	0.44
A218	0.76	0.5	0.64	0.45
avg./total	0.79	0.55	0.70	0.46

TABLE III. RANKING OF CLASSIFICATION PERFORMANCE.

Source	Earth	Sun	Jupiter	Venus
A1	16	16	16	16
A5	3	3	4	4
A6	10	4	11	3
A7	5	11	9	15
A8	15	15	14	14
A9	2	2	7	6
A10	12	9	13	11
A14	6	7	5	2
A18	7	6	2	5
A20	10	10	10	8
A23	1	1	6	12
A25	4	8	1	10
A35	14	13	12	7
A44	9	5	2	1
A204	8	12	8	13
A218	13	14	15	9

of all classifiers are 0.79 for the Earth, 0.70 for Jupiter, 0.55 for the Sun, and 0.46 for Venus. A classifier using those features for the Earth has the highest classification performance presented in this paper. Among our selected seismic sources, the classifier for A23 using the features for the Earth has the highest classification performance reported in this paper. The classification performance ranking is shown in Table III. Table III shows that the classifier for A1 has the lowest classification performance reported herein. For the Earth and Jupiter A5, A23, and A25 are classified very well within the top 6.

The number of classifiers with classification performance of 0.8 or more are 70/120 (number of classifiers is 120) for Earth, 30/120 for Jupiter, 5/120 for the Sun, and 0/120 for Venus in Table II. These results demonstrate that an orbit parameter of the Earth and Jupiter relative to the Moon is effective for deep moonquake classification. Particularly, the features based on the Earth are the most effective. As described in previous papers, this fact indicates that the tidal stress caused by the Earth in the lunar interior can affect the occurrences of deep moonquakes.

The features based on the Sun and Venus are ineffective, as show in Table II. These results show that some features based on the Earth and Jupiter are effective to classify seismic sources, nonetheless some features based on the Sun and Venus are not. There are some sources, such as A5, A23 and A25, which are easy to classify by using orbit parameters. A subject of future work is analysis of why these features contribute well to the classification or not.

TABLE IV. FEATURE IMPORTANCE FOR EACH SEISMIC SOURCE: EARTH.

Source	x	y	z	vx	vy	vz	Distance	Velocity
A1	0.13	0.11	0.13	0.11	0.13	0.16	0.14	0.09
A5	0.14	0.1	0.11	0.13	0.16	0.12	0.17	0.07
A6	0.14	0.12	0.13	0.12	0.14	0.14	0.14	0.08
A7	0.12	0.14	0.17	0.13	0.12	0.12	0.12	0.08
A8	0.15	0.12	0.12	0.11	0.14	0.12	0.15	0.09
A9	0.09	0.12	0.14	0.13	0.1	0.25	0.09	0.09
A10	0.14	0.11	0.11	0.11	0.14	0.14	0.15	0.09
A14	0.12	0.14	0.12	0.14	0.12	0.14	0.13	0.09
A18	0.12	0.13	0.12	0.13	0.13	0.16	0.13	0.09
A20	0.11	0.13	0.15	0.12	0.12	0.14	0.12	0.12
A23	0.08	0.11	0.23	0.12	0.08	0.21	0.08	0.08
A25	0.1	0.17	0.09	0.18	0.11	0.15	0.12	0.07
A35	0.11	0.15	0.12	0.14	0.11	0.15	0.11	0.1
A44	0.11	0.14	0.17	0.14	0.11	0.14	0.11	0.09
A204	0.15	0.14	0.1	0.14	0.14	0.11	0.13	0.08
A218	0.14	0.13	0.13	0.13	0.13	0.11	0.13	0.09

TABLE V. FEATURE IMPORTANCE FOR EACH SEISMIC SOURCE: SUN.

Source	x	y	z	vx	vy	vz	Distance	Velocity
A1	0.12	0.12	0.13	0.12	0.12	0.14	0.13	0.13
A5	0.12	0.13	0.12	0.13	0.12	0.14	0.12	0.12
A6	0.12	0.12	0.12	0.12	0.12	0.14	0.13	0.13
A7	0.12	0.12	0.13	0.12	0.12	0.14	0.13	0.13
A8	0.12	0.12	0.13	0.12	0.12	0.13	0.13	0.13
A9	0.12	0.12	0.13	0.12	0.12	0.14	0.14	0.12
A10	0.12	0.12	0.13	0.12	0.12	0.14	0.13	0.13
A14	0.12	0.12	0.13	0.12	0.12	0.14	0.13	0.13
A18	0.12	0.12	0.13	0.12	0.12	0.14	0.13	0.13
A20	0.12	0.12	0.12	0.12	0.12	0.13	0.14	0.14
A23	0.12	0.12	0.13	0.12	0.12	0.14	0.13	0.12
A25	0.12	0.12	0.12	0.12	0.12	0.14	0.13	0.12
A35	0.13	0.11	0.13	0.11	0.13	0.13	0.13	0.13
A44	0.12	0.12	0.13	0.12	0.12	0.13	0.14	0.13
A204	0.12	0.12	0.12	0.12	0.12	0.14	0.14	0.12
A218	0.12	0.13	0.13	0.12	0.12	0.13	0.12	0.12

Table II and Table III show that orbit features are useful for classification of deep moonquakes as well as waveforms studied in an earlier paper [7]. As a result, our experimental results show that orbit features can classify deep moonquakes. Therefore, when we try to classify unclassified deep moonquakes or moonquakes with noise and small amplitude of the waveforms, the orbit features are effective to classify the moonquakes. In addition, the relation between the Moon and other planets includes some knowledge to analyze the occurrence of deep moonquakes.

D. Feature Importances

The average of feature importances in each seismic source for each planet are shown in Table IV, Table V, Table VI, and Table VII. Among all lists, vz of the Earth in A9 based on the Earth is the highest score. Also, z of the Earth in A23 based on Earth is the second highest score. The velocity of the Earth in A5 is the lowest score. In Table IV, the score related to velocity is low in all sources. The score difference in all sources is small in Table V and Table VII. Also, x and vy of A204 are the highest scores in Table VI. The feature importances of distance and velocity are low in all sources in Table VI.

We discuss a reason of high feature importances related to vz of the Earth in A9 and z of the Earth in A23. Figure 1 and Figure 2 are box plots that present values of the feature for each seismic source. Figure 1 shows that distribution of the position in the z coordinate at occurrence time of A23 events is from about -45,000 km to about -20,000 km. That of A7 events is from about 0 km to about 50,000 km. Other sources,

TABLE VI. FEATURE IMPORTANCE FOR EACH SEISMIC SOURCE: JUPITER.

Source	x	y	z	vx	vy	vz	Distance	Velocity
A1	0.14	0.14	0.13	0.14	0.14	0.12	0.1	0.1
A5	0.18	0.13	0.11	0.13	0.17	0.1	0.09	0.09
A6	0.14	0.15	0.13	0.14	0.13	0.12	0.1	0.1
A7	0.12	0.16	0.13	0.16	0.13	0.11	0.09	0.09
A8	0.14	0.15	0.13	0.15	0.14	0.11	0.09	0.1
A9	0.13	0.17	0.12	0.17	0.13	0.11	0.09	0.09
A10	0.13	0.16	0.12	0.16	0.13	0.11	0.09	0.09
A14	0.13	0.16	0.12	0.17	0.14	0.11	0.09	0.09
A18	0.16	0.14	0.12	0.14	0.17	0.11	0.09	0.09
A20	0.13	0.14	0.14	0.14	0.14	0.12	0.1	0.1
A23	0.17	0.14	0.12	0.14	0.17	0.11	0.09	0.08
A25	0.14	0.17	0.11	0.18	0.14	0.1	0.08	0.08
A35	0.13	0.15	0.13	0.15	0.13	0.13	0.09	0.09
A44	0.14	0.15	0.15	0.15	0.14	0.1	0.09	0.09
A204	0.17	0.13	0.12	0.13	0.18	0.1	0.08	0.09
A218	0.15	0.13	0.13	0.13	0.16	0.11	0.09	0.1

TABLE VII. FEATURE IMPORTANCE FOR EACH SEISMIC SOURCE: VENUS.

Source	x	y	z	vx	vy	vz	Distance	Velocity
A1	0.12	0.12	0.13	0.12	0.12	0.13	0.12	0.12
A5	0.13	0.12	0.12	0.12	0.13	0.13	0.12	0.12
A6	0.12	0.12	0.13	0.12	0.12	0.13	0.12	0.12
A7	0.12	0.12	0.14	0.12	0.13	0.13	0.12	0.12
A8	0.12	0.12	0.13	0.13	0.12	0.13	0.12	0.12
A9	0.13	0.12	0.13	0.12	0.13	0.13	0.12	0.12
A10	0.12	0.12	0.13	0.12	0.12	0.14	0.12	0.12
A14	0.13	0.12	0.13	0.12	0.13	0.13	0.12	0.12
A18	0.13	0.12	0.13	0.12	0.13	0.13	0.12	0.12
A20	0.13	0.12	0.13	0.12	0.13	0.13	0.12	0.12
A23	0.12	0.12	0.14	0.12	0.13	0.13	0.12	0.12
A25	0.13	0.12	0.13	0.12	0.13	0.13	0.12	0.12
A35	0.12	0.12	0.13	0.12	0.13	0.13	0.13	0.12
A44	0.12	0.13	0.13	0.13	0.12	0.13	0.12	0.12
A204	0.13	0.12	0.13	0.12	0.13	0.13	0.12	0.12
A218	0.13	0.12	0.13	0.12	0.13	0.13	0.12	0.12

such as those of A1, A8, and A10, have a wider range than A23 or A7. Conversely, Figure 2 shows that the distribution of the velocity in the z coordinate at occurrence time of A9 events is from about 0.06 km/s to about 0.13 km/s. That of A5 is from about -0.13 km/s to about -0.02 km/s. Other sources, such as A8, A20, and A35, have a wider range than A9 or A5.

Figure 1 and Figure 2 show differences in the distribution of the features for each seismic source. We can show that the features with high importance have a narrow distribution and that seismic sources have features which have high feature importances; A1 does not have these features.

Moreover, the position and velocity in z coordinate at occurrence time of each seismic event in a few sources are shown in Figure 3 and Figure 4. Figure 3 shows that fluctuation of z position at occurrence time of A23 events is small through the observation period and that the occurrence frequency of A23 from about 1975 to about 1976 is less frequent than in other periods. The distribution of z position at occurrence time of A1 events changed from about 1973 to about 1975. Conversely, Figure 4 shows that fluctuation of z velocity at occurrence time of A9 events is small through the observation period. The distribution of z velocity at occurrence time of A1 events changed from about 1973 to about 1975.

The results show that there is a time variation of the features for each source. Therefore, the classification performance of A1 might be improved if features with time variation could be considered.

Next, we discuss the velocity of the Earth and the distance of Jupiter as examples of the features with low feature importance.

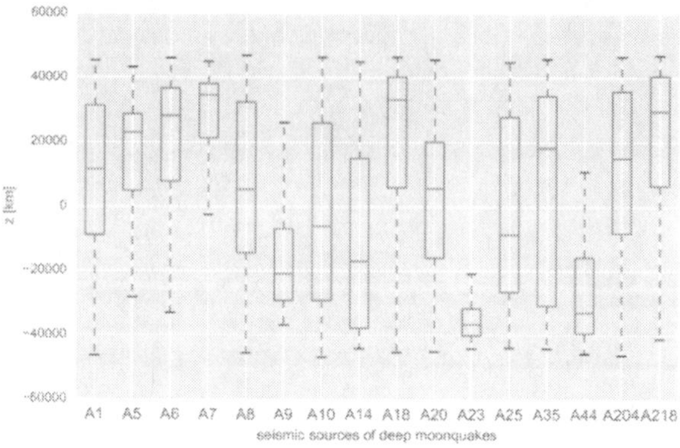

Figure 1. Box plots showing the position of z coordinate for each seismic source,
where red line is the median, and the box is a value of 25%–75 %, where top and bottom bars are the maximum and minimum, and "+" is an outlier, which is more than 1.5 times the interquartile range.

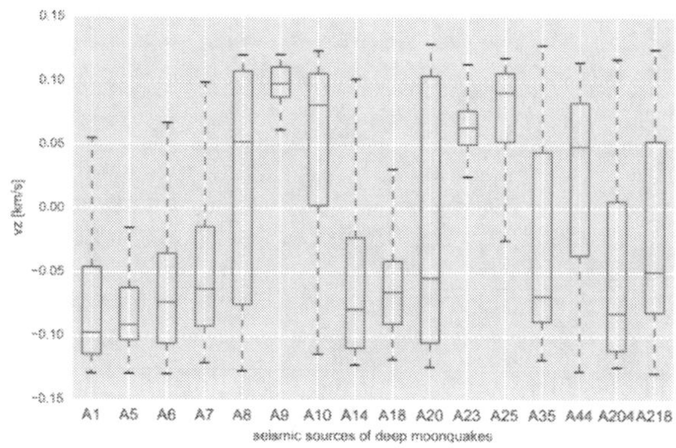

Figure 2. Box plots showing Earth velocity of z coordinate for each seismic source.

portance. Figure 5 and Figure 6 are box plots that indicate values of these features for each seismic source. Figure 5 and Figure 6 show that the low feature importances are caused by small difference among values of the features for each seismic source.

Time variations of the velocity of Earth and distance of Jupiter are presented in Figure 7 and Figure 8. Figure 7 shows that the velocity of Earth greatly varies with time. Figure 8 shows that the period of distance is about 1 year. Figure 7 and Figure 8 show that it is difficult to extract tendencies of the features because, this time, the variation is very different from Figure 3 or Figure 4. These results show that we may be able to improve classification if we apply methods and features considering the time variation or periodicity.

E. Methods and Features

Using Balanced Random Forest, we easily calculated the feature importance in addition to the classification perfor-

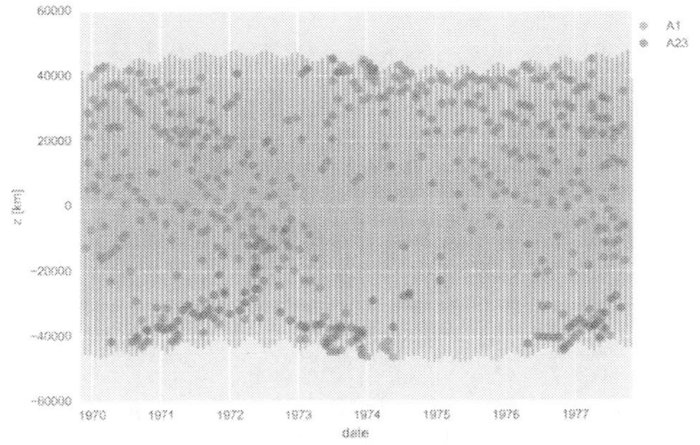

Figure 3. Time series of Earth position of z coordinate for each seismic source.

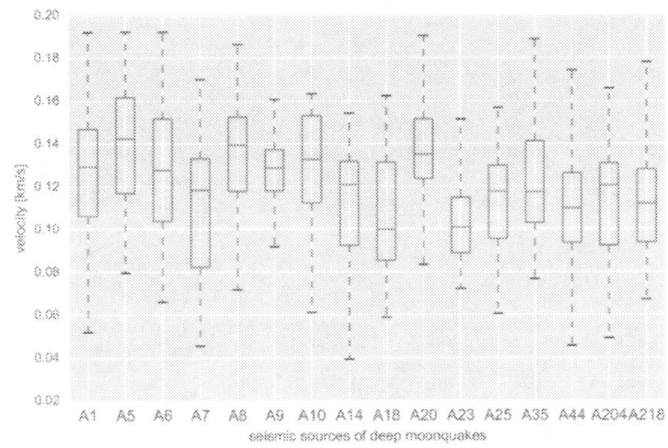

Figure 5. Box plots showing Earth velocity for each seismic source.

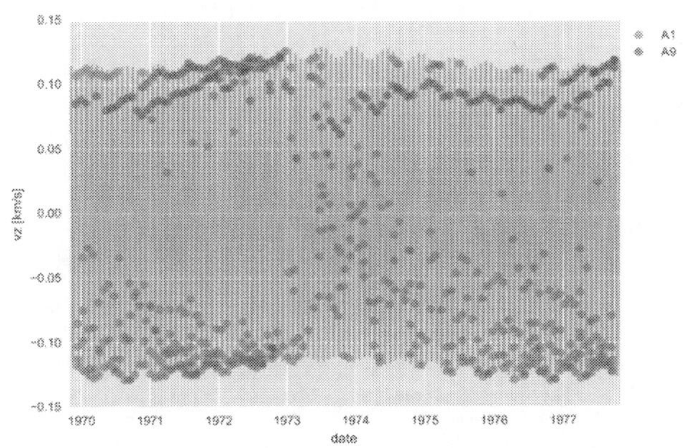

Figure 4. Time series of Earth velocity of z coordinate for each seismic source.

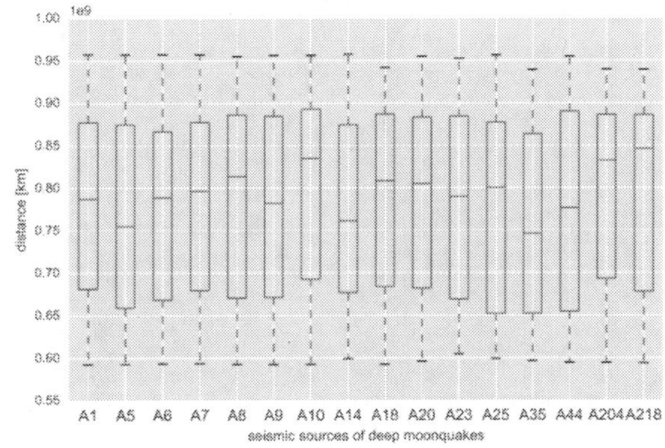

Figure 6. Box plots showing the Jupiter distance for each seismic source.

mance. As a result, some orbit parameters are useful for the classification of deep moonquakes. However, we did not do fine-tuning to improve the classification performance. We need to apply other machine learning methods, fine tuning of parameters, and waveforms to classify more precisely.

We avoided analyzing all features to limit multicollinearity. Therefore, it is difficult to declare decisive features to characterize seismic sources. Additionally, in this paper, it is difficult to estimate causal relationship.

Accordingly, we must verify new features or preprocess features with multicollinearity considering features leading to elucidation of the causes of deep moonquakes. However, the features in our approach are effective for new analyses and for creating knowledge of experts. Our findings show the causal relations between seismic sources and outer space for occurrence of deep moonquakes.

V. CONCLUSION

This study evaluated the spatial and temporal features for classification of deep moonquake sources using Balanced Random Forest. The findings reported in this paper are presented below.

- Seismic sources are classifiable using temporal and spatial features without using the waveforms used in conventional classification.
- Results of the classification performance using orbit parameters of objects in our Solar System (Earth, Sun, Jupiter, and Venus) suggest that the Earth orbit parameter is the most effective feature among them. The Jupiter orbit parameter is effective for classification of some seismic sources.
- Features of seismic sources with low time variation have high feature importance.

Our experimental results show that the orbit features are effective when we try to classify unclassified deep moonquakes or moonquakes with noise and small amplitude of the waveforms. These findings are expected to be useful for new analyses and for knowledge creation by experts. Further progress of this study can generate new knowledge about deep moonquake occurrence mechanisms. Future works are described below.

- Verification considering correlation and confounding among some features.

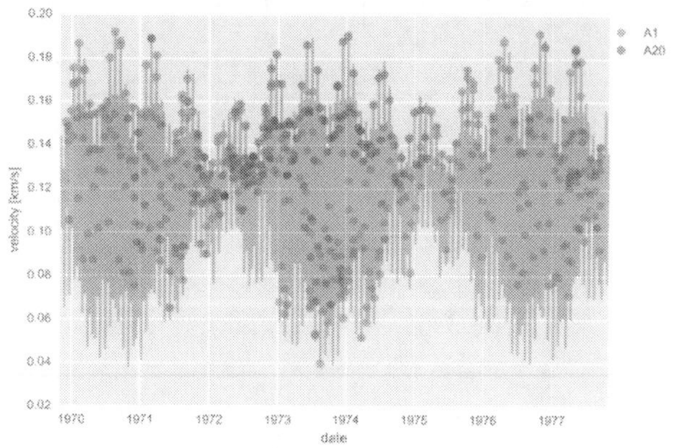

Figure 7. Time series showing Earth velocity for each seismic source.

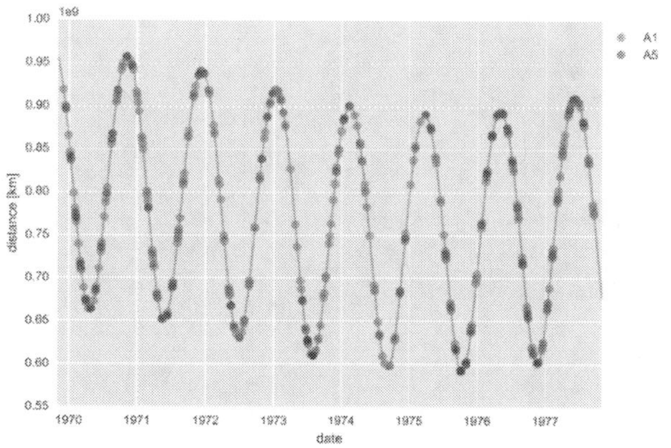

Figure 8. Time series of the Jupiter distance for each seismic source.

- Analysis considering time variation and interplanetary relations.

We can address future issues and problems from the standpoint of planetary interpretation.

ACKNOWLEDGMENT

We are grateful to Dr. Yoshiyuki Shoji for helpful discussions.

This work was supported by JSPS KAKENHI Grant Numbers 16K00157, 16K16158, and a Tokyo Metropolitan University Grant-in-Aid for Research on Priority Areas "Research on social big data."

REFERENCES

[1] R. Yamada, Y. Yamamoto, J. Kuwamura, and Y. Nakamura, "Development of an online retrieval system of apollo lunar seismic data," Journal of Space Science Informatics Japan, no. 1, 2012, pp. 121–131.

[2] C-SODA at ISAS/JAXA. DARTS. [Online]. Available: http://darts.jaxa.jp [retrieved: 3, 2017]

[3] Y. Nakamura, G. V. Latham, and H. J. Dorman, "Apollo lunar seismic experiment—final summary," Journal of Geophysical Research: Solid Earth (1978–2012), vol. 87, no. S01, 1982, pp. A117–A123.

[4] P. Lognonné, J. Gagnepain-Beyneix, and H. Chenet, "A new seismic model of the moon: implications for structure, thermal evolution and formation of the moon," Earth and Planetary Science Letters, vol. 211, no. 1, 2003, pp. 27–44.

[5] R. C. Bulow, C. L. Johnson, B. G. Bills, and P. M. Shearer, "Temporal and spatial properties of some deep moonquake clusters," Journal of Geophysical Research: Planets (1991–2012), vol. 112, no. E9, 2007.

[6] D. R. Lammlein, G. V. Latham, J. Dorman, Y. Nakamura, and M. Ewing, "Lunar seismicity, structure, and tectonics," Reviews of Geophysics, vol. 12, no. 1, 1974, pp. 1–21.

[7] Y. Nakamura, "New identification of deep moonquakes in the apollo lunar seismic data," Physics of the Earth and Planetary Interiors, vol. 139, no. 3, 2003, pp. 197–205.

[8] Y. Goto, R. Yamada, Y. Yamamoto, S. Yokoyama, and H. Ishikawa, "Som-based visualization for classifying large-scale sensing data of moonquakes," in P2P, Parallel, Grid, Cloud and Internet Computing (3PGCIC), 2013 Eighth International Conference on. IEEE, 2013, pp. 630–634.

[9] R. Weber, B. Bills, and C. Johnson, "Constraints on deep moonquake focal mechanisms through analyses of tidal stress," Journal of Geophysical Research: Planets, vol. 114, no. E5, 2009.

[10] J. Koyama and Y. Nakamura, "Focal mechanism of deep moonquakes," in Lunar and Planetary Science Conference Proceedings, vol. 11, 1980, pp. 1855–1865.

[11] Y. Nakamura, "A1 moonquakes-source distribution and mechanism," in Lunar and Planetary Science Conference Proceedings, vol. 9, 1978, pp. 3589–3607.

[12] Y. Nakamura, G. V. Latham, H. J. Dorman, and J. Harris, "Passive seismic experiment long-period event catalog," Galveston Geophysics Laboratory Contribution, vol. 491, 1981.

[13] R. C. Bulow, C. L. Johnson, and P. Shearer, "New events discovered in the apollo lunar seismic data," Journal of Geophysical Research: Planets (1991–2012), vol. 110, no. E10, 2005.

[14] B. Knapmeyer-Endrun and C. Hammer, "Identification of new events in apollo 16 lunar seismic data by hidden markov model-based event detection and classification," Journal of Geophysical Research: Planets, vol. 120, no. 10, 2015, pp. 1620–1645.

[15] C. Chen, A. Liaw, and L. Breiman, "Using random forest to learn imbalanced data," University of California, Berkeley, 2004, pp. 1–12.

[16] L. Breiman, "Random forests," Machine learning, vol. 45, no. 1, 2001, pp. 5–32.

[17] NASA. SPICE. [Online]. Available: https://naif.jpl.nasa.gov/naif/ [retrieved: 3, 2017]

[18] F. Pedregosa et al., "Scikit-learn: Machine learning in Python," Journal of Machine Learning Research, vol. 12, 2011, pp. 2825–2830.

Measurement-based Cost Estimation Method of a Join Operation for an In-Memory Database

Tsuyoshi Tanaka* and Hiroshi Ishikawa†

Faculty of System Design, Tokyo Metropolitan University, Tokyo, Japan
Email: *tanaka-tsuyoshi@ed.tmu.ac.jp and †ishikawa-hiroshi@tmu.ac.jp

***Abstract*—Non-volatile memory is applied not only to storage subsystems but also to main memory to improve performance and increase capacity. Some in-memory database systems use non-volatile main memory as a durable medium instead of using existing storage devices such as hard disk drives or solid state drives. For such in-memory database systems, the cost of memory access instead of I/O processing decreases, and the CPU cost increases relatively for cost calculation to select the most suitable access path for a database query. Therefore, a high-precision cost calculation method of query execution is required. In particular, when the database system cannot select a proper join method, the query execution time increases. Accordingly, we propose a database join operation cost model using statistics information measured by a performance monitor embedded in the CPU and evaluated the accuracy of estimating the change point of join methods. As a result, the proposed method can estimate more accurately than the existing method to within one significant figure. In conclusion, the in-memory database system using the proposed cost calculation method is able to select the best join method.**

Keywords*–*Non-volatile memory; In-memory database systems; Query optimization; Query execution cost.

I. INTRODUCTION

Improving the performance and expanding the capacity of non-volatile memory (NVM) is made applicable to both high-speed disk drives and main memory units. Intel and Micron developed the NVM named 3D Xpoint memory [1] for such use. NVM is implemented as byte-addressable memory and is assigned as a part of the main memory space. An application programming interface (API) [2] [3] for accessing NVM is proposed to make the development of applications easier. Roughly speaking, the API provides two types of access methods to NVM from software. The first is "load/store type:" it is the same method used to access conventional main memory from user applications. The other is "read/write type:" this is the method used by existing I/O devices, such as hard disk drives (HDDs) or solid state drives (SSD) through operating system (OS) calls such as read/write functions. There are two types of implementations of in-memory databases through the application of NVM to main memory. The load/store type must be implemented using array structures or list structures on a main memory address area such as the durable media of the database (Figure 1(c)). The read/write type can be easily applied to the existing database management system (DBMS) because the database files stored on disk drives (Figure 1(a)) are moved to files on NVM defined by the API for NVM (Figure 1(b)). The performance when accessing the database using the former type is better than the latter type because the DBMS directly accesses the database without any I/O device emulation operation. However, operations of the database administration (e.g., system configuration, backup, etc.) do not have to be changed. That means that it is easy for the administrators to introduce the in-memory database system.

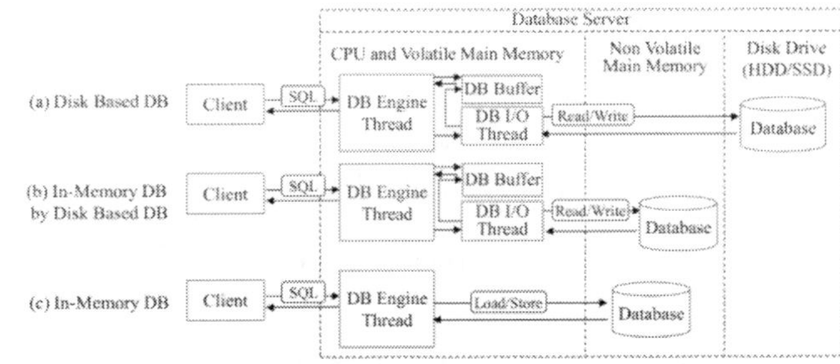

Figure 1. Disk-based database and in-memory database

The DBMS has a problem in preparation for executing a query. In general, the DBMS executes several steps before executing a query. First, the DBMS analyzes the query. Next, it creates multiple execution plans. Then, it estimates the query processing cost for each execution plan. Finally, it selects a minimum execution plan from a plurality of candidates. For example, when the DBMS joins two tables, such as the R table and S table shown in Figure 2(a), it generates the execution plan (Figure 2(b)) that minimizes the number of rows to be referenced. At this time, the execution time depends on which join method the DBMS selects. The DBMS estimates the cost of each join method by using statistical information from the database and chooses the join method with the minimum cost. In general, the cost of a join operation is a function of the ratio of the extracted records to all records. Hereafter, we refer to this ratio as the selectivity. In Figure 2, the selectivity is determined by the condition x for the column R.C in Figure 2(c). In Figure 2(c), two cost functions cross at X_{cross}. Join method 2 must be chosen from the left side of X_{cross} and join method 1 should be chosen from the right side of X_{cross}. If the DBMS cannot estimate the selectivity X_{cross} accurately, it will choose the wrong join method.

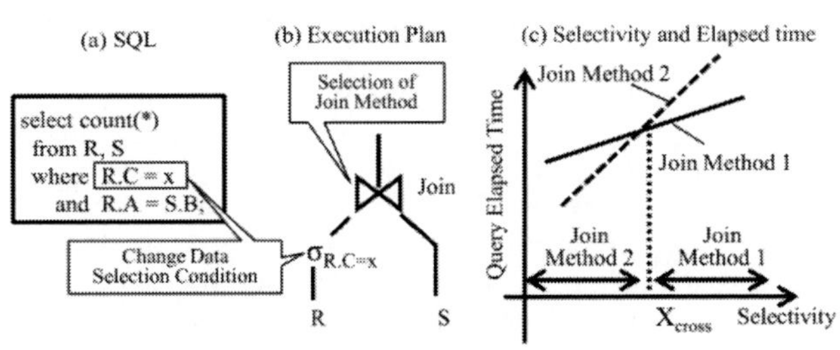

Figure 2. Cost estimation problem for the selection of join methods

On the other hand, the query execution cost ($cost$) is generally expressed as the sum of the Central Processing Unit (CPU) cost (cpu_cost) and the I/O cost (io_cost) [4] [5]. The CPU cost is the CPU time, and the I/O cost is the latency when accessing the disk drive:

$$cost = cpu\_cost + io\_cost \quad (1)$$

For example, the cost formula for MySQL is given below [6]. The cost of scanning a table R is given by

$$table\_scan\_cost(\mathrm{R}) = record(\mathrm{R}) \times CPR + page(\mathrm{R}) \times CPIO \quad (2)$$

where $record(\mathrm{R})$ is the number of records of table R, CPR is the CPU cost per record, $page(\mathrm{R})$ is the number of pages of table R and $CPIO$ is the I/O cost per page stored record for DBMS access. When table R (inner table) and table S (outer table) are joined, the cost of a join operation is given by

$$table\_join\_cost(\mathrm{R}, \mathrm{S}) = table\_scan\_cost(\mathrm{R}) + record(R) \times selectivity \times records\_per\_key(\mathrm{S}) \times (CPIO + CPR) \quad (3)$$

where $selectivity$ is the selectivity ratio given by the distribution of attributes, and the condition for selection such as a where-clause definition in SQL, and $records\_per\_key(\mathrm{S})$ is the number of join keys specified by table S's records. Here $CPR = 0.2$ and $CPIO = 1$ are the default defined values. However, this cost model is established under the condition that I/O performance is the bottleneck of the query execution time. A further improvement in disk performance increases the CPU cost relative to the I/O cost. When the I/O cost itself disappears ultimately in a native in-memory database (Figure 1(c)), it becomes necessary to more accurately predict the CPU cost.

To improve the accuracy of the CPU processing cost prediction, the estimation of CPU processing time must become more accurate than the conventional method mentioned above. In general, the CPU processing time can be predicted by the product of the number of executed instructions and the latency until the instruction is completed. To estimate the latency with high accuracy, it is necessary to consider the structure of the hardware, such as instruction execution parallelism, cache miss ratio, and memory hierarchy. These are problems that cannot be solved by the software algorithm alone.

In this study, we propose a method to improve the accuracy of CPU cost estimation of in-memory databases applied to existing DBMSs (Figure 1(b)). It is easy to apply our method to native in-memory databases (Figure 1(c)). Our contribution can be summarized as follows.

- First, we propose a method for modeling CPU cycles and estimating the join operation cost for a database. While considering the CPU pipeline architecture, we classify CPU cycles into three components: a pipeline stall cycle caused by instruction cache misses, a pipeline stall cycle caused by branch misprediction, and an access cycle of data caches or main memory. By using this classification, we propose a CPU cycle modeling method, which can express the total CPU execution time. In addition, to estimate the processing time of the join operation of a database, we decompose the pattern of the join processing into four parts and estimate the join operation cost by using a combination of these parts (Section II).
- Next, we analyze the behavior of measurement results of join operation by using a performance monitor embedded on the CPU and determine the cost estimation formulas (Section III).
- Finally, we verify the accuracy of the proposed CPU cost estimation formulas by comparing the actual CPU processing cycle and the conventional CPU cost estimation formula of MySQL (Section IV).

II. Proposed CPU Cost Model

In this section, first, we analyze the CPU pipeline architecture and categorize pipeline events. We propose the CPU operation cycle estimation method, which can express whole CPU process cycles by considering the categorized events. Next, we categorize join operations of the DBMS and divide the join operation into several parts. We propose an estimation model based on a combination of these parts. Finally, we create the CPU cost formula for estimating each part of the join operations using statistics information measured by the performance monitor embedded in the CPU and assemble those join parts formulas into the complete CPU cost estimation formula.

A. Model of CPU Operation Time

We chose the Intel Nehalem processor as a typical model of a CPU for application to the database server because all of the processors developed after Nehalem, namely Sandy Bridge, Haswell, and Skylake, are based on the pipeline architecture of Nehalem. Partial enhancements, such as additional cache for the micro-operations (uOPs), increased reorder buffer entries, and increased instruction execution units, were added to the successor CPUs of Nehalem.

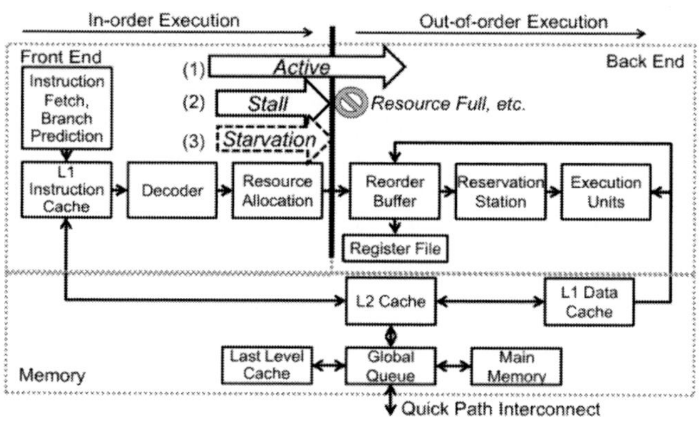

Figure 3. Focus point of the CPU pipeline

The pipeline is composed of a front-end and a back-end in Figure 3 [7]. The front-end fetches instructions from the L1 instruction cache (L1I) and decodes them into uOPs in-order. The term "in-order" means that a subsequent instruction cannot overtake preceding instructions in the pipeline. After decoding instructions, the front-end issues uOPs to the back-end. Conversely, the back-end executes the uOPs in execution units out-of-order. The back-end can execute the uOPs in a different order than issued by the front-end to improve the throughput of operating uOPs. An L1I miss causes the pipeline of the front-end to stall until the missing instruction is fetched from the lower level of cache or main memory. A branch prediction miss causes a dozen cycles of the instructions executed speculatively to be flashed, and the front-end cannot issue uOPs. In this paper, such a condition is referred to as an *instruction-starvation state* (Figure 3(3)). There are cases in which the uOP issued in the front-end is not executed because of the saturation of the reorder buffer or the reservation station in the back-end, or the data dependency with the preceding instructions. We refer to this state as a *stall state* in this paper (Figure 3(2)). In addition, we refer to the state in which the uOPs are issued without an *instruction-starvation state* or a *the stall state* as an *active state*.

A summary of the related notation of the CPU cost calculation to be used afterward is shown in Table I before creating the CPU cost calculation model.

TABLE I. NOTATION FOR THE CPU COST CALCULATION MODEL

Symbol	Description
I	Number of instructions to complete a query
$CPI0$	Cycle per instruction (CPI) on the condition that all of instructions and data are stored in L1 cache
Li	Level i cache memory (Maximum value of "i" varies depending on the CPU. In this paper, the maximum is "3". L3 is represented by "last-level cache" (LLC).
M_{mem}, L_{mem}	Number of references of instructions and data to the main memory, main memory latency
M_{memI}, M_{memD}	Number of references of instructions to the main memory, number of references of data to the main memory
M_{Li}, L_{Li}	Number of references of instructions and data to Li cache, Li cache latency
M_{LiI}, M_{LiD}	Number of references of instructions to Li cache, the number of references of data to Li cache
BF_{mem}, BF_{Li}	Blocking factor of main memory, Li cache reference
BF_{memI}, BF_{LiI}	Blocking factor of instruction references to the main memory, Li cache
BF_{memD}, BF_{LiD}	Blocking factor of data references to the main memory, Li cache
BF_{MP}	Blocking factor when branch misprediction and instruction cache miss occur simultaneously
H_{mem}	Ratio of the number of references to the main memory to the number of instructions ($H_{mem} = M_{mem}/I$)
H_{Li}	Ratio of the number of references to Li cache to the number of instructions ($H_{Li} = M_{Li}/I$)
H_{LiI}	Ratio of instruction references to Li cache to the number of instructions
H_{LiD}	Ratio of data references to Li cache to the number of instructions
C_{Total}	Total CPU cycles to execute a query
$C_{Active}, C_{Stall}, C_{Starvation}$	CPU cycles in *active state, stall state, starvation state*
$C_{ICacheMiss}$	CPU cycles from the occurrence of L1I miss until the acquisition of an instruction from other cache or the main memory
$C_{DCacheAcc}$	CPU cycles in *active state*
M_{MP}	Number of branch mispredictions
L_{MP}	Recovering latency from a branch misprediction
C_{MP}	Total CPU cycles when recovering from branch mispredictions
P	Selectivity of the outer table
R_O, R_I	Number of outer table records, number of inner table records
T_{NLJ}, T_{HJ}	Nested loop join (NLJ) execution time, hash join (HJ) execution time
T_{build}, T_{probe}	Execution time of the HJ build phase, execution time of the HJ probe phase
C_{NLJ_Total}	Total CPU cycles of NLJ
$C_{NLJ\_ICacheMiss}$	CPU cycles from the occurrence of L1I miss on executing NLJ until acquisition of an instruction from other cache or the main memory
C_{NLJ_MP}	Total CPU cycles when recovering from branch mispredictions on executing NLJ
$C_{NLJ\_DCacheAcc}$	CPU cycles in *active state* on executing NLJ
$C_{Build\_Total}, C_{Probe\_Total}$	Total CPU cycles of the build phase of HJ, probe phase of HJ
$C_{Build\_ICacheMiss}, C_{Probe\_ICacheMiss}$	CPU cycles from the occurrence of L1I miss until the acquisition of an instruction from other cache or the main memory on executing the build phase of HJ, probe phase of HJ
$C_{Build\_MP}, C_{Probe\_MP}$	Total CPU cycles of recovering from branch mispredictions on executing the build phase of HJ, probe phase of HJ
$C_{Build\_DCacheAcc}, C_{Probe\_DCacheAcc}$	CPU cycles in data cache or main memory Access on executing the build phase of HJ, probe phase of HJ
I_{Load}	Number of load instructions
M_{LMMI}, M_{LMMD}	Number of instruction references to local main memory, number of data references to local main memory
L_{LMM}	Latency of local main memory
M_{LLLCI}, M_{LLLCD}	Number of instruction references to local LLC, number of data references to local LLC
L_{LLLC}	Latency of local LLC
M_{RLLCI}, M_{RLLCD}	Number of instruction references to remote LLC, number of data references to remote LLC
L_{RLLC}	Latency of remote LLC

In this paper, we focus on the boundary between the front-end and the back-end in the CPU pipeline (Figure 3) to model the overall operation of the CPU. The uOPs are issued from front-end to back-end and are stored in the buffers, namely the reorder buffer and reservation station. The buffers allow us to change the processing order of uOPs from in-order to out-of-order across the boundary. The CPU-embedded performance monitor can measure events such as the saturation of buffers, dequeues from buffers by the completion of uOPs, and the existence of uOPs to issue to back-end [7]. Any CPU cycle situation can be modeled by the performance monitor to analyze these events. Therefore, we propose measurement-based estimation of the query execution cost. The *active state* is estimated from the number of the events that the uOP is issued without delay in the back-end buffer. The buck-end buffer holds the uOPs until the execution of the uOPs is completed and the uOPs are deleted from the buffer. The *stall state* is estimated from the number of the events for which the buffer cannot receive uOPs. The *starvation state* is inferred from the event count in which there are no uOPs to be issued to the back-end buffer. The total CPU cycle is composed of the *active state* cycle, the *stall state* cycle and the *starvation state* cycle. Therefore, the following equation can be obtained:

$$C_{Total} = C_{Active} + C_{Stall} + C_{Starvation} \tag{4}$$

Cycle Per Instruction (CPI), which refers to the number of CPU clock cycles per instruction, is widely used as a metric for evaluating CPU processing efficiency [8]. CPI is calculated as the product of the number of references to the memory and the latency of the memory access. Latency is the delay time when fetching an instruction or data from memory. CPI is given by

$$CPI = CPI0 + \{ \sum_{i=2}^{last\_level} (H_{Li} \times L_{Li} \times BF_{Li}) + (H_{mem} \times L_{mem} \times BF_{mem}) \} \tag{5}$$

where last-level cache (LLC) means the lowest cache in the cache memory hierarchy and the blocking factor [8] is a correction coefficient for concealing the latency by executing instructions in parallel. The second term on the right-hand side of (5) is the product of the number of memory references, the latency, and the blocking factor, i.e., the *stall state*. The product of the second term on the right-hand side of (5) and the number of instructions I is the pipeline stall cycle (C_{Stall}):

$$C_{Stall} = \sum_{Li=L2}^{LLC} (M_{Li} \times L_{Li} \times BF_{Li}) + (M_{mem} \times L_{mem} \times BF_{mem}) \tag{6}$$

$$C_{Total} = CPI \times I = CPI0 \times I + C_{Stall} \tag{7}$$

From (5)–(7), we can show that *CPI0* includes the *active state* and *starvation state*:

$$CPI0 \times I = C_{Active} + C_{Starvation} \tag{8}$$

The *starvation state* is mainly caused by instruction cache misses or branch mispredictions, and can be classified as the number of CPU cycles from the occurrence of one of these events until the acquisition of the next instruction to be executed:

$$C_{Starvation} = C_{ICacheMiss} + M_{MP} \times L_{MP} \times BF_{MP} \tag{9}$$

$$C_{ICacheMiss} = \sum_{Li=L2}^{LLC} (M_{LiI} \times L_{Li} \times BF_{LiI}) + (M_{memI} \times L_{mem} \times BF_{memI}) \quad (10)$$

Here BF is a correction coefficient for considering that both branch misprediction and instruction cache miss occur simultaneously. $ICacheMiss$ is expressed as 10 by modifying 6 because operations after instruction cache misses and data cache misses are the same. Only terms relating to branch misprediction are defined:

$$C_{MP} = M_{MP} \times L_{MP} \times BF_{MP} \quad (11)$$

According to the previous research [9], the CPI of the decision support system benchmark is 1.5–2.5. In general, when the CPI is 1, this means that one instruction is completed in one cycle, so the instructions are executed sequentially in query execution. In addition, since the indices and tables of the database are usually implemented with list structures or tree structures, it is not until the stored data which the pointer refers to is read out that the next reference address becomes clear. Thus, it is difficult for the CPU to predict the destination of the next reference. In particular, the characteristics of such a memory reference in the list structure are applied to a benchmark program for measuring memory latency [10]. Therefore, *stall state* occurs because the operation of the stalled instruction waits for the preceding data reference processing to be completed. From the viewpoint of memory reference, the *active state* can be considered as an L1 data cache (L1D) reference, and the *stall state* can be considered as a reference to a cache level lower than L1 or a main memory reference. Therefore, CPU cycles in the *active state* and those in the *stall state* can be integrated as $C_{DCacheAcc}$ in

$$C_{DCacheAcc} = C_{Active} + C_{Stall} \quad (12)$$

$$C_{DCacheAcc} = \sum_{i=1}^{last_level} (M_{LiD} \times L_{Li} \times BF_{LiD}) + (M_{memD} \times L_{mem} \times BF_{memD}) \quad (13)$$

where (6)(13) use the same symbols for latency and the blocking factor for convenience, but the contents are different.

From the above discussion, the total number of CPU cycles is calculated using

$$C_{Total} = C_{DCacheAcc} + C_{ICacheMiss} + C_{MP} \quad (14)$$

In this paper, each term on the right-hand side of (14) uses statistical information obtained from actual measurements.

B. DBMS Operation Model

DBMS queries perform operations including selection, projection, and join. Queries performing the join operation depend on the join method chosen by the DBMS's optimizer. The optimizer selects the join method to minimize the operation cost of the join operation. The cost depends on the selectivity of records defined by the clause of the SQL and the statistics of the attribute value of the database. Most DBMSs calculate the statistics during data loading to the database. This paper focuses on the cost estimation for the optimization of join operations. There are three basic joins: nested loop join (NLJ), hash join (HJ), and sort–merge join (SMJ).

NLJ searches records from the inner table every time it reads one record from the outer table. The generalized operation model of NLJ is shown in Figure 4. The process involves tracing multiple tables and indices from the point of view of memory access, which means repeatedly traversing linked lists. Therefore, NLJ can be regarded as searching between the outer table and the huge internal table created by tracing multiple tables in the same way as loop expansion by a compiler. Moreover, it is possible to calculate the cost of NLJ of multiple tables using the cost estimation function with two typical NLJs (Figure 4(a)), which is the function of the number of total records to be referenced in the multi-table join. NLJ and HJ are regarded as part of our proposed cost estimation method. In this paper, we do not examine SMJ because it is possible to apply the proposed method using the steps from the other join methods, specifically dividing parts into sorting and merging operations and calculating the measured statistics values for each model. Figure 4 also shows that HJ is decomposed into a build phase (Figure 4(b-1)) and a probe phase (Figure 4(b-2)) because each operation of HJ is executed sequentially and can be modeled separately in the cost calculation formula based on measurement results.

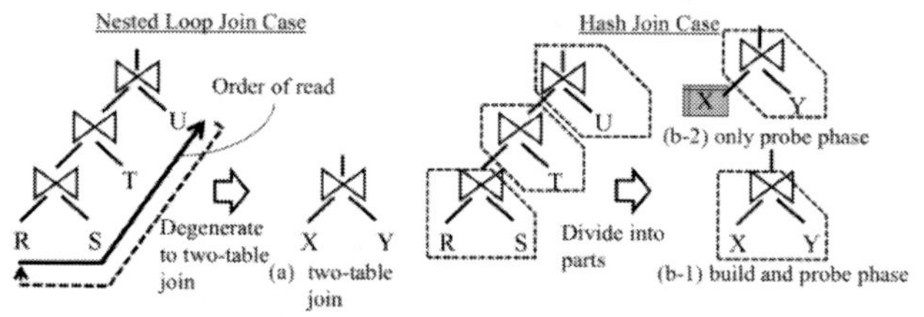

Figure 4. Degradation and split cost calculation method

C. Cost Calculation Formula

Before considering the cost calculation formulas, we define the inputs and outputs as in Table II. The information input to the cost calculation formulas is recorded in the database for management as statistical information, which is collected generally by the DBMS when storing or updating the record. Information regarding memory latency and I/O response time is also required. This information can be measured with a simple benchmark program [10].

TABLE II. PARAMETER LIST FOR COST CALCULATION

Input	Selectivity of outer table to join and number of records of tables
Output	Calculated cost expressed by number of CPU cycles
Parameters of cost calculation formulas	*Static information*: Memory latency and I/O response time *Information obtained from measurement*: Relational formula between the input information and number of CPU cycles of the events on the right-hand side of (14) (e.g., slope and intercept if the input information and the number of cycles of the interested event can be linearly approximated.)

In this section, we derive the cost calculation formula for NLJ and HJ in two tables (14) where each element of (14) is obtained as a function of the selectivity from the outer table and the number of records. The cost formula of NLJ

$$C_{NLJ\_Total}(P,R_O,R_I) = C_{NLJ\_ICacheMiss}(P,R_O,R_I) + C_{NLJ\_MP}(P,R_O,R_I) + C_{NLJ\_DCacheAcc}(P,R_O,R_I) \quad (15)$$

is obtained by combining (10)(11)(13)(14). The cost related to each element of the instruction cache miss, the branch misprediction, and the data reference are expressed by

$$C_{NLJ\_ICacheMiss}(P,R_O,R_I) = M_{L2I}(P,R_O,R_I) \times L_{L2} \times BF_{L2I} + M_{LLCI}(P,R_O,R_I) \times L_{LLC} \times BF_{LLCI} + M_{memI}(P,R_O,R_I) \times L_{mem} \times BF_{memI} \quad (16)$$

$$C_{NLJ\_MP}(P,R_O,R_I) = M_{MP}(P,R_O,R_I) \times L_{MP} \times BF_{MP}(P,R_O,R_I) \quad (17)$$

$$C_{NLJ\_DCacheAcc}(P,R_O,R_I) = M_{L1D}(P,R_O,R_I) \times L_{L1} \times BF_{L2D}(P,R_O,R_I) + M_{L2D}(P,R_O,R_I) \times L_{L2} \times BF_{L2D}(P,R_O,R_I) + M_{LLCD}(P,R_O,R_I) \times L_{LLC} \times BF_{LLCD}(P,R_O,R_I) + M_{memD}(P,R_O,R_I) \times L_{mem} \times BF_{mem}(P,R_O,R_I) \quad (18)$$

respectively. The structure of the cost calculation formulas is basically a product-sum formula of the number of occurrences of the event, its latency, and the correction coefficient. The number of data references from the L1D cache, the L2 cache, the LLC cache, and the main memory (M_{L1D}, M_{L2}, M_{LLC}, and M_{mem}), the number of branch mispredictions (M_{MP}), and the blocking factor BF are expressed as a function of the selectivity P and the number of rows of the table, R_O, R_I. The data references include L1D hits because they target all data accesses.

The cost calculation formula of HJ is obtained in the same way as NLJ:

$$C_{Phase\_Total}(P,R) = C_{Phase\_ICacheMiss}(P,R) + C_{Phase\_MP}(P,R) + C_{Phase\_DCacheAcc}(P,R) \quad (19)$$

$$C_{Phase\_ICacheMiss}(P,R) = M_{L2I}(P,R) \times L_{L2} \times BF_{L2I}(P,R) + M_{LLCI}(P,R) \times L_{LLC} \times BF_{LLCI}(P,R) + M_{memI}(P,R) \times L_{mem} \times BF_{memI}(P,R) \quad (20)$$

$$C_{Phase\_MP}(P,R) = M_{MP}(P,R) \times L_{MP} \times BF_{MP}(P,R) \quad (21)$$

$$C_{Phase\_DCacheAcc}(P,R) = M_{L1D}(P,R) \times L_{L1} \times BF_{L2D}(P,R) + M_{L2D}(P,R) \times L_{L2} \times BF_{L2D}(P,R) + M_{LLCD}(P,R) \times L_{LLC} \times BF_{LLCD}(P,R) + M_{memD}(P,R) \times L_{mem} \times BF_{memD}(P,R) \quad (22)$$

where

$$\{Phase, R\} = \begin{cases} \{Build, R_O\} & \text{build phase} \\ \{Probe, R_I\} & \text{probe phase} \end{cases}$$

In the build phase, cache and main memory references, branch misprediction, and the blocking factor are expressed as functions of the selectivity P and the number of records of the outer table (R_O). In the probe phase, they are expressed as functions of the selectivity P and the number of records of the inner table (R_I).

The aim of this paper is to improve the accuracy of the CPU cost calculation. Therefore, we use a method to statistically obtain the parameters of the calculation formula from the measured values using the performance monitor. One of the parameters, the memory latency, depends on the hardware configuration, which includes the number of CPUs, the slot position in which the main memory modules are installed, etc. According to the literature [11], the memory access concentration is low when executing analytic queries such as the TPC-H benchmark and does not increase the memory latency.

III. Evaluation of Obtaining Parameters of the Cost Formula

To obtain the parameters in Table II, actual measurements are made. The measurement environment is shown in Table III. We used Westmere CPUs as they are the same architecture as Nehalem. The servers are equipped with two CPUs. The main memory is connected to each CPU. The memory connected to one CPU is called local memory and the other is called remote memory. In general, such a memory architecture is known as non-uniform memory access (NUMA). The latency of local and remote memory is different. In this study, main memory modules are installed to only one CPU to simplify the examination of measurement results. An NVM Flash SSD is used as a disk device to store the database to improve the experimental efficiency. We used the open-source MariaDB [12] as the DBMS in this study as it supports multithreading and asynchronous I/O, can utilize the latest hardware characteristics, and, moreover, supports multiple join methods. In a precise sense, the NLJ that MariaDB supports is BNL (block nested loop join), which is an improvement on NLJ; however, in the condition of the query and index used in this study, it behaves like the general NLJ. The version of MariaDB used in this study does not select the effective join method automatically; it is specified based on the configuration parameters.

TABLE III. EVALUATION ENVIRONMENT

CPU	Xeon L5630 2.13 GHz 4-core, LLC 12 MB [Westmere-EP]) ×2
Memory	DDR3 12 GB (4 GB ×3) physically attached to only one CPU
Disk (DB)	PCIe NVMe Flash SSD 800 GB ×1 (Note: max throughput suppressed by server's PCIe I/F(ver.1.0a), about 1/4 of max throughput)
Disk (OS)	SAS 10,000 rpm 600 GB, RAID5 (4 Data + 1 Parity)
OS	CentOS 6.6 (x64)
DBMS	MariaDB 10.1.8 with InnoDB storage engine

The query to be evaluated and its measurement conditions are shown in Figure 5. In the SQL statement, we modified Query 3 of TPC-H for an evaluation of two-table join and extracted only join processing (Figure 5(a)). The size of database is scale factor (SF) 5 defined in the TPC-H specification. SF5 means that the total size of the database is 5 GB. To allow us to apply the proposed technology to the actual system, we used small-scale data to reduce the measurement time as much as possible. The indices of the database are created on the primary keys and the foreign keys are defined in the specification of TPC-H [13].

We changed the search condition of the query against the c_acctbal column of the outer table to change the selectivity of the data to be referenced (Figure 5(c)). As for NLJ, the selectivity and the number of records of the inner table are changed (Figure 5(c) and (d)). The purpose of changing the selectivity is to change the total number of records accessed by the DBMS. In addition, the purpose of changing the number of records of the inner table is to change the number of records that have the same key as the record selected from the outer table. This means changing the length of the linked lists that have the key for join with the inner table. As for HJ, only the outer table is accessed in the build phase, and the number of records of the outer table is changed (Figure 5(e)). In the probe phase, only the inner table is accessed, and the number of records of the inner table is changed (Figure 5(d)).

The CPU performance counter data is collected by using Intel® Vtune™ Amplifier XE. We refer to the literature [7] for a description of the content of those counters. The measured data is mainly related to the number of accesses to cache and main memory, the state of the pipeline such as the number of stall cycles, and the number of cache hits or misses.

It is necessary to analyze not only CPU time but also I/O operation time to estimate the whole execution time of a query (1). We measure the I/O count and response time using systemtap and construct I/O cost calculation formulas by analyzing the relation between I/O and the selectivity or the number of records.

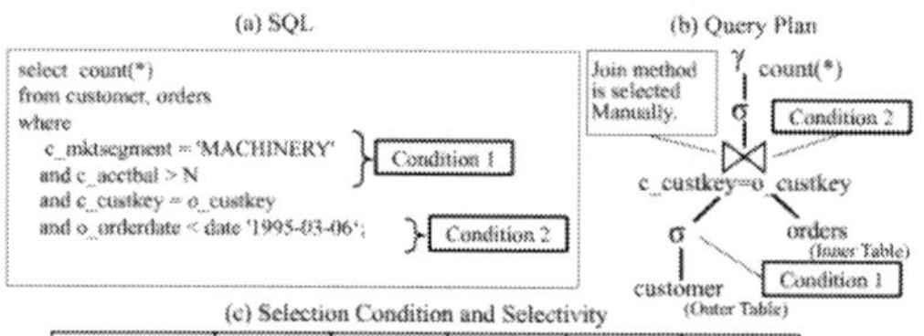

(c) Selection Condition and Selectivity

N	9998	9978	9798	9200	9000
Selectivity (Condition 1)	3.62×10^{-05}	4.00×10^{-04}	3.67×10^{-03}	1.45×10^{-02}	1.82×10^{-02}

(d) Inner Table

Number of Records	7,500,000	5,625,000	3,750,000	1,875,000

(e) Outer Table

Number of Records	750,000	562,500	375,000	187,500

Figure 5. Target query of measurement and cost estimation

IV. Measurement Results and Cost Calculation Formulas

In this paper, we investigate the relations among the selectivity, the number of instructions, the number of events related to memory reference, and the number of branch mispredictions. Regarding NLJ, it is expected that the number of instructions and the number of memory references will increase because the number of records accessed by the DBMS increases in proportion to the increase in the selectivity. Based on the assumptions, we now analyze the measurement results and create formulas using linear regression. Regarding HJ, all of the records of the outer table or inner table are accessed in both the build phase and probe phase. The cost formulas are presumed to not have selectivity as a variable. We analyze the measurement results based on this presumption.

The CPU cost calculation formulas are obtained through the following steps. First, the number of instructions, references of each cache memory and main memory, and branch mispredictions are analyzed using regression analysis, and the regression models are created. In addition, the relation between the sum of the product of the references to each memory and its latency and $C_{ICacheMiss}$ (10) and $C_{DCacheAcc}$ (13) are modeled. Here C_{MP} (11) is obtained from the product of the number of pipeline stages of the front-end, which is 12 in Nehalem, and the number of mispredictions from the measurement results. Each value of memory latency is referred to [14]. The number of disk I/O is modeled using the measured I/O access count and I/O response time. Finally, the cost calculation formulas are evaluated from the point of the accuracy of intersection of two join methods (X_{cross} in Figure 2) with the conventional method.

Figure 6(1) shows the relation between the number of records the DBMS accessed and load instructions. Figure 6(7) shows the relation between the total number of accessed records and the number of instructions. The number of records is the product of the number of outer table records, the number of inner table records, and selectivity. The dotted line is the linear regression line, and its slope and intercept are shown in Table IV. The coefficient of determination (R^2) is near 1 and the P value on the F test is less than 0.05. Therefore, the regression model is highly accurate. The slope and the intercept are used for creating the cost calculation model. Figure 6(2) and (8) show the relation between the number of instructions executed by the DBMS and the number of L1 cache hits. Figure 6(3)–(6) and (9)–(12) show the relation between the number of accesses to L2, LLC, and main memory accesses and the number of cache misses of the upper-level cache. These relations can be linearly approximated because each R^2 is near 1 and each P value is less than 0.05 in Table IV. In this paper, a two-CPU server is used and the LLC and main memory are connected to each CPU. The LLC and main memory on the CPU on which BMS threads are running are called the *local LLC* and *local main memory*. The others are called *remote LLC* and *remote main memory*. The upper-level cache is the local LLC. There exist no references to the remote main memory because the main memory is connected to only one CPU. Figure 6(13) shows the relation between the number of records accessed for the join operation and the branch miss prediction cycles, C_{MP}. Figure 6(14) shows the relation between the product of the number of instruction accesses and latency, and the L1I miss cycles, $C_{ICacheMiss}$. Figure 6(15) shows the relation between the product of the number of data accesses and the latency, and the data cache and main memory access, $C_{DCacheAcc}$. Each graph can be approximated by a regression line because each R^2 is near 1 and each P value is less than 0.05 in Table IV. Figure 7(13) shows the tendency of instructions, cache or main memory accesses, branch misprediction cycles, instruction cache miss cycles, and data cache access cycles. Each graph is linearly approximated by a regression line because each R^2 is near 1 and each P value is less than 0.05 in Table IV. In particular, the slope of the regression line in Figure 6(2)–(5) and (9)–(11) and Figure 7(a2)–(a5), (a9)–(a11), (b2)–(b5), and (b9)–(b11) represents the cache hit rate because the definition of cache hit rate is the quotient of the number of cache hits and the number of cache references, and the upper-level cache miss becomes the lower-level cache reference.

Based on the above considerations, the formula for calculating the cost of join methods is

$$I = A1 \times R + B1 \quad (23)$$

$$M_{L1I} = A2 \times I + B2 \quad (24)$$

$$M_{L2I} = A3 \times (I - M_{L1I}) + B3$$

$$M_{LLLCI} = A4 \times (I - M_{L1I} - M_{L2I}) + B4 \quad (25)$$

$$M_{RLLCI} = A5 \times (I - M_{L1I} - M_{L2I} - M_{LLLCI}) + B5 \quad (26)$$

$$M_{LMMI} = A6 \times (I - M_{L1I} - M_{L2I} - M_{LLLCI}) + B6 \quad (27)$$

$$I_{Load} = A7 \times R + B7 \quad (28)$$

$$M_{L1D} = A8 \times I_{Load} + B8 \quad (29)$$

$$M_{L2D} = A9 \times (I - M_{L1DI}) + B9 \quad (30)$$

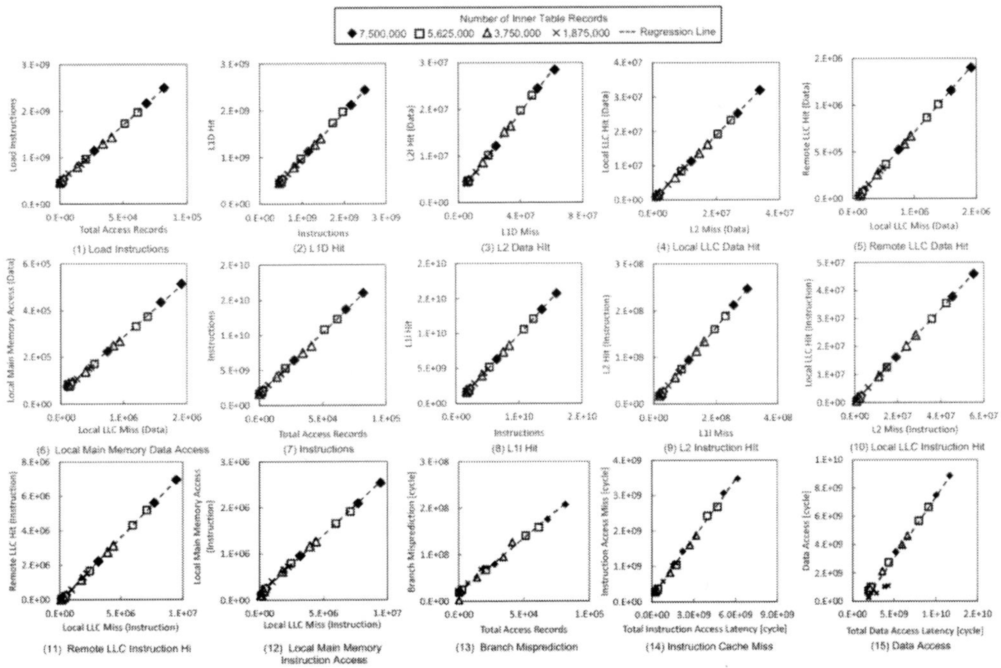

Figure 6. CPU event count on executing NLJ

$$M_{LLLCD} = A10 \times (I - M_{L1D} - M_{L2DI}) + B10 \quad (31)$$

$$M_{RLLCD} = A11 \times (I - M_{L1D} - M_{L2D} - M_{LLLCD}) + B11 \quad (32)$$

$$M_{LMMD} = A12 \times (I - M_{L1D} - M_{L2D} - M_{LLLCD}) + B12 \quad (33)$$

$$C_{ICacheMiss} = A13 \times (M_{L2I} \times L_{L2} + M_{LLLCI} \times L_{LLLC} + M_{RLLCI} \times L_{RLLC} + M_{LMMI} \times L_{LMM}) + B13 \quad (34)$$

$$C_{DCacheAcc} = A14 \times (M_{L1D} \times L_{L1} + M_{L2D} \times L_{L2} + M_{LLLCD} \times L_{LLLC} + M_{RLLCD} \times L_{RLLC} + M_{LMMD} \times L_{LMM}) + B14 \quad (35)$$

$$C_{MP} = A15 \times R + B15 \quad (36)$$

where

$$R = \begin{cases} R_O \times R_I \times P & \text{NLJ} \\ R_O & \text{Build phase of HJ} \\ R_I & \text{Probe phase of HJ} \end{cases}$$

Table IV lists the definitions of the parameters given in (23)-(36). In the case of NLJ, the calculation formula of the number of the disk I/Os is created by using the regression line shown in Figure 8(a). The measured I/O response time ($io_responcetime$) was 154 μs. The I/O cost of NLJ is

$$io\_cost = A16 \times R_O \times R_I \times P \times io\_responce\_time + B16 \quad (37)$$

However, in the case of HJ, the ratio of the processing time of disk I/O and the query execution time of HJ is less than 1% in Figure 8(b). In this paper, the cost calculation formula is composed of only the CPU cost and the disk I/O cost.

To evaluate the cost calculation formulas, we used a larger TPC-H database than the database used for measurement, SF100, and chose a combination of the following two tables, *customer* and *orders*, *supplier* and *lineitem*, and *part*

TABLE IV. SLOPE AND INTERCEPT OF THE REGRESSION MODELS

Type		Slope		Intercept	R^2	P value on F test	Reference
NLJ	A1	1.745×10^{5}	B1	1.64×10^{9}	9.99×10^{-1}	1.30×10^{-29}	Figure 6(1)
	A2	9.802×10^{-1}	B2	1.26×10^{7}	1.00	2.18×10^{-58}	Figure 6(2)
	A3	8.077×10^{-1}	B3	2.68×10^{6}	1.00	2.91×10^{-40}	Figure 6(3)
	A4	8.318×10^{-1}	B4	5.23×10^{4}	1.00	3.93×10^{-39}	Figure 6(4)
	A5	7.425×10^{-1}	B5	-1.18×10^{5}	1.00	3.77×10^{-34}	Figure 6(5)
	A6	2.575×10^{-1}	B6	1.18×10^{5}	9.98×10^{-1}	7.05×10^{-26}	Figure 6(6)
	A7	2.464×10^{4}	B7	4.63×10^{8}	9.99×10^{-1}	5.97×10^{-31}	Figure 6(7)
	A8	9.723×10^{-1}	B8	7.05×10^{6}	1.00	3.85×10^{-53}	Figure 6(8)
	A9	4.342×10^{-1}	B9	1.95×10^{6}	9.99×10^{-1}	5.17×10^{-28}	Figure 6(9)
	A10	9.442×10^{-1}	B10	-2.87×10^{4}	1.00	2.06×10^{-44}	Figure 610)
	A11	7.609×10^{-1}	B11	-4.84×10^{4}	1.00	2.80×10^{-35}	Figure 6(11)
	A12	2.391×10^{-1}	B12	4.84×10^{4}	9.98×10^{-1}	3.10×10^{-26}	Figure 6(12)
	A13	5.526×10^{-1}	B13	1.44×10^{8}	9.98×10^{-1}	9.85×10^{-26}	Figure 6(13)
	A14	8.595×10^{-1}	B14	-1.25×10^{9}	9.67×10^{-1}	9.00×10^{-15}	Figure 6(14)
	A15	2.321×10^{3}	B15	1.92×10^{7}	9.90×10^{-1}	1.35×10^{-19}	Figure 6(15)
HJ Build	A1	2.045×10^{3}	B1	1.58×10^{7}	1.00	4.21×10^{-40}	Figure 7(a1)
	A2	9.879×10^{-1}	B2	2.53×10^{5}	1.00	2.19×10^{-61}	Figure 7(a2)
	A3	9.708×10^{-1}	B3	-7.48×10^{4}	1.00	1.79×10^{-49}	Figure 7(a3)
	A4	9.191×10^{-1}	B4	-6.57×10^{4}	9.99×10^{-1}	7.76×10^{-31}	Figure 7(a4)
	A5	3.317×10^{-1}	B5	-1.64×10^{4}	9.29×10^{-1}	8.38×10^{-12}	Figure 7(a5)
	A6	6.683×10^{-1}	B6	1.64×10^{4}	9.82×10^{-1}	4.49×10^{-17}	Figure 7(a6)
	A7	6.099×10^{2}	B7	2.85×10^{5}	9.99×10^{-1}	4.46×10^{-30}	Figure 7(a7)
	A8	9.902×10^{-1}	B8	-1.89×10^{3}	1.00	1.05×10^{-57}	Figure 7(a8)
	A9	8.033×10^{-1}	B9	-2.39×10^{4}	1.00	6.00×10^{-33}	Figure 7(a9)
	A10	9.042×10^{-1}	B10	1.58×10^{2}	1.00	8.94×10^{-46}	Figure 7(a10)
	A11	2.131×10^{-1}	B11	-2.74×10^{3}	9.80×10^{-1}	1.13×10^{-16}	Figure 7(a11)
	A12	7.869×10^{-1}	B12	2.74×10^{3}	9.98×10^{-1}	8.16×10^{-27}	Figure 7(a12)
	A13	1.226	B13	-8.36×10^{6}	9.98×10^{-1}	1.55×10^{-25}	Figure 7(a13)
	A14	3.691×10^{-1}	B14	2.02×10^{7}	1.00	6.83×10^{-32}	Figure 7(a14)
	A15	2.351×10^{1}	B15	5.12×10^{5}	9.97×10^{-1}	2.86×10^{-24}	Figure 7(a15)
HJ Probe	A1	1.900×10^{3}	B1	2.33×10^{7}	1.00	3.46×10^{-46}	Figure 7(b1)
	A2	9.883×10^{-1}	B2	3.88×10^{5}	1.00	3.69×10^{-62}	Figure 7(b2)
	A3	9.750×10^{-1}	B3	-1.76×10^{4}	1.00	6.81×10^{-52}	Figure 7(b3)
	A4	8.131×10^{-1}	B4	-2.44×10^{4}	1.00	1.12×10^{-41}	Figure 7(b4)
	A5	9.455×10^{-1}	B5	-2.44×10^{4}	1.00	8.30×10^{-36}	Figure 7(b5)
	A6	5.449×10^{-2}	B6	2.44×10^{4}	9.56×10^{-1}	1.15×10^{-13}	Figure 7(b6)
	A7	5.763×10^{2}	B7	-3.57×10^{7}	9.99×10^{-1}	6.14×10^{-27}	Figure 7(b7)
	A8	9.892×10^{-1}	B8	-3.89×10^{5}	1.00	6.68×10^{-54}	Figure 7 (b8)
	A9	7.288×10^{-1}	B9	1.58×10^{5}	9.88×10^{-1}	7.30×10^{-19}	Figure 7(b9)
	A10	7.946×10^{-1}	B10	2.81×10^{4}	1.00	5.98×10^{-33}	Figure 7 (b10)
	A11	9.341×10^{-1}	B11	-6.04×10^{4}	1.00	7.79×10^{-34}	Figure 7 (b11)
	A12	6.595×10^{-2}	B12	6.04×10^{4}	9.52×10^{-1}	2.69×10^{-13}	Figure 7(b12)
	A13	1.503	B13	2.58×10^{07}	9.89×10^{-1}	5.80×10^{-19}	Figure 7(b13)
	A14	3.576×10^{-1}	B14	6.61×10^{7}	9.98×10^{-1}	1.75×10^{-25}	Figure 7(b14)
	A15	2.761×10^{1}	B15	-1.12×10^{7}	9.35×10^{-1}	3.83×10^{-12}	Figure 7(b15)
NLJ (I/O)	A16	1.016	B16	2.52×10^{3}	1.00	1.85×10^{-15}	Figure 8(a)
HJ (I/O)	A16	0.000	B16	0.000	N/A	N/A	N/A

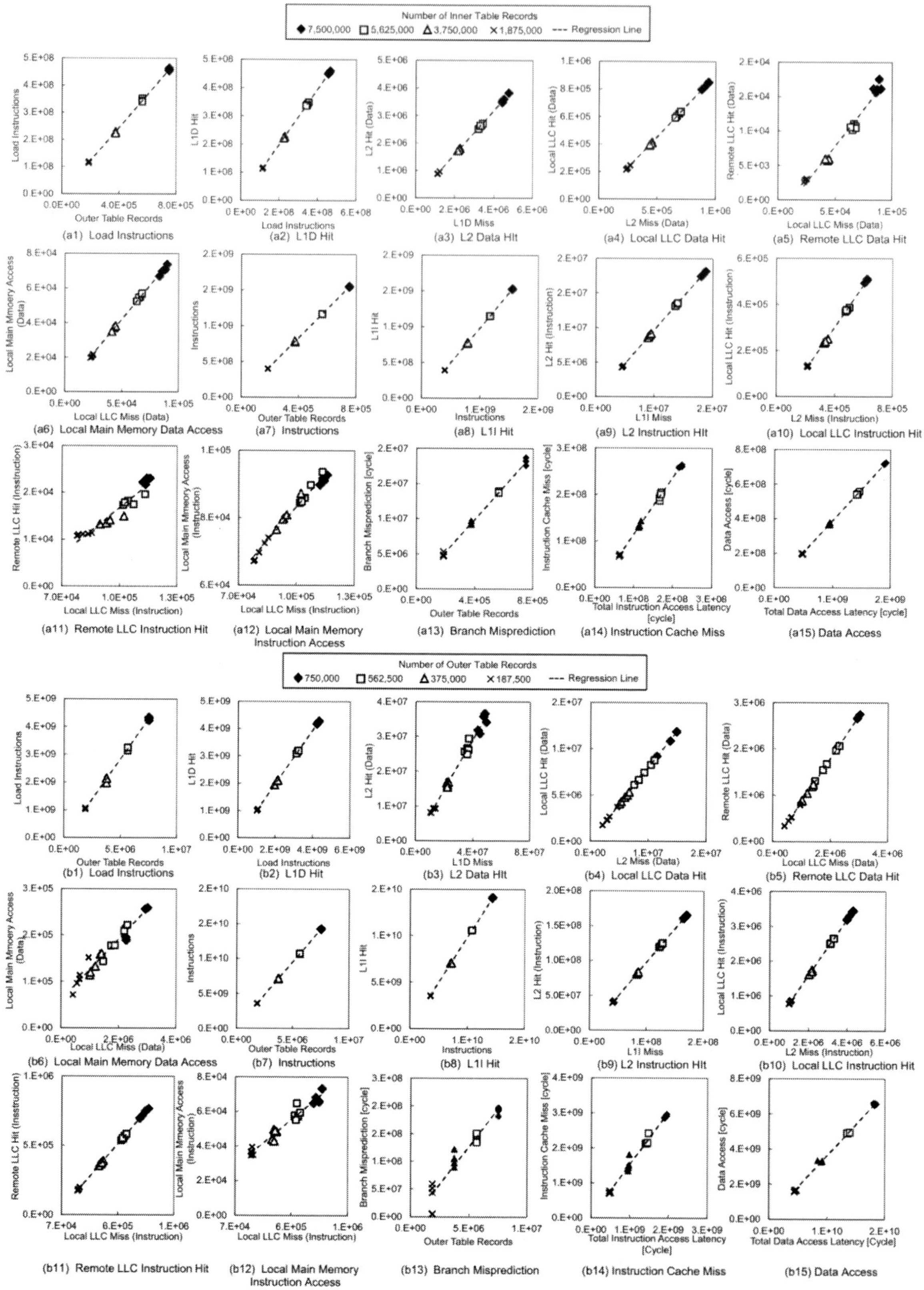

Figure 7. CPU event count on executing HJ

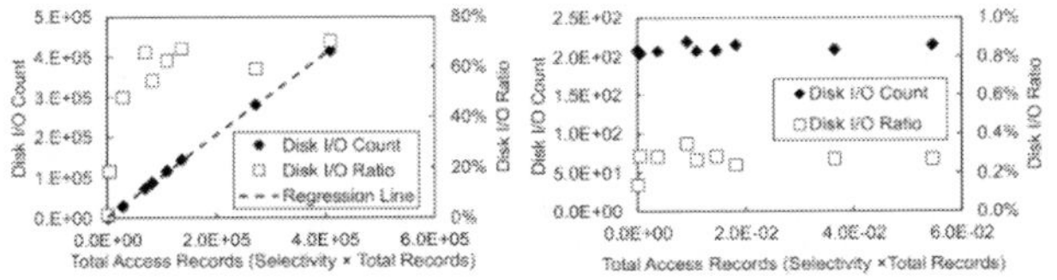

Figure 8. Number of disk I/O and disk I/O processing time per query execution time

and *lineitem*. The parameters setting of the cost calculation formulas is generated from the measurement values when joining *customer* and *orders*, whose size is SF5. The I/O processing time is added to allow a comparison with the query execution time. The proposed cost calculation method is compared with the measured query execution time and the conventional method (2)(3). We evaluate whether the selectivity where the join method is switched can be estimated accurately. However, because the conventional method does not support HJ, single table scans of the outer table and inner table are used. Moreover, MariaDB, as used in this experiment, cannot use the function to automatically select the join method, and only the join method set by the user is selected. The goal of this study is to accurately find the intersection point of the NLJ and HJ graphs. As a result, in all of the cases evaluated in this study, the proposed method was able to find the intersection point with an accuracy of one significant figure or better compared with the conventional method (Figure 9).

V. Discussion

In the acquisition of measurement data for constructing the cost calculation formula, since the type of counters that the hardware monitor can collect at one time is limited to four, it is necessary to measure many times in order to perform an accurate measurement of 40 events. Therefore, a certain amount of time must be secured for measurement. For example, it takes about 5 hours and 30 minutes for the measurement of this study. From the point of securing time for measurement and the point that the CPU cost calculation formula does not need to change the CPU cost calculation formula unless there is a change in the hardware configuration or join operation codes of DBMS, it is appropriate to create the proposed CPU cost calculation formula at integrating or updating a system. Next, in the use of the cost calculation formula, the proposed CPU cost formula is used in the optimization process to be executed before executing a query. The CPU cost of executing the query is calculated from the number of records to be searched. As shown in the reference [15] [16], in a general DBMS, histograms representing the relationship between the attribute value and the appearance frequency are automatically acquired when inserting or updating records. From the histogram and the condition of the where clause of the query, it is possible to estimate the number of records accessed by the DBMS. In this way, CPU costs can be calculated with only the data already acquired by the DBMS, so cost can be calculated by the cost calculation formula before query execution.

In this study, we have proposed a cost calculation method for the in-memory DBMS using a disk-based DBMS. The calculation formulas have been created using the data measured by the CPU-embedded performance monitor. The study revealed that the proposed method estimated the intersection point of the join methods more accurately than the conventional method. We used TPC-H for measuring CPU activities. TPC-H has the advantage that it is easy to analyze the evaluation results because the distribution of data is uniform. However, the actual data has a skew in the distribution of keys. The premise of the technique in this paper is the accuracy of selectivity. Even if the distribution of data varies, if the selectivity is the same, the same measurement result is obtained. Since a general DBMS acquires attribute values and their distribution in a database in the form of a histogram when loading data to the database, the prerequisite for application of the proposed technique is considered to be satisfactory. However, it is necessary to develop a technique to derive histogram information and input it as an input parameter of the cost formulas.

Since this technique sets parameters based on actual measurements, it is difficult to deal with various patterns such as the presence or absence of indices and complicated queries. Although we have focused on the operation of all CPU cycles, it is necessary for practical use to simplify the model omitting some parameters. For the collection of statistical data, it is conceivable that actual measurement could be performed at the time of initial installation and parameter setting. However, when the code of the DBMS is modified, it is difficult to change in real time, so separate complementary technology is required. As a breakthrough measure, it is possible to reduce the amount of data to be verified and to reduce measurement points.

VI. Related Work

Evaluating CPU performance using the performance monitor for behavior analysis of a DBMS has long been performed. In particular, in the evaluation of the benchmark TPC-D for e decision support systems, the L1 miss and the processing delay due to L2 cache occupy a large part as the components of the CPI, and it is important in terms of performance. However, it is only used for bottleneck analysis [17].

There is research that applied a CPI calculation method focusing on a memory reference to cost calculation (5) for an in-memory database [18] [19]. This previous research targets DBMS that use the load/store type memory access (Figure 1(c)).

In this research, the number of cache hits or main memory accesses is predicted from the data access pattern of the database, and the cost is calculated as the product of the number of the cache hits or main memory accesses and the memory latency. Modeling of *CPI0*, which is the state that all data exists in the L1 cache, and modeling of instruction cache misses have not been considered in previous studies. Although not explicitly mentioned in the literature, it was presumed that it was impossible to reproduce and measure the state in which all instructions and data are on the L1 cache, which is the definition of *CPI0*, by means such as a CPU-embedded performance monitor.

VII. Conclusions and Future Work

In this study, we have proposed a cost calculation method for the in-memory DBMS using disk-based DBMS. We focused on a CPU pipeline architecture and classified CPU cycles into three types based on the characteristics of operation of the front-end and back-end. The calculation formulas are created using the data measured by the CPU-embedded performance monitor. In the evaluation, the difference in selectivity corresponding to the intersection points of NLJ and HJ between the calculated cost and the measured time was less than 1%;

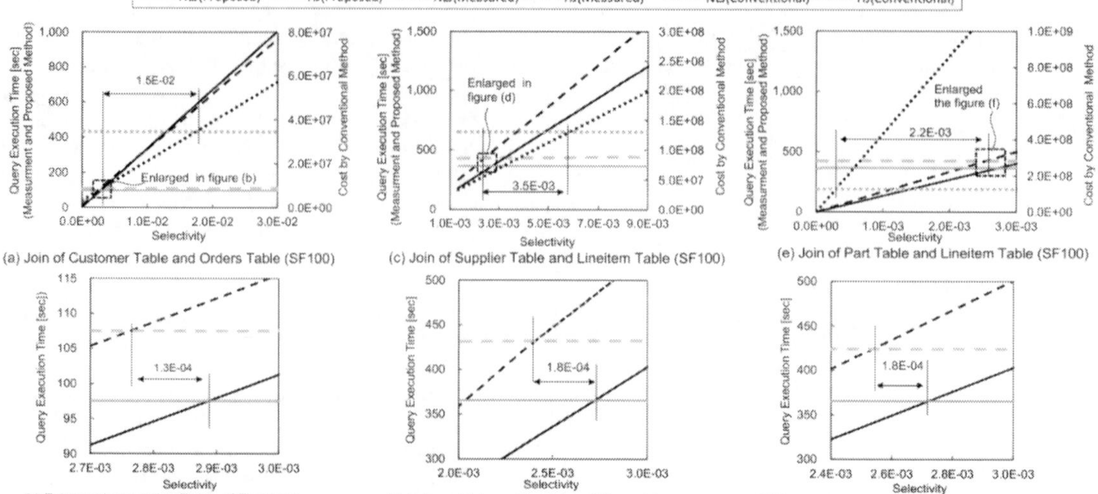

(a) Join of Customer Table and Orders Table (SF100)
(c) Join of Supplier Table and Lineitem Table (SF100)
(e) Join of Part Table and Lineitem Table (SF100)
(b) Enlarged Intercection Points of Figure (a)
(d) Enlarged Interception Point of Figure (c)
(f) Enlarged Interception Point of Figure (e)

Figure 9. Comparison of measured results, the proposed cost model, and the conventional cost model

that is, the cost formulas can model the actual join operation with high accuracy. As a result, by applying the proposed cost calculation formulas, we can select the join method appropriately and reduce the risk of unexpected query execution delay to users of the DBMS. In the future, we will consider joins of three or more tables. Furthermore, we will evaluate different generation CPUs and analyze how the differences in CPU architecture affect the cost formulas and implement a DBMS that automatically distinguishes CPU differences from the analysis results and automatically corrects the parameters for cost calculation or the calculation model itself.

REFERENCES

[1] A. Foong and F. Hady, "Storage as fast as rest of the system," in 2016 IEEE 8th International Memory Workshop (IMW), May 2016, pp. 1–4.

[2] A. Rudoff, "Programming models to enable persistent memory," Storage Developer Conference, SNIA, Santa Clara, CA, USA, September, 2012, https://www.snia.org/sites/default/orig/SDC2012/presentations/Solid_State/AndyRudoff_Program_Models.pdf [retrieved: March, 2017].

[3] A. Rudoff, "The impact of the nvm programming model," Storage Developer Conference, SNIA, Santa Clara, CA, USA, September, 2013, https://www.snia.org/sites/default/files/files2/files2/SDC2013/presentations/GeneralSession/AndyRudoff_Impact_NVM.pdf [retrieved: March, 2017].

[4] P. G. Selinger, M. M. Astrahan, D. D. Chamberlin, R. A. Lorie, and T. G. Price, "Access path selection in a relational database management system," in Proceedings of the 1979 ACM SIGMOD International Conference on Management of Data, ser. SIGMOD '79. New York, NY, USA: ACM, 1979, pp. 23–34. [Online]. Available: http://doi.acm.org/10.1145/582095.582099

[5] W. Wu et al., "Predicting query execution time: Are optimizer cost models really unusable?" in Data Engineering (ICDE), 2013 IEEE 29th International Conference on, April 2013, pp. 1081–1092.

[6] O. Sandsta, "Mysql cost model," http://www.slideshare.net/olavsa/mysql-optimizer-cost-model [retrieved: March, 2017], October 2014.

[7] D. Levinthal, "Performance analysis guide for intel core i7 processor and intel xeon 5500 processors," Intel Performance Analysis Guide, vol. 30, 2009, p. 18.

[8] P. Apparao, R. Iyer, and D. Newell, "Towards modeling & analysis of consolidated cmp servers," SIGARCH Comput. Archit. News, vol. 36, no. 2, May 2008, pp. 38–45. [Online]. Available: http://doi.acm.org/10.1145/1399972.1399980

[9] N. Hardavellas et al., "Database servers on chip multiprocessors: Limitations and opportunities," in Proceedings of the Biennial Conference on Innovative Data Systems Research (CIDR), Asilomar, CA, USA, January 2007, pp. 79–87.

[10] L. McVoy et al., "lmbench: Portable tools for performance analysis," in USENIX annual technical conference, San Diego, CA, USA, 1996, pp. 279–294.

[11] J. L. Lo et al., "An analysis of database workload performance on simultaneous multithreaded processors," in ACM SIGARCH Computer Architecture News, vol. 26, no. 3. IEEE Computer Society, 1998, pp. 39–50.

[12] The mariadb foundation - ensuring continuity and open collaboration in the mariadb ecosystem. [Online]. Available: https://mariadb.org/ (2017)

[13] "TPC BENCHMARK™ H (decision support) standard specification revision 2.17.1, Transaction Processing Performance council (TPC)," http://www.tpc.org/tpc_documents_current_versions/pdf/tpch2.17.1.pdf [retrieved: March, 2017], 2014.

[14] D. Molka, D. Hackenberg, R. Schone, and M. S. Muller, "Memory performance and cache coherency effects on an intel nehalem multiprocessor system," in 2009 18th International Conference on Parallel Architectures and Compilation Techniques, Sept 2009, pp. 261–270.

[15] A. Aboulnaga et al., "Automated statistics collection in db2 udb," in Proceedings of the Thirtieth International Conference on Very Large Data Bases - Volume 30, ser. VLDB '04. VLDB Endowment, 2004, pp. 1158–1169. [Online]. Available: http://dl.acm.org/citation.cfm?id=1316689.1316788

[16] I. Babae, "Engine-independent persistent statistics with histograms in mariadb," Percona Live MySQL Conference and Expo 2013, April, 2013, https://www.percona.com/live/london-2013/sites/default/files/slides/uc2013-EIPS-final.pdf [retrieved: March, 2017].

[17] A. Ailamaki, D. J. DeWitt, M. D. Hill, and D. A. Wood, "Dbmss on a modern processor: Where does time go?" in VLDB" 99, Proceedings of 25th International Conference on Very Large Data Bases, September 7-10, 1999, Edinburgh, Scotland, UK, no. DIAS-CONF-1999-001, 1999, pp. 266–277.

[18] S. Manegold, P. A. Boncz, and M. L. Kersten, "Optimizing database architecture for the new bottleneck: memory access," The VLDB Journal, vol. 9, no. 3, 2000, pp. 231–246.

[19] S. Manegold, P. Boncz, and M. L. Kersten, "Generic database cost models for hierarchical memory systems," in Proceedings of the 28th international conference on Very Large Data Bases. VLDB Endowment, 2002, pp. 191–202.

A Proposal of Activation Mechanism for User Communication based on User Behavior Analysis on Wedding Community Sites

Toshinori Hayashi*, Yuanyuan Wang†, Yukiko Kawai‡, and Kazutoshi Sumiya*
*Kwansei Gakuin University,
2–1 Gakuen, Sanda, Hyogo 669–1337, Japan
Email: den82687@kwansei.ac.jp, sumiya@kwansei.ac.jp
†Yamaguchi University,
2–16–1 Tokiwadai, Ube, Yamaguchi 755–8611, Japan
Email: y.wang@yamaguchi-u.ac.jp
‡Kyoto Sangyo University,
Kamigamo Motoyama, Kita-ku, Kyoto 603–8555, Japan
Email: kawai@cc.kyoto-su.ac.jp

***Abstract*—In this paper, we present an active communication mechanism based on a user behavior analysis on wedding community sites. To this end, we propose a novel mechanism for activation of user communication that provides related comments and users by detecting knowledge and interests from archived comments; this information from a wedding community website evokes conversations among users. The proposed mechanism has three components: 1) profiling static user information such as users' age and location and active user information like her dynamic interest and intention to communicate, 2) detecting and recommending users who are likely to communicate with each other, and 3) recommending comments that may be of interest to a user. Through the proposed activation mechanism, users on a wedding community site can communicate with each other easily and efficiently. We discuss our proposed user characteristic extraction and user recommendation methods using actual user posts from a wedding community website.**

Keywords–user behavior analysis; wedding community site; communication.

I. INTRODUCTION

In recent years, research has been conducted using data from Social Networking Services (SNSs) [1][2]. It is important to collect as much data as possible from SNS community sites, such as Facebook, LINE, and other Q&A sites. However, such services that focus on data collection cannot promote user communication on community websites because of differences in values. In this paper, we focus on a wedding community site, and we aim to promote user communication by recommending appropriate users and comments.

Specifically, we propose a novel active communication mechanism that shares comments of users by considering their knowledge and interests by analyzing their behavior on community websites. To this end, we first extract all posts of each user and extract their feature words using the term frequency–inverse document frequency (*tf-idf*) method. Next, we calculate the similarities among users to detect appropriate users. Finally, we recommend their comments by generating links to them in posts (Fig. 1). To use this mechanism, users can communicate with other users that are recommended to them about wedding planning; furthermore, it promotes communication among users on a wedding community site.

The remainder of the paper is organized as follows. Section II provides an overview of our system and reviews related work. Section III explains how to recommend users and their comments on a wedding community site. Section IV illustrates the experimental results obtained using a real dataset from a wedding community site. Finally, Section V concludes the paper and outlines our future work.

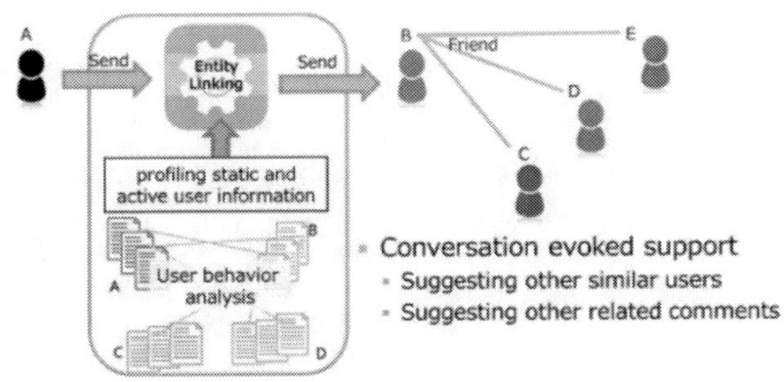

Figure 1. User and comment recommendations for activation of user communication based on a user behavior analysis.

II. SYSTEM OVERVIEW AND RELATED WORK

A. Active Communication Mechanism

We present an active communication mechanism based on a user behavior analysis on wedding community sites. This mechanism has three steps: 1) user login information and user characteristic extraction, 2) user detection and recommendations, and 3) comment recommendations (Fig. 1).

To use this mechanism, users are required to install a toolbar (a browser plug-in) on an existing wedding community site in Japan. Wedding community sites are generally utilized by couples that plan to hold a wedding and are intended to assess a couples' needs regarding marriage. On this website, there are threads for wedding planning in different marriage statuses, and users can freely post their comments to each thread. The only way to communicate with other users is by replying to other users' comments on a thread. To improve replies, we propose a method that recommends both users and their comments by analyzing user behavior and their profile information on a wedding community site. Our goal is for our active communication mechanism to determine which users may want to communicate with other users.

A wedding community site is not a "Question & Answer site"; rather, it is a website where users can share their positive opinions and experiences about weddings. The proposed system will recommend other users who have had similar situations or values of marriage to evoke communication between users. This system can also be used on other community websites; however, since the proposed system is considered on a wedding community site, it uses static information entered by a user during their initial user registration regarding their ideal wedding ceremony.

Fig. 1 shows the overview of our proposed mechanism. After a user posts, the mechanism analyzes the user behavior and recommends other users by calculating the similarities between them.

B. Related Work

Issac et al. [3] noted that communication is important to discuss different topics and work with others as a group. They mentioned that communication makes people more willing to contribute to society. Moreover, it is also effective for communication on websites, not only face-to-face communication. Ellison et al. [4] focused on SNS communities. According to these studies, communicating with others on SNSs makes more people feel happy.

In our previous work [5], users communicated with each other when they searched for web pages. In this work, we extend our previous work to recommend users and comments based on the link generation for a wedding community site. Although several automatic link generation methods for websites have been studied [6][7], they have primarily focused on web pages for knowledge support only; they did not consider communication among users. To address this deficiency, our proposed method recommends users to evoke communication. Other studies that have recommended analyzing user behavior on news sites [8] did not consider the relationships between users. In this paper, we first extract user posts to analyze user behavior and detect users to recommend by extracting the relationships between users.

Akihiro et al. [9] conducted an experiment for active communication in e-lectures through a chat system. However, it did not work very well because it was a burden for students to chat with others during the lectures. In this paper, we propose a new active communication mechanism by recommending appropriate users for different marriage statuses of users.

III. Active Communication Mechanism for Wedding Sites

A. User Behavior Analysis on a Wedding Community Site

To evoke communication among users, our active communication mechanism recommends users and their comments by analyzing user behavior on a wedding community site. According to our previous work [5], users can help other users when they search for the same web pages. Furthermore, in general, users communicate with each other easily when they are in similar statuses or situations. Therefore, in order to recommend users, we analyze to make 3 profiles based on aspects of wedding community site (see Fig. 2); in particular, we consider the axes of "Static Profile Information", "Marriage Status", and "Active Profile Information".

1) User Login Information Extraction: We extract user login information by acquiring user registration information on a wedding community site that users input upon site registration. Users input information such as their ages, places where they live, and marriage status. We divide the user login information as user static profile information and marriage status.

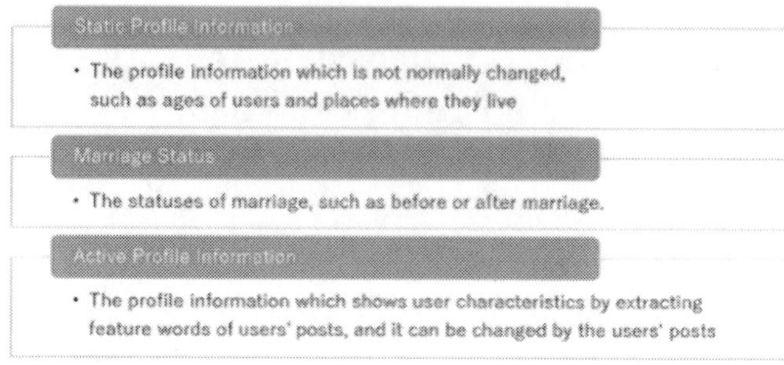

Figure 2. Profiling based on user's aspects.

2) User Characteristic Extraction: We extract user characteristics by extracting all posts of each user. Next, we calculate the term frequency and document frequency based on the *tf-idf* method; specifically, we use the following formulas:

$$tf_{i,j} = \frac{n_{i,j}}{\sum_k n_{k,j}}, \tag{1}$$

$$idf_i = \log \frac{|D|}{df_i}, \tag{2}$$

where $n_{i,j}$ denotes the term frequency of the word t_i in document d_j. In this work, d_j denotes the document that is integrated by all posts of one user. Therefore, the number of documents is equal to the number of users on the wedding community site. Furthermore, $\sum_k n_{k,j}$ denotes the sum of the term frequencies of all words in document d_j, and $|D|$ denotes the total number of documents, which is also equal to the number of users. Finally, df_i denotes the number of the documents that include the word t_i.

Based on the above, we use the obtained *tf-idf* values and feature words of each user to determine a users' active profile information.

B. User Detection and Recommendation

1) User Detection: We detect users based on the similarities of "Active Profile Information" between users by using the cosine similarity as follows:

$$Sim(\overrightarrow{x}, \overrightarrow{y}) = \frac{\sum_{i=1}^{|V|} x_i \cdot y_i}{\sqrt{\sum_{i=1}^{|V|}(x_i)^2} \cdot \sqrt{\sum_{i=1}^{|V|}(y_i)^2}}, \tag{3}$$

where $\overrightarrow{x}$ denotes the feature vector of user x, and $\overrightarrow{y}$ denotes the feature vector of user y; $|V|$ is the number of dimensions of the feature vector.

"Marriage Status" is an absolute value, such as "before marriage" or "after marriage"; therefore, it will not change based on other users. However, "Static Profile Information" and "Active Profile Information" are relative values; they will change depending on each user.

TABLE I. FIVE USER PATTERNS FOR RECOMMENDATION.

Pattern	User (Who)	Marriage Status (to who)	Static Profile Information	Active Profile Information	Purpose
1	After marriage	Before	Neutral	Similar	Give advice
2	After marriage	After	Neutral	Similar	Share
3	Before marriage	Before	Similar	Different	Reference
4	Before marriage	Before	Neutral	Similar	Share
5	Before marriage	After	Neutral	Similar	Get advice

TABLE II. RECOMMENDATION SITUATION FOR EACH USER PATTERN.

Pattern	Purpose	When	How
1	Give advice	Links are generated in the comments	○○ needs some advice from you
2	Share	After Login	○○ is on the same status as you
3	Reference	Links are generated in the comments	You can refer to ○○
4	Share	After Login	○○ is on the same status as you
5	Get advice	Links are generated in the comments	○○ can be a good adviser for you

2) User Recommendation: We recommend users to communicate with others by considering users who have similar situations; such users may easily relate and share their experiences or advice. Based on the three axes described in the previous subsection, we classify five useful patterns of users on a wedding community site (see Table I).

We detect the user that is most similar to each user for Patterns 1, 2, 4, and 5; moreover, we detect the user that is most different from each user for Pattern 3. Based on the above procedure, we propose recommendations to users.

C. Comment Recommendation

1) Comment Extraction: In the previous subsection, we explained how to detect users and make recommendations to stimulate communication on a wedding community site. To recommend user comments, we calculate the most related comments from the recommended users that are derived using Eq. (3).

2) Recommendation Interface: Our active communication mechanism recommends users or user comments in different scenarios; we refer to each user pattern in Table II.

This mechanism has two methods of recommending users. The first method recommends users in the comments by generating links to them. The second method recommends users on the top page after login.

For the first method, the interface of recommendation for Patterns 1, 3, and 5, the mechanism generates links in the comments. To generate links in the comments after users have posted, we attach the links of user information or their comments to related words by extracting user characteristics (feature words).

In the second method, the interface of recommendation for Patterns 2 and 4, the mechanism presents users on the top page of the website after login. This mechanism also recommends users on the top page that are likely to share similar experiences. We assume that users prefer to see more users on the top page than in the links generated in the comments.

IV. Evaluation

In this section, we first extract the actual data from a wedding community site to verify the user characteristic extraction method by extracting feature words of all posts for each user. Second, we detect similar users by comparing the cosine similarity with collaborative filtering.

A. Experiment 1: Verification of User Characteristic Extraction

To evaluate our user characteristic extraction, we extracted feature words of all posts for each user. We compared three methods as follows:

1) *tf*
2) *tf-idf* (*df* = all of users)
3) *tf-idf* (*df* = the users before or after marriage)

We extracted 7,728 terms from 588 user posts.

Table III shows the top-15 feature words for users A, B, C, and D for each method. Bold words denote that feature words are related to these users. We found that many feature words are proper nouns for Methods 2) and 3) such as "Fish paste" and "Limousine". However, for Method 1), we found common words that all users often use, i.e., there are no effective words that can be considered feature words. We determined that

TABLE III. TOP-15 FEATURE WORDS OF USERS A, B, C, AND D.

User \ Method	1)	2)	3)
A	of, a, ceremony, wedding ceremony, to, sister, I will, heart, family, after, because, to, did, et al., that	sister, wedding ceremony, **earthquake disaster**, **Fukushima**, bata, fireplace, chaya, sister, attendance, column, heart, family, safety, stop, name	wedding ceremony, sister, **Earthquake disaster**, bata, attendance, heart, **Fukushima**, chaya, fireplace, family, sister, column, 11, safety, influence
B	of, did, better, object, pull, a marriage, I will, he, now, a student, generation, learning, Toyama, now, chestnut	**fish paste**, Toyama, red snapper, gift, girlfriend, object, luck, a student, surprised, age, pull, mountain, form, chestnut, happiness	Toyama, red snapper, **fish paste**, object, gift, girlfriend, luck, a student, surprised, age, mountain, form, happiness, chestnut, woman
C	did, of, better, reach, day, that, friend, friends, ceremony, wedding ceremony, while, a, before, first, good	it seems intriguing, eve, **limousine**, the eve, first meeting, face to face, a van, friend, the other day, reach, move, the previous day, festival, the best	eve, it seems intriguing, **limousine**, first meeting, friend, face to face, the best, a van, move, the previous day, festival, the other day, Hawaii, fellow, reach
D	a, of, did, one, this, now, better, "", to, about, place, et al., yo, filtration, meeting	reserved, **snow board**, lending, no, alternating current, table, **hair style**, comment, firing, male, rooftop, development, release, frank	reserved, **snow board**, alternating current, male, hair style, table, board, **BGM**, rooftop, firing, girlfriend, in Tokyo, development, comment

calculating with *idf* is a more effective way to extract feature words; however, there are no differences between Methods 2) and 3). The *idf* values imply how the words are generally used by many users; if the *idf* value is high, the word is rarely used among users, and similarly, if it is low, the word is common among users. Therefore, there are no differences between the posts of users before marriage and the posts of users after marriage. Thus, we considered different definitions of document groups, which are not limited to marriage status.

Our results suggest that in the future, we need to remove common words since some generally used words were identified using Methods 2) and 3).

The above discussion confirms that many feature words of users are effectively extracted using *tf-idf* methods, namely, Methods 2) and 3). To detect user characteristics with feature words, more advanced methods are required.

B. Experiment 2: Verification of User Detection

In our active communication mechanism, the similarities between users are the key point for recommending users. In the previous section, we described our classification scheme that classifies users based on similarities of three axes. In this way, we choose the most suitable users to promote communication.

To evaluate the similarities between users, we compared two calculation methods; the first method is the proposed method, specifically, the content-based recommendation method using the cosine similarity with active profile information, and the second method is the item-based recommendation method that uses collaborative filtering with static profile information and marriage status. As mentioned before, we calculated the cosine similarity based on user characteristics, which consist of feature words of each user. Therefore, each user has feature vectors of *tf-idf* values. In Experiment 1, Method 2) is the most useful method for extracting feature words. We also calculated the cosine similarity based on the feature words produced by Method 2). Collaborative filtering is also a method used to calculate similarities between users. This method calculates similarities using user login information as items of each user. It is mainly used to recommend other items to users according to the following formula:

$$Sim(X,Y) = \frac{\sum(x-\bar{x})(y-\bar{y})}{\sqrt{\sum(x-\bar{x})^2\sum(y-\bar{y})^2}}. \quad (4)$$

TABLE IV. COSINE SIMILARITY AMONG 588 USERS.

value	#user combinations
0 - 0.1	154,132
0.1- 0.2	16,158
0.2 - 0.3	2,022
0.3 - 0.4	209
0.4 - 0.5	46
0.5 - 0.6	7
0.6 - 0.7	4
0.7 - 1.0	0

This equation calculates the similarity between users X and Y. On a wedding community site, users create individual accounts by answering questions about their wedding planning. For example, "Do you agree with a simple style marriage?" For each question, a user may choose from one of the following responses: "Strongly disagree," "Disagree," "Neither disagree nor agree," "Agree," or "Strongly agree." Each of these responses was assigned a numerical value ranging from 1 to 5, respectively, for calculation purposes. We then calculated the similarities using these numbers. Note that $\bar{x}$ and $\bar{y}$ denote the averages of the chosen answers, for example, if a user chose answers 1 to 5, the average value would be 3.

The users evaluated for our proposed user characteristic extraction are shown in Table III. For this evaluation, we calculated 172,578 combinations from 588 users; the value of the cosine similarity ranges between 0 and 1.

Table IV shows the distribution of results of the cosine similarity. The average value of all combinations is 0.045. We found that many results of user combinations are below 0.1. This can be attributed to the fact that most users talk about different topics related to their wedding planning. However, some user combinations induce a high cosine similarity.

Table V shows the distribution of results of collaborative filtering. The value of collaborative filtering should be between -1 and 1. For this method, the values are calculated based on the answers from the questions regarding wedding planning when users create accounts on the wedding community site. A high value implies the users have similar wedding planning ideas. For this evaluation, we calculated 435 combinations of 30 users. The average value of all combinations was 0.304, which confirms that many users have similar wedding planning tastes.

TABLE V. COLLABORATIVE FILTERING AMONG 30 USERS.

value	#user combinations
-1.0 - -0.9	0
-0.9 - -0.8	0
-0.8 - -0.7	2
-0.7 - -0.6	4
-0.6 - -0.5	5
-0.5 - -0.4	8
-0.4 - -0.3	8
-0.3 - -0.2	15
-0.2 - -0.1	23
-0.1 - 0	26
0 - 0.1	35
0.1- 0.2	39
0.2 - 0.3	40
0.3 - 0.4	38
0.4 - 0.5	41
0.5 - 0.6	41
0.3 - 0.7	44
0.7 - 0.8	31
0.8 - 0.9	26
0.9 - 1.0	9

Based on these results, we compared two similarity calculation methods. Here, we focused on user E, who has a high cosine similarity with other users and often posts on a wedding community site as a main user. We calculated all combinations with user E; therefore, there were a total of 588 values of the cosine similarity and 588 values of collaborative filtering.

Fig. 3 shows the distribution of the cosine similarity and collaborative filtering for 10 users, specifically, users E, H, I, J, K, L, M, N, O, and P. Each dot corresponds to one user and has two values: the cosine similarity with each user, and the collaborative filtering with each user. The vertical axis corresponds to the values of the cosine similarity, and the horizontal axis corresponds to the values of collaborative filtering. We focused on two users, specifically, F and G for user E. Both of these users have high cosine similarity values above 0.6, but their values of collaborative filtering are 0 and 0.54, respectively.

First, we compared the posts of users E and F. A post by user E describes their cousins' impressive wedding with the grooms' tears. On the other hand, a post of user F describes how their cousins' wedding was organized. Even though common words were used in their posts, the meanings of these sentences and their topics are different.

Second, we compared the posts of users E and G. The post from user E is the same post mentioned above. A post from user G describes their cousins' wedding with tears because of a letter about a grandmother who was gone. These posts both mention the same type of wedding and their cousins' weddings with tears, even though the content of these posts is slightly different.

As a result, we found that only calculating the cosine similarity is not effective to detect similar comments. However, we found that calculating both the cosine similarity and collaborative filtering are effective. Therefore, these two methods can help detect similar user comments to evoke communication among users. However, we still must evaluate other situations of users with other users' axes and marriage statuses.

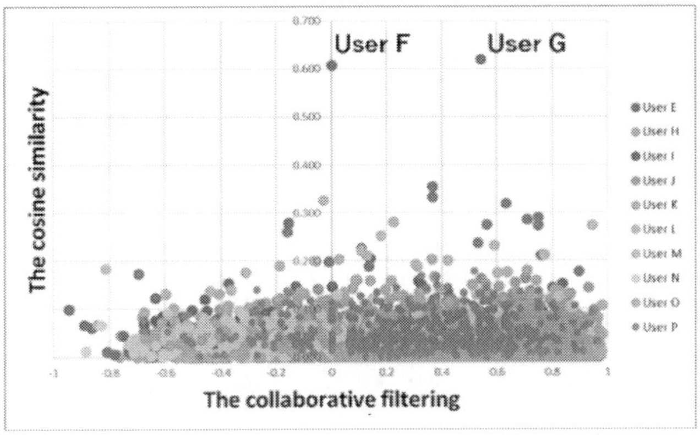

Figure 3. Distribution of the cosine similarity and collaborative filtering 1.

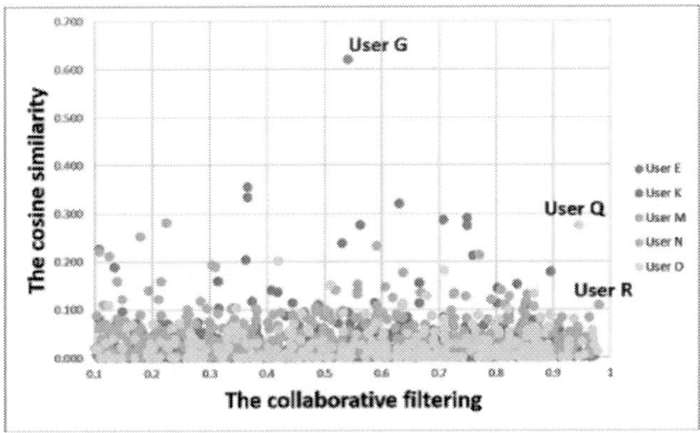

Figure 4. Distribution of the cosine similarity and collaborative filtering 2.

Fig. 4 briefly shows the distribution of the cosine similarity and collaborative filtering for users E, K, M, N, and O. We found several users that are especially similar to these users such as users Q and R. In future, we plan to propose methods for clustering with the cosine similarity and collaborative filtering.

V. CONCLUSION

In this paper, we proposed an active communication mechanism for a wedding community site. This mechanism recommended 1) users who may potentially evoke communication and 2) their comments. To detect users, this mechanism classified all users into three axes, specifically, "Static Profile Information," "Marriage Status," and "Active Profile Information." We then calculated the similarities between users using the cosine similarity. To extract comments that were posted on a wedding community site by recommended users, our mechanism detected the most related comments. Finally, we evaluated the user characteristic extraction from posts by comparing *tf-idf* methods and evaluated similarity calculation methods with the cosine similarity and collaborative filtering.

In the future, we plan to enhance the proposed method based on our experimental results and evaluate the effects of user recommendations. Furthermore, we plan to extract the relationships between users by constructing a matrix based on user behavior, as in our previous work [10].

ACKNOWLEDGMENT

This work was partially supported by JSPS KAKENHI Grant Numbers 15K00162 and 16H01722.

REFERENCES

[1] U. Pfeil, R. Arjan, and P. Zaphiris, "Age differences in online social networking–a study of user profiles and the social capital divide among teenagers and older users in myspace," Computers in Human Behavior, vol. 25, no. 3, 2009, pp. 643–654.

[2] M. D. Roblyer, M. McDaniel, M. Webb, J. Herman, and J. V. Witty, "Findings on facebook in higher education: A comparison of college faculty and student uses and perceptions of social networking sites," The Internet and higher education, vol. 13, no. 3, 2010, pp. 134–140.

[3] R. Isaac and J. Walker, "Communication and free-riding behavior: The voluntary contribution mechanism," Economic Inquiry, vol. 26, no. 4, 1988, pp. 585–608.

[4] N. B. Ellison, C. Steinfield, and C. Lampe, "The benefits of facebook "friends:" social capital and college students' use of online social network sites," Journal of Computer-Mediated Communication, vol. 12, no. 4, 2007, pp. 1143–1168.

[5] Y. Mastsui and Y. Kawai, "Social search system for retrieval and communication based on networks of pages and users," Computer Software, vol. 28, no. 4, 2011, pp. 196–205.

[6] D. Zhou, M. Truran, T. Brailsford, H. Ashman, and A. Pourabdollah, "Llama-b: Automatic hyperlink authoring in the blogosphere," in Proceedings of the Nineteenth ACM Conference on Hypertext and Hypermedia, ser. HT '08. New York, NY, USA: ACM, 2008, pp. 133–138. [Online]. Available: http://doi.acm.org/10.1145/1379092.1379119

[7] R. D. souza, A. Kulkarni, and I. A. Mirza, "Automatic link generation for search engine optimization," International Journal of Information and Education Technology, vol. 2, no. 4, 2012, pp. 401–403, ISSN: 2010-3689.

[8] J. Liu, E. Pedersen, and P. Dolan, "Personalized news recommendation based on click behavior," Proceedings of the 15th International Conference on Intelligent User Interfaces, 2010, pp. 31–40.

[9] H. Akihiro, Y. Madoka, T. Hiroyuki, and K. Yahiko, "Experimental chat sessions to encourage active communication in lectures," IPSJ SIG Notes, vol. 2000, no. 45, 2000, pp. 61–66.

[10] Y. Wang, Y. Kawai, S. Miyamoto, and K. Sumiya, "An automatic scoring system for e-reports based on student peer evaluation using groupware," DBSJ Journal, vol. 13, no. 1, 2015, pp. 71–76.

A Node Access Frequency based Graph Partitioning Technique for Efficient Dynamic Dependency Analysis

Kazuma Kusu
Graduate School of Culture and Information Science, Doshisha University
1-3 Tatara-Miyakodani, Kyotanabe, Kyoto 610-0394, Japan
Email: kusu@ilab.doshisha.ac.jp

Izuru Kume
Graduate School of Information Science, Nara Institute of Science and Technology
8916-5 Takayama, Ikoma, Nara 630-0192, Japan
Email: kume@is.naist.jp

Kenji Hatano
Faculty of Culture and Information Science, Doshisha University
1-3 Tatara-Miyakodani, Kyotanabe, Kyoto 610-0394, Japan
Email: khatano@mail.doshisha.ac.jp

Abstract—**Program execution traces (simply "traces" for short) contain data/control dependency information, and are indispensable to novel kinds of debugging such as back-in-time debugging. However, traces easily become large and complicated. For a practical use, maintainers need to be able to interactively invoke an analysis process when required and obtain rapid feedback. To this end, the authors develop an approach for efficient macroscopic analysis of traces of large sizes with complex data structures. We propose an approach that involves storing graphs in a database that reduces the number of attributes in the main memory during dependency analysis. We also introduce a criterion for the application of this approach that can maximize its effectiveness. Finally, we conduct experiments to assess its effectiveness for efficient dependency analysis.**

Keywords–Dynamic Dependency Analysis; Back-in-time Debugger; Debugging Support; Graph Database; Graph Search; Java.

I. INTRODUCTION

The examination of runtime states and their dependencies are indispensable to program debugging [1] [2]. Debuggers that are currently in use allow maintainers to suspend program execution at specified break points and examine the runtime states at these points. However, such debuggers do not have a provision for maintainers to examine states prior to the designated points for the suspension of execution. Therefore, they cannot trace backwards to detect causes of erroneous states by following the dependency of statements [3].

In the last decade, the so-called *Back-in-time debuggers* have emerged as a new kind of debugging supporting tools. These debuggers use traces containing dependency information [4]–[6]. Such debuggers analyze dependencies to determine the operation that assigns value to a referenced variable [4], to examine the reasons for why a given statement is or is not executed [5], and what happens during the execution of a method that has already been successfully invoked [6]. This kind of dependency analysis is useful for the examination of a particular instruction.

The scalability of process traces containing dependency information has been discussed in the literature [3]. We believe that the recent, rapid developments in hardware and software technologies have made it possible to process the traces of a certain scale of software products. In previous work [7], we demonstrated two kinds of dynamic dependency analysis (simply called dependency analysis in this paper) that detect symptoms of an infection caused by defects in the application of the Java framework application [8].

Although our previous study has raised the prospect of a solution to the scalability problem, yet implementation of our dependency analysis remains inefficient. The main cause of the inefficiency is the richness of data in the model of our traces. The design of our trace proposed here aims not only at the requirements of symptom detection [7], but also at the analysis of other aspects of program execution. Therefore, our trace design incorporates the richness of data to enable various kinds of dependency analysis instead of reducing the amount of data, such as in the approach proposed by Wang et al. [9].

In addition to currently studied Back-In-Time Debuggers [4]–[6], which aim at a microscopic perspective for the dependency analysis of a specific statement, our previous study [7] dealt with all-state updates via *persistent variables* and their value dependency across the entire trace. A persistent variable is either a class variable, an instance variable, or an array component. It implements a state that persists after the invocation of a method is completed [10]. This macroscopic nature of our dependency analysis renders it inefficient, although the algorithm works in practice. In order to solve this problem, an approach is needed to support the efficient analysis of dependency in a large trace.

This study implements an efficient dependency analysis environment for macroscopic dependency analysis similar to that in [7]. Hence, the bottleneck in our dependency analysis environment needs to be resolved. In our previous study [11], we had clarified a factor affecting efficiency in our dependency analysis environment and had proposed a trace-partitioning approach for it. However, our approach did not enhance the efficiency of dependency analysis. In this study, we assess the effectiveness of our proposed approach for efficient dependency analysis.

We will introduce related to dependency analysis, and describe the demands of for dynamic analysis environment in Section II. Then, in Section III, we illustrate our implementation of dynamic analysis environment that consists of a trace generation part and a trace processing part using the graph database. In Section IV, we propose a trace-partitioning approach based on graph database for efficient trace analysis. We will conduct an experiment of dynamic analysis performance for evaluating our proposed approach.

II. RELATED WORK

Debuggers widely used in software development projects support a common feature to suspend program execution at a specified *break point* and show the runtime state at that point. They do not record the execution and, thus, have the common drawback that there is no way to examine the execution of a method whose invocation has been already completed. It is a serious problem because defects and infections are often found in methods that have been completed before the program fails [6]. A defect is an error in program code while an infection, in software engineering, is a runtime error caused by the execution of a defect [1].

Maintainers using a debugger must repeat a task to specify a breakpoint (it is usually very difficult to find a suitable breakpoint in the program code.) and re-execute the program to examine the executions of methods that have been completed. Such a debugging style, forced by the common limitation in current of existing debuggers, leads to inefficient debugging [3].

Using traces for debugging support is a natural idea to overcome the above limitation in existing debuggers [4] [5] [12]. An omniscient debugger [4] examines assignment operations with set values referenced from variables. If a maintainer wants to determine why a statement has or has not been executed, Whyline [5] analyzes related dependencies and generates the results of the analysis using sophisticated Graphical User Interfaces (GUI).

Dynamic Object Flow Analysis [12] aims to understand program execution from the aspect of object references. Its area of application ranges from dependency analysis of methods for software testing [13] to performance engineering for a back-in-time debugger [6].

To the best of our knowledge, no existing dependency analysis approaches to debugging support aims at macroscopic dependency analysis except for our previous proposal [7]. An omniscient debugger deals with only the correspondence between the value of a variable and the assignment operation that has sets this value. Whyline navigates a maintainer along the dependencies among statements to the extent of his/her manual examination. Dynamic object flow analysis performs macroscopic analysis but only deals with object references.

The above approaches to microscopic dependency analysis provide useful debugging aids. However, understanding a program from a macroscopic viewpoint is necessary for debugging [14]; therefore, maintainers have to spend time and effort to obtain this perspective through manual dependency analysis.

We studied several kinds of macroscopic dependency analysis in this context in our last study [7]. Of these, *outdated-state* analysis aims to identify symptoms to suggest possible infections incurred by the accidental use of an old value of a field or array component along with its updated value.

III. IMPLEMENTATION OF DEPENDENCY ANALYSIS ENVIRONMENT

Debugging a program requires various kinds of dependency analysis of statements. Therefore, we developed two kinds of techniques for the analysis of the relevant symptom in our previous study [7]. The proposed trace was designed to execute these symptom analyses. For this reason, our trace tended to be large and complex, and usually led to inefficient processing of analysis. In order to conduct an efficient dependency analysis, an analysis environment is needed that can handle our trace.

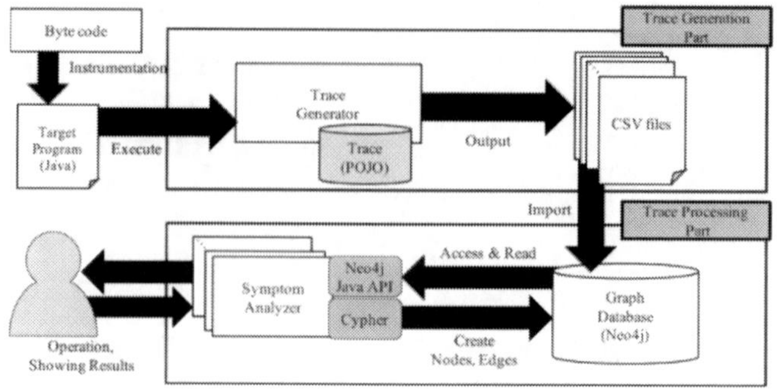

Figure 1. Dependency analysis environment.

Figure 1 illustrates the entire process, which involves the execution of a Java program under instrumentation and several sub-processes of symptom analysis in a dependency analysis environment. In trace generation, our system generates a trace using Java byte code instrumentation technology. In trace processing, on the other hand, it stores the generated trace in a graph database system (GDBS) and supports efficient processing of various kinds of dependency analysis.

A. Trace Data Model

Dependency analysis approaches from various aspects of execution are necessary for practical debugging support. In previous work, we developed two kinds of dependency analysis algorithms to detect symptoms that indicate infections in a failed execution [7].

Both of the proposed algorithms process control data dependency across the entire extent of an execution. One algorithm checks a complex condition that specifies data flow to associate operations in a class instance caused by the invocation of a certain kind of method. The other algorithm keeps track of side effects via fields and array components. We propose a new kind of dependency analysis that aims to abstract the effects of methods and operations on objects based on inputs by the debugger users.

In order to meet the above requirements, our trace model defines the following basic elements of program executions:

- Method execution
- Execution of abstracted byte code instructions to represent statements.
- Creation and reference of values by instructions.
- Values to be created or referenced.

Some abstracted instructions represent "control statements," such as conditional statements, method invocations, and throw and catch. Abstracted instructions contain assignment operations on local variables, fields, and array components. The instruction set also contains constants, instance creations, and array creations, as well as various calculation operations. Values created, calculated, and assigned are referenced by the instructions that use them.

For each executed instruction in an execution, its trace records the control instruction under which it is executed. If

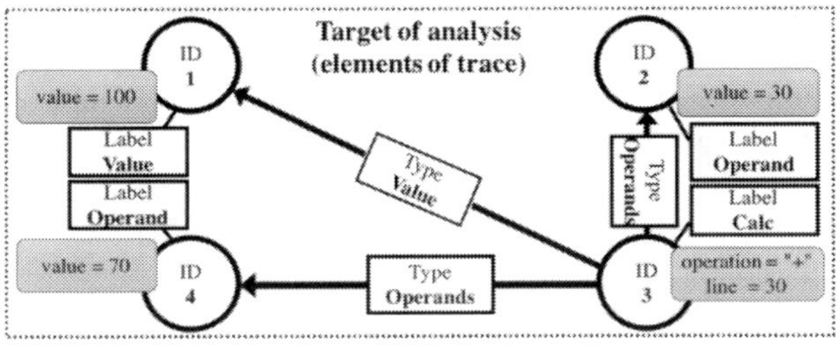

Nodes

Node ID	Attribute Key	Attribute Value
1	value	100
2	value	30
3	operation	"+"
	line	30
4	value	70

Relationships

Start Node ID	End Node ID	Attribute Key	Attribute Value
3	1	-	-
3	2	-	-
3	4	-	-

Figure 2. Property graph model.

the instruction references a value, the trace records from the instruction form which the value originates. In this way, we can obtain control and data dependency information among instructions, including a method invocation structure.

A trace generated by the proposed approach can first be represented using the property graph model shown in Figure 2. This is a data model defined in the TinkerPop project in Apache [15]. This data model features good description capability, and hence can represent various kinds of data.

The proposed data model allows programs to check data/control dependency for a large number of instructions in order to examine state changes on some objects or to find the cause of an infection. Algorithms to check such dependencies, which is represented by links among graph nodes, should be efficient.

B. *Trace Processing*

The requirements stated in Section III-A make it difficult to reduce trace size. Traces are needed not for a particular dependency analysis, but for various kinds of analysis dealing with the conditions of such program elements as classes, fields, and methods related to the four elements described in Section III-A. Therefore, rich data is required for the proposed trace model for such additional information.

For dependency analysis purposes, the instructions between which the analysis is performed cannot be predicted. Therefore, for a failed execution, the trace of the entire extent of execution is first needed. The proposed algorithms then search for instructions that are the targets of dependency analysis.

Dependency analysis usually requires checking of complex conditions for the above four kinds of elements one by one along with their dependency relationships. Furthermore, the results of past condition checks must be stored for reference.

A situation sometimes arises where the Java virtual machine is quite inefficient, or even runs out of memory in applying dependency analysis to the execution of a software system. Hence, data engineering approaches are needed to build a framework that enables efficient access to and processing of massive traces.

In this study, we develop a dependency analysis environment on the GDBS to improve analysis performance. This paper adopts a GDBS called Neo4j following the property graph model [16] because it is suitable for storing traces with complex data structures. Moreover, Neo4j is considered the best for handling graph data for all GDBSs [17] [18].

In order to handle our trace, our dependency analysis environment was implemented using the native Java API of Neo4j and its query language Cypher.

IV. A Trace-partitioning Approach and a Rule for Applying the Proposed Approach

The loading nodes, the edges, and their attributes used for dependency analysis are very important for the efficient use of the main memory. Our environment loads only use nodes and edges. When the nodes and edges are loaded, so are all their attributes. However, not all of the loaded attributes are used for all analyses of dependency. Therefore, this paper focuses on the selection of loading attributes.

In the previous study [11], we proposed an approach for partitioning our trace that can load attributes as needed. However, this did not help improve dependency analysis performance. Therefore, we formulate a rule in this section to determine whether a given attribute should be loaded for a given trace.

A. *Trace-partitioning Method for Memory Reduction*

In order to cope with the problem described above, nodes in GDBS are divided into two categories in order to sort them. One category includes those nodes that are analysis targets, while another includes nodes whose attributes are analysis targets.

In this way, it is possible to load only nodes and attributes that are targets of the dependency analysis and eliminate unnecessary ones. We believe that this is the best approach, as kinds of nodes need to be distinguished more frequently than attributes of nodes in dynamic analysis.

The proposed approach is shown in Figure 3, where a node and an edge are first created. This node stores attributes (the node IDs are 5, 6, 7 and 8 in Figure 3.), which are generated for convenience of an analysis (the node IDs are 1, 2, 3 and 4 in shown Figure 3.). The edge distinguishes the nodes that are used to store attributes. The node is described as one used to store attributes and the edge as one used to access the attributes of the nodes in the trace (this edge is called an attribute relationship in this paper). Therefore, deviations from the property graph model obtain: 1) The number of nodes stored doubles in a GDBS. 2) The number of edges connecting nodes of the trace increases.

B. *Inefficient Processing in Proposed Approach*

We assume that the time required for importing a trace increases due to the above sorting 1). However, graph traversal performance is not influenced by the increase in the number of nodes, intended only for the node where graph traversal is connected to a certain node in Neo4j. On the other hand, instead of preventing the loading of attributes of a node that are unnecessary for analysis, an attribute-relationship is loaded with sorting 2). The fixed-length data size of edge on the Neo4j is larger than node's one. However, we can assume that the data

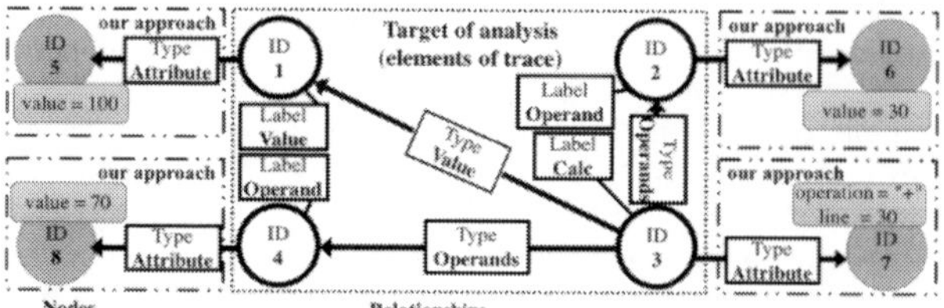

Nodes

Node ID	Attribut Key	Attribute Value
1	-	-
2	-	-
3	-	-
4	-	-
5	value	100
6	value	30
7	operation	"+"
	line	30
8	value	70

Relationships

Start Node ID	End Node ID	Attribute Key	Attribute Value
1	5	-	-
2	6	-	-
3	1	-	-
3	2	-	-
3	4	-	-
3	7	-	-
4	8	-	-

Figure 3. Graph partitioning approach for proposed trace.

Require: N_{node}, N_{attr}, N_{trav}
  for each $l \in L$ **do**
    {Not applying proposed approach to all labels of the node.}
    {Initializing $\boldsymbol{f}$ of the dictionary type.}
    {The key of $\boldsymbol{f}$ is $l \in L$, and let the value be **false**.}
    $\boldsymbol{f}[l] \leftarrow$ **false**
  end for
  for each $l \in L$ **do**
    $before \leftarrow S_{load}(\boldsymbol{f}, N_{attr}, N_{node})$
    $\boldsymbol{f}[l] \leftarrow$ **true** {Applying our approach to l.}
    $after \leftarrow S_{load}(\boldsymbol{f}, N_{attr}, N_{node})$
    $traversal \leftarrow S_{trav}(\boldsymbol{f}, N_{trav}, N_{node})$
    if $before > after$ **and** $traversal = 0$ **then**
      continue
    else
      $\boldsymbol{f}[l] \leftarrow$ **false** {Not applying our approach to l.}
    end if
  end for
  return $\boldsymbol{f}$

Figure 4. Optimization algorithm for the proposed approach.

size of edges loaded in the memory is small because the size of an attribute of edges, such as references and dependencies, is less than that of a nodes. Moreover, the time needed to confirm the edges needed to traverse the graph traversal by sorting 2) increases in all nodes, and we predict that leads to inefficient graph traversal performance.

Furthermore, if it is necessary to access an attribute, the attribute-relationship is traversed during dependency analysis. Since traversing attribute-relationship is not necessary in the case of an original trace, as the number of processes increases, efficiency worsens.

C. Optimization Algorithm for our Previous Approach

The purpose of this approach is to reduce the memory size used by attributes of nodes to improve the efficiency of graph traversal. However, our previous approach [11] has been unable to improve the effectiveness of traversing the proposed trace because we had not considered the situation where the attributes of each node are loaded into the main memory. As a result, the previous approach made additional traversals to analyze attribute relationships. The traversal of attribute relationships does not occur in the original structure of the trace; hence, we propose an algorithm to automatically determine the node needed for the approach in order to avoid creating attributes over and above those that are required. If a minimum number of such attributes can be loaded into the main memory, the effectiveness of the proposed approach will improve.

To automatically determine the node in the proposed approach, the analytical algorithm of the dependency analysis environment needs to be recognized. That is to say, one needs to understand that the algorithm traverses nodes and loads their attributes in the trace using the proposed approach. In this case, the approach requires knowing the number of attributes loaded from all nodes, with each node labeled as N_{trav}. At the same time, it also requires knowing the number of attributes denoted by N_{attr}.

However, we cannot correctly estimate N_{trav}, because dependency analysis is dynamically executed depending on the value of the attribute in the trace. Hence, we assume that all nodes of the trace can be traversed, and the maximum number of loading attributes of nodes is N_{trav}. In short, we decide to partition the attributes of node into extra node when a loading attribute has the potential to obtain the attribute of node.

We developed an algorithm for the automatic application of the proposed, as stated above. This algorithm is shown in Figure 4. Given a set of labels of nodes as L, every node is labelled $l \in L$ as $N_{node}(l)$ in Figure 4, and every attribute is labelled as N_{attr}. We also represent the frequency of the attributes of loading nodes with label $m \in L$ when reaching label $l \in L$ of a node. Note that we take into account the identification of these labels ($l = m$).

We now introduce criteria for applying the proposed approach. S_{load} is the sum of the number of loading attributes while conducting dependency analysis, and S_{trav} is the sum of the number of traversing attribute relationships. We can estimate these criteria using N_{node}, N_{attr} and N_{trav}, respectively. $S_{attr}(L)$ and $S_{trav}(L)$ can be calculated as (1), (2):

$$S_{attr}(L) = \sum_{l \in L} s_{attr}(l, \boldsymbol{f}[\boldsymbol{l}]) \quad (1)$$
$$where:$$
$$s_{load}(l, \boldsymbol{f}[\boldsymbol{l}]) = \begin{cases} N_{attr}(l) \cdot N_{node}(l) & if\ \boldsymbol{f}[l] = false \\ 0 & otherwise \end{cases}$$

$$S_{trav}(L) = \sum_{l \in L} s_{trav}(l, \boldsymbol{f}) \quad (2)$$
$$where:$$
$$s_{trav}(l, \boldsymbol{f}) = \begin{cases} \sum_{m \in L} N_{trav}(l, m) \cdot N_{node}(m) & if\ \boldsymbol{f}[m] = true \\ 0 & otherwise \end{cases}$$

In (1), $s_{load}(l, \boldsymbol{f}[l])$ is calculated to multiply the number of loading attributes of nodes labeled l by the number of nodes labeled l in GDBS. In (2), we also calculate $s_{trav}(l, \boldsymbol{f})$

to multiply the number of traversing attribute relationships connected with nodes labeled m when reaching nodes labeled l. Note that the value of $s_{attr}(l, \boldsymbol{f}[l])$ is zero if the label l is applied because it does not obtain the traversal of an attribute relationship.

Finally, our algorithm produces $\boldsymbol{f}$, which is a combination of whether the proposed approach is applied. This $\boldsymbol{f}$ allows for dependency analysis without traversing attribute relationships and minimizes the sum of loading attributes S_{attr}.

V. Experiment

As described in Section IV-A, we proposed an approach for solving the bottleneck in memory consumption in dependency analysis environments. In this section, we report an experiment to verify the effectiveness of our approach. For the assessment of macroscopic dependency analysis, not only is it necessary that memory consumption be evaluated, the time consumed for it is also a crucial factor to bear in mind. We assessed the improvement in analysis performance using the proposed approach by measuring the memory consumption and analysis time needed for dependency analysis.

We compared the experimental results with the following trace conditions:

- NON: This trace was non-transformational.
- ALL: We employed the approach for all nodes in the trace.
- OPT: We employed the approach for a few nodes selected by the rule in Section IV-C.

The experiments in this section were conducted on a kernel-based virtual machine with 64 GB RAM and the Cent OS 7 operating system.

A. Unified Modeling Language Editor "GEFDemo"

We used trace for the execution of the demonstration program on the Graph Editing Framework (GEFDemo) [8] for dependency analysis in Section V-B. GEFDemo is a simple Unified Modeling Language (UML) editor program that used the application framework as shown in Figure 5(a). A flaw, such as in Figure 5(b), is known to occur during the delete operation, a ternary association, which is a defect in implementation of the GEFDemo.

Accurate inspection of the analysis program was possible because the cause of the defect shown in Figure 5 was manually confirmed. The trace used in this experiment recorded the execution process of GEFDemo that intentionally produced an exception, as shown in Figure 5 in the following procedure:

1) Creating three classes on the editor.
2) Creating an association for other classes from one class.
3) Creating an association for another association from the class that does not create an association.
4) A diamond object expressing the occurrence of a ternary connection occurs.
5) Deleting the diamond object.

The number of nodes in this trace was 510,370 and the number of relationships 4,437,367. Moreover, the trace into the GEFDemo contained 46 kinds of labels for nodes and 44 kinds of relationships. Furthermore, the size of the trace was 63.8 MB as text. Hence, our trace contained a large amount of information about the runtime state of the program. However, it can easily become large and complex.

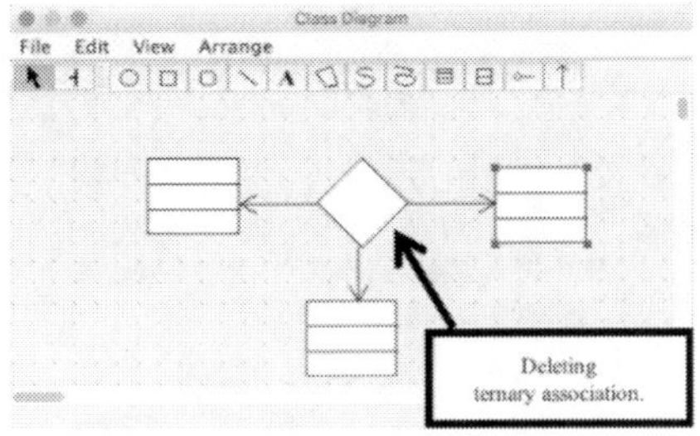

(a) Creating three Classes and a Ternary Association.

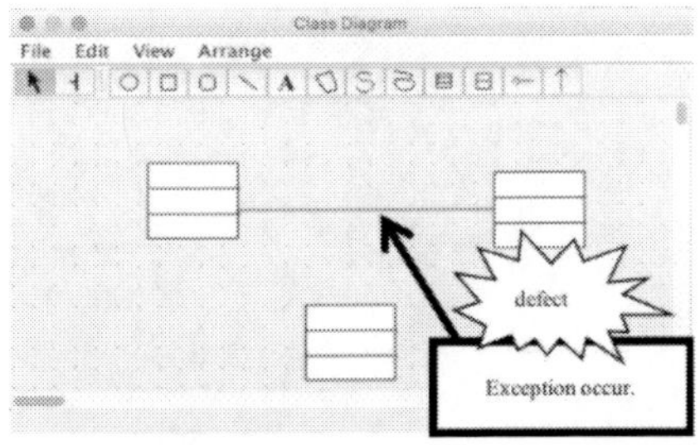

(b) Deleting a Ternary Association.

Figure 5. Operating the GEFDemo Program

B. Outdated-state Analysis

As described in Section V-A, a defect of the GEFDemo is caused by changes in the process of execution of the program during the collection state, which is an object of Java. We used an outdated-state analysis, which is the approach of dependency analysis proposed by Kume et al. [7]. It can detect instructions that use different states of a specified object.

We executed the outdated-state analysis in a dependency analysis environment as described below:

1) Investigating method called in execution order one by one.
2) Investigating dependencies with state of objects with many instructions occurring in each method.
3) When analyzing an instrument concerning the change in the state of the object, a node was created to record the frequency of change of the object for a GDBS.
4) Investigating instructions dependence on the combination of a new state and old states of the same object from nodes that we created by Procedure 3).

In Procedure 1), the outdated-state analysis consumed a large amount of memory because it was necessary to analyze instruments and values in a trace. Moreover, outdated-state analysis is a two-step process: (1) analyzing the trace, (2) creating the nodes and edges to record the status of objects (data generated during dependency analysis) on the database in Procedure 1). Finally, it analyzes data generated using Procedure 3).

C. Measurement of Effects on Entire Dependency Analysis

In order to evaluate the effectiveness of the approach to dependency analysis proposed in this paper, we measured

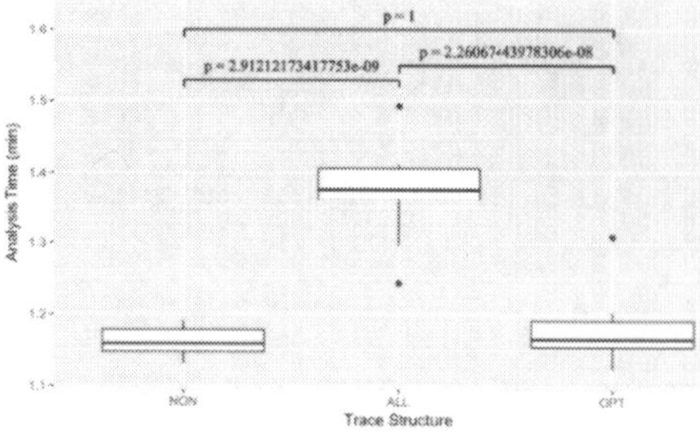

(a) Traversal time.

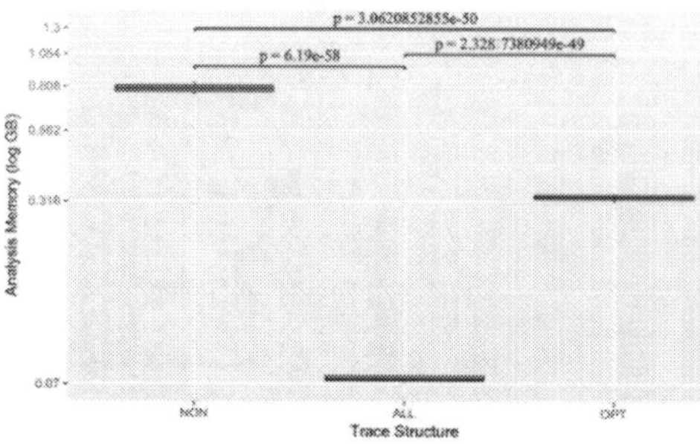

(b) Memory consumption.

Figure 6. Dependency analysis performance.

its processing time and memory consumption. Memory consumptions per second were recorded using vmstat, which is a UNIX command that can report information related to memory, paging, CPU activity, and so on, and can calculate the basic statistics of memory consumption.

Figure 6 shows the results of three approaches. Figures 6(a) and Figure 6(b) show the average value of 10 traversals and instances of memory consumption in the dependency analysis, respectively. In these figures, NON represents our previously approach proposed in [7]. ALL refers to the naïve approach proposed in [11], and OPT represents the approach in this paper.

The six p-values in Figure 6 indicated that OPT could reduce processing time and memory consumption of dependency analysis compared with those of ALL; however, we could not find any difference in traversal times for dependency analysis. In short, OPT can conduct dependency analysis with the same efficiency as NON but consumes less memory using Figure 4. On the other hand, ALL could not conduct dependency analysis with the same efficiency and memory consumption as NON and OPT. Therefore, it can be concluded that Figure 4 can help considerably improve memory consumption for dependency analysis with the same efficiency as NON.

VI. Conclusion

This paper developed a prototype dependency analysis environment for efficient dependency analysis of large traces using complex graph structures. Our analysis environment is built on a graph database system that can efficiently traverse large and complex graph data. For efficient dependency analysis, we introduced a policy to restrict the number of loading operations on node's attributes to the main memory in order to prevent it from being occupied by unnecessary data.

We applied this approach to a trace dealing with dependency across macroscopic program execution. In this experiment, the proposed approach yielded good performance in terms of analysis time and memory consumption during dependency analysis.

Acknowledgment

This work was partially supported by a grant-in-aid from the Science and Engineering Research Institute (the Harris Science Research Institute) of Doshisha University, MEXT/JSPS KAKENHI [Grant-in-Aid for Challenging Exploratory Research (No. 15K12009), and Scientific Research (B) (No. 26280115)], the Artificial Intelligence Research Promotion Foundation, and the Kayamori Foundation of Informational Science Advancement.

References

[1] A. Zeller, Why Programs Fail, Second Edition: A Guide to Systematic Debugging. Morgan Kaufmann, 2009.

[2] M. Weiser, "Program slicing," in International Conference on Software Engineering. IEEE, 1981, pp. 439–449.

[3] J. Ressia, A. Bergel, and O. Nierstrasz, "Object-centric debugging," in International Conference on Software Engineering. IEEE, 2012, pp. 485–495.

[4] B. Lewis, "Debugging backwards in time," in In Proceedings of the Fifth International Workshop on Automated Debugging, pp. 225–235.

[5] A. J. Ko and B. A. Myers, "Designing the whyline: a debugging interface for asking questions about program behavior," in SIGCHI Conference on Human Factors in Computing Systems. ACM, 2004, pp. 151–158.

[6] A. Lienhard, T. Gîrba, and O. Nierstrasz, Practical Object-Oriented Back-in-Time Debugging. Berlin, Heidelberg: Springer Berlin Heidelberg, 2008, pp. 592–615.

[7] I. Kume, M. Nakamura, N. Nitta, and E. Shibayama, "A Case Study of Dynamic Analysis to Locate Unexpected Side Effects Inside of Frameworks," International Journal of Software Innovation, vol. 3, no. 3, 2015, pp. 26–40.

[8] "gefdemo project," http://gefdemo.tigris.org/, [retrieved: 1 Mar. 2017].

[9] T. Wang and A. Roychoudhury, "Using compressed bytecode traces for slicing java programs," in International Conference on Software Engineering. IEEE, 2004, pp. 512–521.

[10] J. Hogg, "Islands: Aliasing protection in object-oriented languages," in OOPSLA, 1991, pp. 271–285.

[11] K. Kusu, I. Kume, and K. Hatano, "A trace partitioning approach for efficient trace analysis," in Proceedings of the 4th International Conference on Applied Computing & Information Technology, 2016 4th Intl Conf on Applied Computing and Information Technology / 3rd Intl Conf on Computational Science/Intelligence and Applied Informatics / 1st Intl Conf on Big Data, Cloud Computing, Data Science & Engineering, 2016, pp. 133 – 140.

[12] A. Lienhard, Dynamic Object Flow Analysis. Lulu.com, 2008.

[13] A. Lienhard, T. Gîrba, O. Greevy, and O. Nierstrasz, "Exposing side effects in execution traces," in International Workshop on Program Comprehension through Dynamic Analysis, 2007, pp. 11–17.

[14] D. J. Agans, Debugging: the 9 Indispensable Rules for Finding Even the Most Elusive Software and Hardware Problems. AMACOM, 2002.

[15] "The property graph model," http://github.com/tinkerpop/blueprints/wiki/Property-Graph-Model, [retrieved: March 2017].

[16] "Graph database neo4j," http://neo4j.com/, [retrieved: 1 Mar. 2017].

[17] V. Kolomičenko, M. Svoboda, and I. H. Mlýnková, "Experimental comparison of graph databases," in Proceedings of International Conference on Information Integration and Web-based Applications & Services, ser. IIWAS '13. ACM, 2013, pp. 115:115–115:124.

[18] S. Jouili and V. Vansteenberghe, "An empirical comparison of graph databases," in Proceedings of the 2013 International Conference on Social Computing, ser. SOCIALCOM '13. IEEE Computer Society, 2013, pp. 708–715.

A Message Passing Approach for Decision Fusion of Hidden-Markov Observations in the Presence of Synchronized Attacks

Andrea Abrardo*†, Mauro Barni*, Kassem Kallas*, Benedetta Tondi*
*Department of Information Engineering and Mathematics, University of Siena
Via Roma 56, 53100 - Siena, ITALY
†CNIT - Consorzio Nazionale Interuniversitario per le Telecomunicazioni
abrardo@diism.unisi.it, barni@dii.unisi.it, k_kallas@hotmail.com, benedettatondi@gmail.com

***Abstract*—We consider a setup in which a Fusion Center (FC) makes a binary decision on the sequence of system states by relying on local observations provided by both honest and byzantine nodes, i.e., nodes that deliberately alter the result of the local decision to induce an error at the fusion center. In this setting, we assume a Markovian information model for the status with a given transition probability that can be perfectly estimated at the FC. Hence, we consider an attacking strategy where the byzantine nodes can coordinate their attacks by producing correlated reports, with the aim of mimicking the behavior of the original information and at the same time minimizing the information conveyed to the FC about the sequence of states. In this scenario, we derive a nearly-optimal fusion scheme based on message passing (MP) and factor graphs. Experimental results show that, although the proposed detector is able to mitigate the effect of Byzantines, the coordination of the efforts is very harmful and significantly impairs the detection performance.**

Keywords–Decision Fusion in Adversarial Settings; Adversarial Signal Processing; Byzantine attacks; Message Passing Algorithm; Markovian Sources.

I. Introduction

We address a decision problem in which a Fusion Center (FC) is required to make a decision about the status of an observed system by relying on the information provided by the nodes of a sensor network. In the adversarial version of this problems, some of the nodes, commonly referred to as Byzantines, malevolently alter their reports to induce a decision error [1]. This is a recurrent problem in many scenario wherein the nodes may take advantage from a decision error, e.g., in cognitive radio networks [2] or online reputation systems [3]. In this paper, we focus on a binary version of the fusion problem, wherein the system can assume only two states. Specifically, the nodes observe the system over an observation window of m time instants and make a local decisions about the sequence of system states. Honest nodes send their decisions to the FC, while Byzantines try to induce a decision error by flipping their observations with a certain probability. When the FC makes its decision on the system state at a certain time instant j by relying only on the corresponding report, the Bayesian optimal fusion rule for the non-adversarial version of this case has been derived in [4] and it is known as Chair-Varshney. In the presence of Byzantines, Chair-Varshney rule requires the knowledge of Byzantines' positions along with their flipping probability P_{mal}. However, this information is rarely available and then the FC needs to resort to suboptimal fusion strategies. In order to improve the estimation of the system states, the FC can gather a sequence of reports and make a global decision. In this way, it is possible for the FC to perform *isolation* of the Byzantines by identifying the malevolent nodes and discarding their reports [5][6]. Isolation is achieved by counting the mismatches between the reports and the global decision. In [7], a soft isolation scheme is proposed where the reports from suspect byzantine nodes are given a lower importance rather than being discarded.

In [8], the optimum fusion rule under a bunch of observations is first derived assuming to know the malicious probability P_{mal} of the Byzantines along with the probability that a node is Byzantine. Then, the knowledge of P_{mal} at the FC is relaxed as it is strategically chosen in a game-theoretic framework. In this work, the authors show that, differently from what commonly expected, always flipping the local decision is not necessarily the best option for the Byzantines. In fact, in some cases, in order to prevent identification, it is better for the Byzantines to minimize the mutual information between the reports submitted to the FC and the system states. One of the main inconvenience of the optimal fusion rule proposed in [8] is that the computational cost grows exponentially with the size of the observation window. A nearly-optimum fusion scheme based on message passing (MP) and factor graphs is proposed in [9], where an iterative algorithm based on the so called Generalised Distributive Law (GLD, [10]), permits to achieve a linear complexity. Besides, whereas in [8] the analysis is limited to the case of independent system states, in [9] it is extended to the case of sequences with Markovian distribution, which is rather common model in many practical scenarios; for instance, in cognitive radio networks the primary user occupancy of the spectrum is often modelled as a Hidden Markov Model (HMM), e.g., [11][12].

In this paper, by focusing on the case of Markovian system states, we consider the scenario in which the Byzantines can cooperate by synchronizing their efforts to push forth more powerful attacks. Specifically, the contribution of this paper is twofold: we first propose two types of synchronized attacks; then, we refine the detection scheme based on message passing proposed in [9] and devise the nearly-optimal decision rule for the synchronized case. Finally, we demonstrate the effectiveness of the proposed scheme by means of numerical simulations. The results show that, upon knowing the attacking strategy, the new detector can mitigate the effect of the Byzantines. Nevertheless, synchronization among Byzantines is very harmful and significantly impairs the detection performance with respect to the non-synchronized case.

The rest of this paper is organized as follows: in Section II, we formalize the problem at hand and we propose the synchronized attack models, while in Section III the message passing algorithm is proposed. In Section IV we use simulations to analyze the performance of the synchronized Byzantine attacks and the message passing algorithm. The paper is concluded in Section V.

II. Problem Formulation

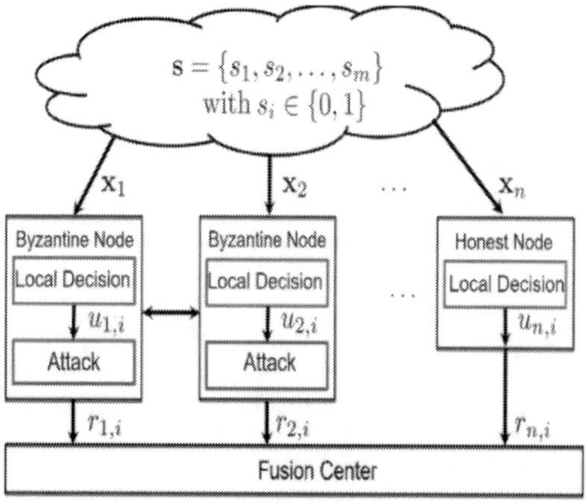

Figure 1. Sketch of the adversarial decision fusion scheme.

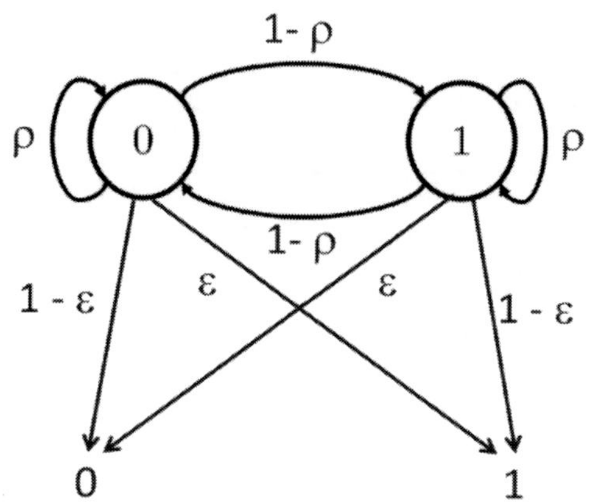

Figure 2. Hidden-Markov model for the local decisions.

1) Problem Setup: The adversarial decision fusion scheme considered in this paper is depicted in Figure 1. We let $\mathbf{s} = \{s_1, s_2, \ldots, s_m\}$ with $s_i \in \{0, 1\}$ indicate the sequence of system states over an observation window of length m. We assume that the sequence of states $\mathbf{s}$ follows a *Markov model* of order 1, with transition probabilities $p(s_i|s_{i-1}) = 1 - \rho$ if $s_i = s_{i-1}$ and $p(s_i|s_{i-1}) = \rho$ when $s_i \neq s_{i-1}$. Then, the probability of a sequence is given by $p(\mathbf{s}) = \prod_i p(s_i|s_{i-1})$, where for $i = 1$ we have $p(s_1|s_0) = p(s_1) = 0.5$.

The nodes collect information about the system through the vectors $\mathbf{x}_1, \mathbf{x}_2 \ldots \mathbf{x}_n$, with $\mathbf{x}_j$ indicating the observations available at node j. Based on such observations, a node j makes a local decision $u_{i,j}$ about system state s_i. We assume that the local error probability is $p(u_{i,j} \neq s_i) = \varepsilon$, which does not depend on either i or j. Then, the sequence of the local decisions follows a Hidden-Markov distribution [13], as shown in Figure 2. The state of the nodes in the network is given by the vector $\mathbf{h} = \{h_1, h_2, \ldots, h_n\}$ with $h_j = 1/0$ indicating that node j is honest or Byzantine, respectively. Finally, the matrix $\mathbf{R} = \{r_{i,j}\}$, $i = 1, \ldots, m$, $j = 1, \ldots, n$ contains all the reports received by the FC. Specifically, $r_{i,j}$ is the report sent by node j relative to s_i. For honest nodes we have $u_{i,j} = r_{i,j}$ while, for Byzantines, possibly $u_{i,j} \neq r_{i,j}$. Then, by assuming an error-free transmission between nodes and FC, according to the local decision error model, for honest nodes we have:

$$p(r_{i,j}|s_i, h_j = 1) = (1-\varepsilon)\delta(r_{i,j} - s_i) + \varepsilon(1 - \delta(r_{i,j} - s_i)), \quad (1)$$

where $\delta(a)$ is equal to 1 when its argument is 0 and 0 otherwise. On the other hand, the probability that the FC receives a wrong report from a Byzantine depends on the attack strategy and is discussed in the following section.

2) The Attacks Model: In the general context of synchronized attacks, we consider two different strategies. In the first case, the Byzantines generate a fake states sequence $\hat{\mathbf{s}}$ and decide to flip the reports only when $\hat{s}_i = 0$. The rationale of this attack is to reduce the mutual information conveyed by the Byzantines towards the FC with respect to the classical $P_{mal} = 1$ case, thus reducing the identification probability. The generation of the fake sequence can be achieved for instance by using a pseudo random generator with a common seed to synchronize the local clocks of the sensors.

In the second attack strategy, the Byzantines generate a fake sequence which follows the statistic of the original sequence, namely a Markovian sequence $\hat{\mathbf{s}}$ with transition probability $\hat{\rho}$. Then, they introduce some intentional i.i.d errors with probability ε thus mimicking the behavior of the honest nodes. In this case, the mutual information between the system states and the malicious reports is completely canceled. To elaborate, for the first attack, we have

$$\begin{aligned} &p(r_{i,j}|s_i, \hat{s}_i, h_j = 0) = \\ &\hat{s}_i[(1-\varepsilon)\delta(r_{i,j} - s_i) + \varepsilon(1 - \delta(r_{i,j} - s_i))] \\ &- (\hat{s}_i - 1)[\varepsilon\delta(r_{i,j} - s_i) + (1-\varepsilon)(1 - \delta(r_{i,j} - s_i))] \end{aligned} \quad (2)$$

where ε is the error probability of the local decisions at the nodes. For the second case, the report conditional probabilities depend on the fake states only:

$$\begin{aligned} &p(r_{i,j}|\hat{s}_i, h_j = 0) = \\ &\quad (1-\varepsilon)\delta(r_{i,j} - \hat{s}_i) + \varepsilon(1 - \delta(r_{i,j} - \hat{s}_i)), \end{aligned} \quad (3)$$

where this time ε is the probability of the i.i.d. errors introduced intentionally.

Eventually, we consider that nodes' state are independent of each other and the state of each node is a Bernoulli random variable with parameter α, that is $p(h_j = 0) = \alpha, \forall j$. In this way, the number of byzantine nodes in the network is a random variable following a binomial distribution, corresponding to the maximum entropy case [8] with $p(\mathbf{h}) = \prod_j p(h_j)$, where $p(h_j) = \alpha(1 - h_j) + (1-\alpha)h_j$.

III. MP-based Decision Fusion with Synchronized Byzantines

Given the sequence of reports, the optimum decision at the FC can be taken by looking at the *bitwise* Maximum A

Posteriori Probability (MAP) estimation of the system states $\{s_i\}$ which reads as follows:

$$
\begin{aligned}
s_i^* &= \arg\max_{s_i \in \{0,1\}} \; p(s_i|\mathbf{R}) \\
&= \arg\max_{s_i \in \{0,1\}} \sum_{\{\mathbf{s},\hat{\mathbf{s}},\mathbf{h}\}\setminus s_i} p(\mathbf{s},\hat{\mathbf{s}},\mathbf{h}|\mathbf{R}) \\
&= \arg\max_{s_i \in \{0,1\}} \sum_{\{\mathbf{s},\hat{\mathbf{s}},\mathbf{h}\}\setminus s_i} p(\mathbf{R}|\mathbf{s},\hat{\mathbf{s}},\mathbf{h})\, p(\mathbf{s})p(\hat{\mathbf{s}})p(\mathbf{h}) \\
&= \arg\max_{s_i \in \{0,1\}} \sum_{\{\mathbf{s},\mathbf{q},\mathbf{h}\}\setminus s_i} \prod_{i,j} p(r_{i,j}|s_i,\hat{s}_i,h_j) \prod_i p(s_i|s_{i-1}) \\
&\prod_i p(\hat{s}_i|\hat{s}_{i-1}) \prod_j p(h_j) \qquad (4)
\end{aligned}
$$

where the notation $\sum_{\setminus}$ denotes a summation over all the variables contained in the expression except the one listed after the operator. For a given $\mathbf{h}$, the matrix of the observations $\mathbf{R}$ at the FC follows a HMM.

The objective function in the optimal fusion rule expressed in (4) can be seen as a marginalization of a sum product of functions of binary variables, and, as such, it falls within the MP framework [14]. Specifically, in our problem, the variables are the system states s_i, the fake system states $\hat{s}_i$, and the status of the nodes h_j, while the functions are the probabilities of the reports $p(r_{i,j}|s_i,\hat{s}_i,h_j)$, the conditional probabilities $p(s_i|s_{i-1})$, $p(\hat{s}_i|\hat{s}_{i-1})$, and the a-priori probabilities $p(h_j)$. The resulting bipartite graph along with all the messages exchanged are shown in Figure 3. These messages are exchanged to parallely estimate each state s_i in the vector $\mathbf{s}$. Specifically, we have:

$$
\begin{aligned}
&\tau_i^{(l)}(s_i) = \varphi_i^{(l)}(s_i) \prod_{j=1}^{n} \nu_{i,j}^{(u)}(s_i) \\
&\qquad i = 1,\ldots,m \\
&\tau_i^{(r)}(s_i) = \varphi_i^{(r)}(s_i) \prod_{j=1}^{n} \nu_{i,j}^{(u)}(s_i) \\
&\qquad i = 1,\ldots,m \\
&\varphi_i^{(l)}(s_i) = \sum_{s_{i+1}=0,1} p(s_{i+1}|s_i)\, \tau_{i+1}^{(l)}(s_{i+1}) \\
&\qquad i = 1,\ldots,m-1 \\
&\varphi_i^{(r)}(s_i) = \sum_{s_{i-1}=0,1} p(s_i|s_{i-1})\, \tau_{i-1}^{(r)}(s_{i-1}) \\
&\qquad i = 2,\ldots,m \\
&\varphi_1^{(r)}(s_1) = p(s_1) \\
&\nu_{i,j}^{(u)}(s_i) = \sum_{h_j=0,1} \sum_{\hat{s}_i=0,1} p(r_{i,j}|s_i,\hat{s}_i,h_j)\, \lambda_{j,i}^{(u)}(h_j) \hat{\nu}_{i,j}^{(d)}(\hat{s}_i) \\
&\qquad i = 1,\ldots,m, \quad j = 1,\ldots,n \\
&\nu_{i,j}^{(d)}(s_i) = \varphi_i^{(r)}(s_i)\varphi_i^{(l)}(s_i) \prod_{\substack{k=1 \\ k\neq j}}^{n} \nu_{i,k}^{(u)}(s_i) \\
&\qquad i = 1,\ldots,m-1, \quad j = 1,\ldots,n \\
&\nu_{m,j}^{(d)}(s_m) = \varphi_i^{(r)}(s_m) \prod_{\substack{k=1 \\ k\neq j}}^{n} \nu_{m,k}^{(u)}(s_m) \\
&\qquad j = 1,\ldots,n \\
&\hat{\tau}_i^{(l)}(\hat{s}_i) = \hat{\varphi}_i^{(l)}(\hat{s}_i) \prod_{j=1}^{n} \hat{\nu}_{i,j}^{(u)}(\hat{s}_i) \\
&\qquad i = 1,\ldots,m \\
&\hat{\tau}_i^{(r)}(\hat{s}_i) = \varphi_i^{(r)}(\hat{s}_i) \prod_{j=1}^{n} \nu_{i,j}^{(u)}(\hat{s}_i) \\
&\qquad i = 1,\ldots,m \\
&\hat{\varphi}_i^{(l)}(\hat{s}_i) = \sum_{\hat{s}_{i+1}=0,1} p(\hat{s}_{i+1}|\hat{s}_i)\, \hat{\tau}_{i+1}^{(l)}(\hat{s}_{i+1}) \\
&\qquad i = 1,\ldots,m-1 \\
&\hat{\varphi}_i^{(r)}(\hat{s}_i) = \sum_{\hat{s}_{i-1}=0,1} p(\hat{s}_i|\hat{s}_{i-1})\, \hat{\tau}_{i-1}^{(r)}(\hat{s}_{i-1}) \\
&\qquad i = 2,\ldots,m \\
&\hat{\varphi}_1^{(r)}(s_1) = p(\hat{s}_1) \\
&\hat{\nu}_{i,j}^{(u)}(\hat{s}_i) = \sum_{h_j=0,1} \sum_{s_i=0,1} p(r_{i,j}|s_i,\hat{s}_i,h_j)\, \lambda_{j,i}^{(u)}(h_j) \nu_{i,j}^{(d)}(s_i) \\
&\qquad i = 1,\ldots,m, \quad j = 1,\ldots,n \\
&\hat{\nu}_{i,j}^{(d)}(\hat{s}_i) = \hat{\varphi}_i^{(r)}(\hat{s}_i)\hat{\varphi}_i^{(l)}(s_i) \prod_{\substack{k=1 \\ k\neq j}}^{n} \hat{\nu}_{i,k}^{(u)}(s_i) \\
&\qquad i = 1,\ldots,m-1, \quad j = 1,\ldots,n \\
&\hat{\nu}_{m,j}^{(d)}(\hat{s}_m) = \hat{\varphi}_i^{(r)}(\hat{s}_m) \prod_{\substack{k=1 \\ k\neq j}}^{n} \hat{\nu}_{m,k}^{(u)}(\hat{s}_m) \\
&\qquad j = 1,\ldots,n \\
&\lambda_{j,i}^{(d)}(h_j) = \sum_{s_i=0,1} \sum_{\hat{s}_i=0,1} p(r_{i,j}|s_i,\hat{s}_i,h_j)\, \nu_{i,j}^{(d)}(s_i)\hat{\nu}_{i,j}^{(d)}(\hat{s}_i) \\
&\qquad i = 1,\ldots,m, \quad j = 1,\ldots,n \\
&\lambda_{j,i}^{(u)}(h_j) = \omega_j^{(u)}(h_j) \prod_{\substack{q=1 \\ q\neq i}}^{m} \lambda_{j,q}^{(d)}(h_j) \\
&\qquad i = 1,\ldots,m, \quad j = 1,\ldots,n \\
&\omega_j^{(d)}(h_j) = \prod_{i=1}^{m} \lambda_{j,i}^{(d)}(h_j) \\
&\qquad j = 1,\ldots,n \\
&\omega_j^{(u)}(h_j) = p(h_j) \\
&\qquad j = 1,\ldots,n
\end{aligned}
\qquad (5)
$$

As for the scheduling policy, the MP procedure starts by initializing the messages $\lambda_{j,i}^{(u)}(h_j) = p(h_j)$ and $\hat{\nu}_{i,j}^{(d)}(\hat{s}_i) = 1$ and sending them to all $p(r_{i,j}|s_i,\hat{s}_i,h_j)$ factors, and by sending the messages $p(s_1)$ and $p(\hat{s}_1)$ to the variable nodes s_1 and $\hat{s}_1$, respectively. Hence, the MP proceeds according to the general message passing rules, until all variable nodes are able to compute the respective marginals, thus concluding the first iteration. Successive iterations are carried out by starting from leaf nodes and by taking into account the messages received at the previous iteration for the evaluation of new messages. The algorithm stops when convergence of messages is achieved, or after a maximum number of iterations.

This version of the MP algorithm described above is an extension of the one proposed in [9], which does not take into account the possibility of synchronized attacks. More specifically, in the attack model considered in [9], the Byzantines independently flip the observations with a given probability P_{mal}, thus yielding

$$p(r_{i,j}|s_i, h_j = 0) = \\ (1-\eta)\delta(r_{i,j} - s_i) + \eta(1 - \delta(r_{i,j} - s_i)) \quad (6)$$

where $\eta = \varepsilon(1 - P_{mal}) + (1 - \varepsilon)P_{mal}$ is the probability of receiving a wrong report from a Byzantine. For the honest nodes, the probability model was the same as in Equation (1).

In order to evaluate the complexity of the algorithm shown in Figure 3, we consider the number of operations performed to estimate the vector of system states s. By number of operations we mean the number of additions, substractions, multiplications and divisions done at the FC for the state estimation.

By looking at equation (5), we see that running the message passing algorithm requires the following number of operations:

- $n+1$ operations for each of $\tau_i^{(l)}(s_i)$, $\tau_i^{(r)}(s_i)$, $\nu_{i,j}^{(d)}(s_i)$, $\hat{\tau}_i^{(l)}(\hat{s}_i)$, $\hat{\tau}_i^{(r)}(\hat{s}_i)$, and $\hat{\nu}_{i,j}^{(d)}(\hat{s}_i)$.
- 3 operations for each of $\varphi_i^{(l)}(s_i)$, $\varphi_i^{(r)}(s_i)$, $\hat{\varphi}_i^{(l)}(\hat{s}_i)$ and $\hat{\varphi}_i^{(r)}(\hat{s}_i)$.
- n operations for each of $\nu_{m,j}^{(d)}(s_m)$ and $\hat{\nu}_{m,j}^{(d)}(\hat{s}_m)$.
- 8 operations for each of $\nu_{i,j}^{(u)}(s_i)$, $\hat{\nu}_{i,j}^{(u)}(\hat{s}_i)$ and $\lambda_{j,i}^{(d)}(h_j)$.
- m operations for each of $\lambda_{j,i}^{(u)}(h_j)$ and $\omega_j^{(u)}(h_j)$.

summing up to $8n+2m+41$ operations for each iteration over the factor graph. Therefore, we can argue that the complexity of the algorithm increases linearly with both n and m in contrast to the complexity the optimum fusion rule presented in [8] which grows exponentially with n.

IV. Simulation Results and Discussion

In this section, we evaluate the performance of the proposed synchronized attacks. We denote the two attack strategies described in Section II-2 as ATTACK_SYNC_FLIP and ATTACK_SYNC_FAKE, respectively. We also compare the performance of these attacks with the unsynchronized attack considered in [8] where the Byzantines act independently from each other and flip the decisions with a given P_{mal}. Specifically, we consider the two cases $P_{mal} = 1.0$ and $P_{mal} = 0.5$, which are the most meaningful cases, as shown in [8]. Simulation results are provided for both the MP-based detector proposed in [9] (referred to as MP_UN) and the MP-based detector proposed in this paper (referred to as MP_SYNC).

We consider the following settings: a sensor network with $n = 20$ nodes, transition probability of the Markovian states $\rho = 0.95$, an observation window $m = 10$, local error probability $\varepsilon = 0.15$, the fraction of Byzantines in the network $\alpha \in [0, 0.45]$ and $\hat{\rho} = \{0.5, 0.95\}$. To evaluate the performance of the MP algorithm, we consider three performance metrics: the probability of decision error P_e, the probability of correct identification of byzantines nodes $P(B|B)$, and the probability of mis-identifying a byzantine node as honest $P(B|H)$. The performance metrics are estimated over 20000 simulations.

Figure 4 shows the performance of the detectors subject to different attacks. As first observation, we can note that both the synchronized attacks have a much more detrimental effect on the system performance than the un-synchronized attacks (bottom-most curves displayed in Figure 4). Moreover, the worst performance is provoked by the ATTACK_SYNC_FAKE strategy with perfect information model estimation, i.e., $\hat{\rho} = \rho$ (upper-most curves displayed in Figure 4). The rationale is twofold: on one side, the sequence of reports sent from the Byzantines does not convey any information to the FC concerning the true states' values (zero-mutual information case); on the other side, in the ATTACK_SYNC_FAKE case, when the fake sequence $\hat{s}$ perfectly matches the state model, the identification of the byzantine nodes become very difficult at the FC. When instead $\hat{\rho} \neq \rho$, the effectiveness of the attack decreases. Indeed, since the Byzantines's reports do not follow exactly the same model as that of the honest nodes, the identification becomes easier. As an example, in Figure 4, it is shown that for $\hat{\rho} = 0.5$, the efficiency of the ATTACK_SYNC_FAKE is considerably reduced and it gives almost the same results of the ATTACK_SYNC_FLIP. Finally, it is worth noting from Figure 4 that the MP_SYNC significantly outperforms the MP_UN in the presence of synchronized attacks. In Figure 5, we report the performance of the MP_SYNC in terms of $P(B|B)$ and $P(B|H)$ to understand how well the MP algorithm can correctly identify the nodes' status. Upon inspection of the figure, we see that identification of the Byzantines is quite good when they adopt the ATTACK_SYNC_FLIP strategy ($P(B|B)$ is around 0.9 and $P(B|H)$ is lower than 0.1). Similar results are obtained for the mismatched ATTACK_SYNC_FAKE case with $\hat{\rho} = 0.5$ and that is why the curves of both cases are superposed on each other. When instead the Byzantines adopt the ATTACK_SYNC_FAKE strategy with perfect estimation of the model, the mission of the detector as expected becomes harder than before (for $\alpha = 0.45$ we have $P(B|B) = 0.7$ and $P(B|H) = 0.25$).

V. Conclusion

We presented two types of synchronized attacks capable to affect the performance of decision fusion in sensor networks. Then, we propose a nearly-optimum detector for coping with synchronized attacks by extending the message passing approach proposed in [9]. Experimental results show that, although the proposed detector is able to mitigate the effect of Byzantines, the coordination of the efforts is very harmful and significantly impairs the detection performance.

References

[1] A. Vempaty, T. Lang, and P. Varshney, "Distributed inference with byzantine data: State-of-the-art review on data falsification attacks," IEEE Signal Processing Magazine, vol. 30, no. 5, Sept 2013, pp. 65–75.

[2] A. S. Rawat, P. Anand, H. Chen, and P. K. Varshney, "Collaborative spectrum sensing in the presence of byzantine attacks in cognitive radio networks," IEEE Transactions on Signal Processing, vol. 59, no. 2, February 2011, pp. 774–786.

[3] Y. Sun and Y. Liu, "Security of online reputation systems: The evolution of attacks and defenses," IEEE Signal Processing Magazine, vol. 29, no. 2, March 2012, pp. 87–97.

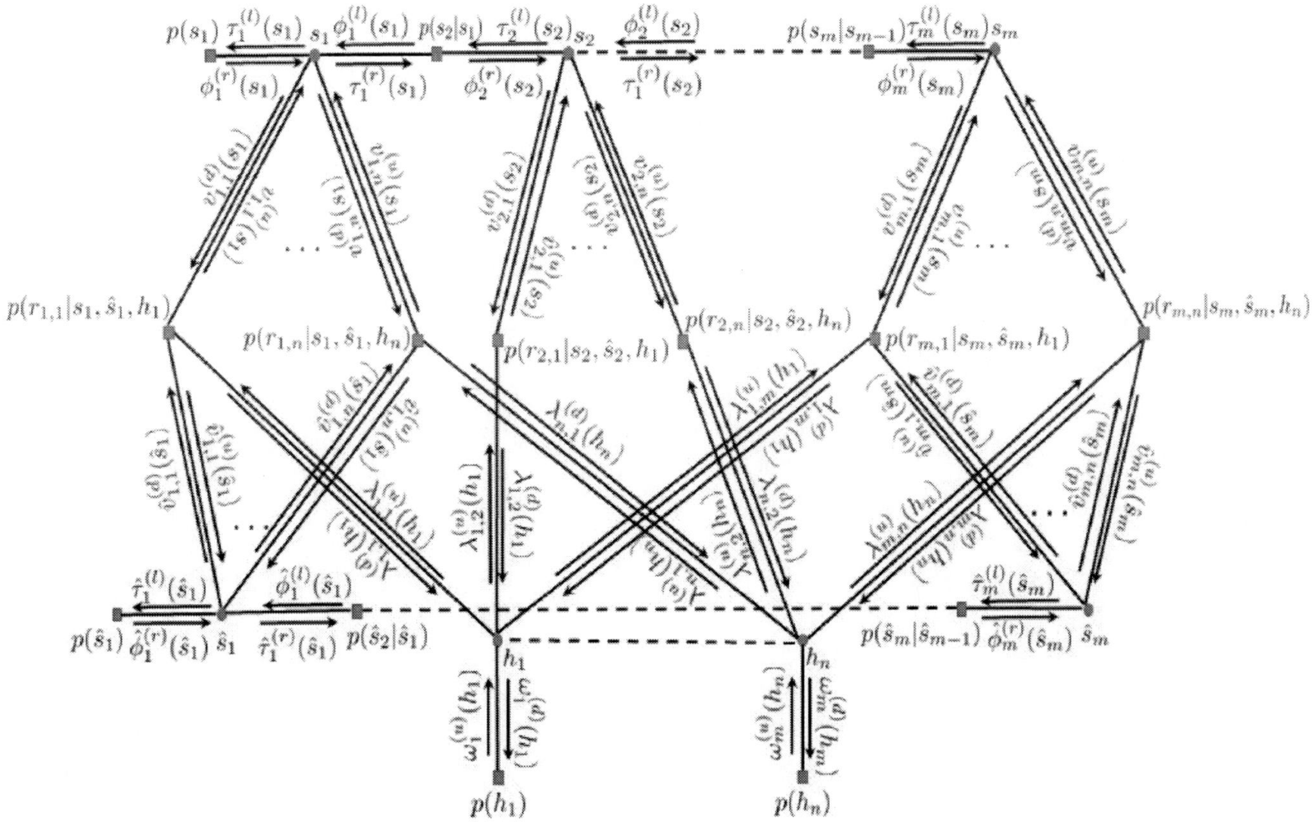

Figure 3. Factor graph for the problem at hand with the illustration of all the exchanged messages.

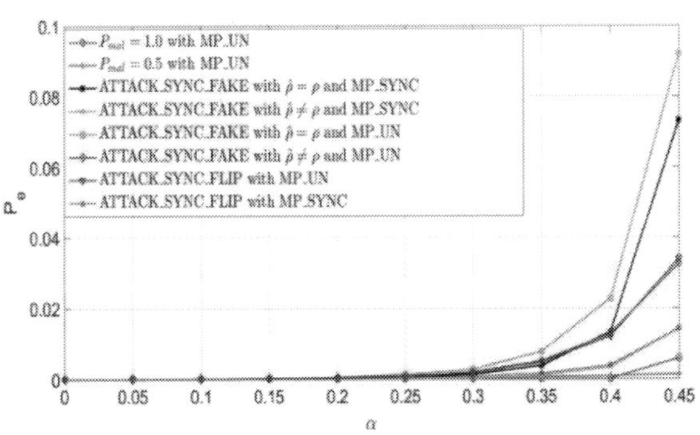

Figure 4. P_e vs. α for various attacks with MP_SYNC and MP_UN for $n = 20$, $\varepsilon = 0.15$, $\rho = 0.95$, $\hat{\rho} = \{0.5, 0.95\}$, and $m = 10$.

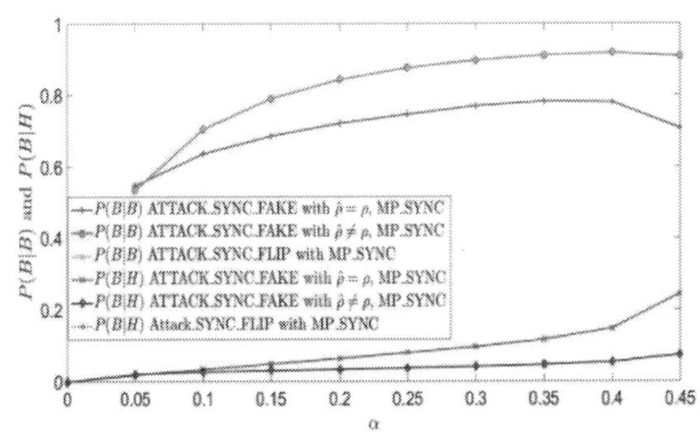

Figure 5. $P(B|B)$ and $P(B|H)$ vs. α for various attacks with MP_SYNC for $n = 20$, $\varepsilon = 0.15$, $\rho = 0.95$, $\hat{\rho} = \{0.5, 0.95\}$, and $m = 10$.

[4] P. K. Varshney, Distributed Detection and Data Fusion. Springer-Verlag, 1997.

[5] S. Marano, V. Matta, and L. Tong, "Distributed detection in the presence of byzantine attacks," IEEE Transactions on Signal Processing,, vol. 57, no. 1, 2009, pp. 16–29.

[6] A. S. Rawat, P. Anand, H. Chen, and P. K. Varshney, "Collaborative spectrum sensing in the presence of byzantine attacks in cognitive radio networks," IEEE Transactions on Signal Processing, vol. 59, no. 2, Feb 2011, pp. 774–786.

[7] A. Abrardo, M. Barni, K. Kallas, and B. Tondi, "Decision fusion with corrupted reports in multi-sensor networks: A game-theoretic approach," in 53rd IEEE Conference on Decision and Control, Dec 2014, pp. 505–510.

[8] A. Abrardo, M. Barni, K. Kallas, and B. Tondi, "A game-theoretic framework for optimum decision fusion in the presence of byzantines," IEEE Transactions on Information Forensics and Security, vol. 11, no. 6, June 2016, pp. 1333–1345.

[9] A. Abrardo, M. Barni, K. Kallas, and B. Tondi, "A Message Pass-

ing Approach for Decision Fusion in Adversarial Multi-Sensor Networks," submitted to the Information Fusion Journal. ArXiv e-prints 1702.08357, Feb 2017.

[10] S. M. Aji and R. J. McEliece, "The generalized distributive law," IEEE Transactions on Information Theory, vol. 46, no. 2, Mar 2000, pp. 325–343.

[11] K. W. Choi and E. Hossain, "Estimation of primary user parameters in cognitive radio systems via hidden markov model," IEEE Transactions on Signal Processing, vol. 61, no. 3, Feb 2013, pp. 782–795.

[12] I. A. Akbar and W. H. Tranter, "Dynamic spectrum allocation in cognitive radio using hidden markov models: Poisson distributed case," in IEEE Proceedings of SoutheastCon, March 2007, pp. 196–201.

[13] L. Rabiner and B. Juang, "An introduction to hidden markov models," IEEE ASSP Magazine, vol. 3, no. 1, Jan 1986, pp. 4–16.

[14] F. R. Kschischang, B. J. Frey, and H.-A. Loeliger, "Factor graphs and the sum-product algorithm," IEEE Transactions on Information Theory, vol. 47, no. 2, 2001, pp. 498–519.

Modelling Temporal Structures in Video Event Retrieval using an AND-OR Graph

Maaike H.T. de Boer
TNO and Radboud University
The Hague and Nijmegen, The Netherlands
Email: maaike.deboer@tno.nl

Camille Escher
Institut Superieur d'Electronique de Paris
Paris, France
Email: escherCamille@gmail.com

Klamer Schutte
TNO
The Hague, The Netherlands
Email: klamer.schutte@tno.nl

Abstract—**One of the challenges in Video Event Retrieval, the field in which (a sequence of frames with) high-level events are retrieved from a set of videos, is to model the temporal structure. One way to incorporate this information is using AND-OR graphs, which is a type of graphical model consisting of layers with AND nodes and OR nodes. We introduce new nodes, such as the BEFORE and WHILE node, for AND-OR graphs to explicitly model temporal information. The advantage of these nodes is that the graph is insightful and transparent for a user. Additionally, the graph can both be created by a user or with the use of training examples. We perform initial experiments on a video surveillance dataset named VIRAT, which contains temporally inverse events with the same concepts, such as entering and exiting a building. We compare performance to state of the art Support Vector Machine and Hidden Markov Model methods. We show that our proposed graph with WHILE and BEFORE nodes outperforms the state of the art methods.**

***Keywords*–AND-OR graph; Temporal Information; Event Retrieval.**

I. Introduction

Nowadays, the most common way to search for a video is to type a textual query in a search engine. Most general search engines, such as Youtube, contain videos with added textual information or *metadata*. In the security domain, this information is often not available. The content of the video should be analyzed to be able to search through those videos. This field of research is named *content-based visual information retrieval*. Within content-based visual information retrieval, we focus on Video Event Retrieval. A complex or high-level event is defined as 'long-term spatially and temporally dynamic object interactions that happen under certain scene settings' [1]. An open challenge in Video Event Retrieval is to model the temporal structure. The difference between videos and images is the temporal structure. It is, however, not directly clear how this temporal structure should be incorporated in image retrieval systems.

Current state of the art methods use Convolutional Neural Networks (CNNs) to train concept detectors [2][3]. Implicitly the temporal structure can be modelled by for example a 3D CNN model [4]. The drawback of the CNN models is that a huge amount of training examples should be available, training of the detectors takes a lot of time and the results are not insightful in why a detector did select a certain action.

Instead of training a neural network for each event, other state of the art methods often use pre-trained concept detectors on images and combine them temporally to represent an event. This combination can be done using some kind of pooling, such as average or max pooling or the more sophisticated Fisher vector or Vector of Locally Aggregated Descriptors (VLAD) pooling [5], and a classifier such as an Support Vector Machine (SVM) [6][7]. This method works well when certain objects or actions are highly indicative for a certain event, but temporally distinctive events, such as the difference between *entering a building* and *exiting a building*, are hard for this type of methods.

Another branch in classification is that of graphical models. Graphical models use probability and graph theory to find structure in sequential data [1]. Examples of such models are Hidden Markov Models (HMM), Conditional Random Fields (CRFs) and AND-OR graphs. The main contribution of this paper is the introduction of BEFORE and WHILE nodes, which support the explicit modelling of the temporal information in an AND-OR graph. The advantage of these nodes is that the graph is insightful and can easily be created by a user or by training examples.

In Section 2, we provide some related work on graphical models in the field of content-based visual information retrieval. Section 3 explains the details of our proposed model with the BEFORE and WHILE nodes. Section 4 contains the experiments on the Video and Image Retrieval and Analysis Tool (VIRAT) 2.0 dataset in which we compare our proposed model with an SVM and HMM model. Section 5 consists of the discussion, conclusion and future work.

II. Related Work on Graphical Models

The simplest case of graphical models are HMMs. HMMs are often used in human action recognition and event retrieval. An overview is provided by Jiang et al. [1]. For example, Li et al. [8] use salient poses as hidden states to form a model for an action. Tang et al. [9] use a latent structural SVM to learn the feature vectors to feed an HMM. Chen et al. [10] present a framework for video event classification using probabilistic HMM event classification. An advantage of these models is that temporal information can be modelled by these types of models and the models are transparent, but a disadvantage is that causality cannot be modelled and the probability of an event being present is based on a final state. When multiple events have the same end state, these cannot easily be distinguished.

Other types of graphical models are Conditional Random Fields (CRFs) and Dynamic Bayesian Networks (DBNs). Although Vail et al. [11] have shown that CRFs can outperform HMMs in action recognition, these models are disadvantagenous in situations where the dependency between events and subevents needs to be modelled [1]. DBNs are a solution to the causality problem of HMMs, but they assume that states are conditionally independent. This makes temporal structure harder to model.

The final type of graphical model is the AND-OR graph. These graphs are often used in the context of grammars. In our previous work, we have proposed a system with a more extended grammar [12], a stochastic grammar to model a temporal sequence [13] and a grammar model that is robust to noisy inputs [14]. In these grammars, AND-OR graphs can represent hierarchical components by using alternating layers of AND and OR nodes. The AND nodes represent entities that should occur together. An example is the *Part-Of* relation with a person and its parts, such as arms and legs. An example in the event retrieval is the co-occurrence of several objects, such as a car and a person that have to be present at the same time. The OR nodes represent alternative configurations of a certain entity. An example is the skin color, the gender or the type of hair of a person. Each graph has LEAF nodes at the bottom of the graph, which represent the smallest components and one ROOT node, which represents the whole entity that is modelled. Commonly, the AND-OR graphs are formalized by $G = (V, E)$ in which V represents the set of vertices or nodes, and E is the set of undirected edges expressing the relation between two nodes of consecutive layers. During inference, the LEAF nodes are filled with their values. In video retrieval, these values are often binary or a value between zero and one. The values travel bottom up to the ROOT node. The AND nodes take the (normalized) sum of the values and the OR node takes the maximum value of its decendants. The value at the ROOT node represents the score for that modelled entity, such as an event.

Within event retrieval, Tang et al. [15] use the AND-OR graph to fuse multi-modal features. A special type of AND-OR graphs, named Spatial-Temporal AND-OR graphs (ST-AOGs) are previously used to recognize cars [16] and to combine image information with textual information [17]. A very related work is presented by Pei et al. [18]. They use a stochastic context sensitive grammar to present a hierarchical composition of events and temporal relations. They use an AND of temporally related ORs. They represent all events in one model. The disadvantage of this model is that the graph should be re-trained in cases of new events. In general, the advantage of AND-OR graphs is that they are insightful and they can be used on top of grammar models, but a disadvantage is the computational cost of the large number of possible configurations. As a solution structural constraints are often chosen to limit the computational complexity of the learning process.

III. MODEL REPRESENTATION

Our model is represented by an undirected graph G, of which an example is shown in Figure 1. We propose a graph that contains a BEFORE node, followed by WHILE nodes. These WHILE nodes are connected to ID(entity) and/or NOT nodes. The LEAF nodes represent the objects at certain time points. This graph can be created by a user that can visualize the query in the graph, or the graph can be created using positive and negative training examples.

A. Inference

To infer whether the event presented by the graph is present in a certain sequence, we use a bottom-up approach to calculate the value at the root node. The value of the leaf nodes is the concept classifier score at a certain time point. The root value can be interpreted as a probability or a score.

The formulas for the nodes are formalized as:

$$v_{ID}(l_{a,t}) = l_{a,t} \tag{1}$$

where $l_{a,t}$ is the value of leaf node a at time point t and v_{ID} is the ID node connected to one of the objects at time t.

$$v_{NOT}(l_{a,t}) = 1 - l_{a,t} \tag{2}$$

where v_{NOT} is the NOT node connected to one of the objects at time t.

$$v_{WHILE}(v_{1,t}, .., v_{m,t}) = \frac{\sum_{i=1,...,m} v_{i,t}}{m} \tag{3}$$

where $v_{1,t}$ to $v_{m,t}$ are the nodes connected to the v_{WHILE} node at time t.

$$v_{BEFORE}(v_1, .., v_n) = \prod_{i=1,...,n} v_i \tag{4}$$

where v_1 to v_n are the nodes connected to the v_{BEFORE} node.

The WHILE node is, thus, an OR node. The BEFORE node is different from the AND node, because the BEFORE node takes the product and the AND node takes one of the values. Although we do not state that the subevents connected by the BEFORE node are independent, our formula equals a joint probability of the subevents assuming independency.

When the length of the test sequence is not comparable to the expected sequence length of the graph, a simple dynamic time warping algorithm is applied. In this algorithm, we delete all redundancies in the consecutive frames and create subsequences of the proper length. These subsequences are all subsequences that can be created with length t, in which t is the amount of time points in the created graph. The highest root node score is used to present the event.

B. Training

In training, we initialize the ID/NOT layer with ID(entity) nodes. The amount of BEFORE nodes is based on the amount of time warped time points of the positive instances for the event. Our current model only has one BEFORE node. The amount of WHILE and ID nodes is the amount of objects that are relevant for this event. Currently, each BEFORE node is connected to two WHILE nodes. Each WHILE node is connected to half the amount of objects in the bag of objects. The ID nodes are randomly pointing to one of the LEAF nodes at their time point.

The graph is trained using the ratio R between the root score of the positive examples ($\overrightarrow{P}_{c,r}$) for class c (in our case an event) on root node r and the negative examples ($\overrightarrow{N}_{c,r}$):

$$R = \frac{1 - ||\overrightarrow{N}_{c,r}||^2 + \overrightarrow{P}_{c,r}}{2} \tag{5}$$

During training, three types of moves are possible:

- Pivot: change the object ($l_{a,t}$) in the bag of objects that the ID/NOT node is pointing to.
- Polarity inversion: replace the ID node by a NOT node or vice versa.

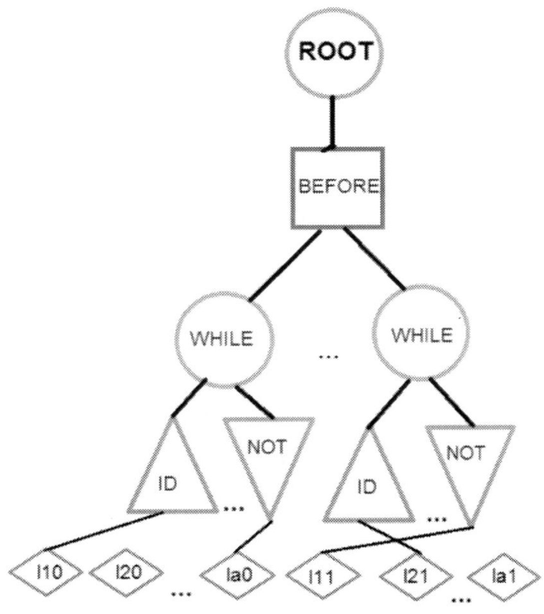

Figure 1. Proposed BEFORE-WHILE Graph model

- Pivot + polarity inversion: first apply a pivot and then a polarity inversion before processing the bottom-up inference.

In a more generalized system, some moves can be added, such as addition of an ID/NOT, WHILE or BEFORE node, as well as removing parts of the graph. During the training process, the following procedure is repeated until convergence of R.

- start with graph G, which has ratio R
- a vertex v is randomly selected in the ID-NOT layer
- one move is randomly selected among the 3 type of moves and new values for $\overrightarrow{P}_{c,v}$ and $\overrightarrow{N}_{c,v}$ are assigned to v.
- the bottom-up inference is applied to propagate the new values to $\overrightarrow{P}_{c,i}$ and $\overrightarrow{N}_{c,i}$ of each node of the graph
- the ratio R is calculated
- if the ratio R' of new G' is higher than R of G, G' becomes the new G, otherwise continue with the old G

IV. Experiments

We use the VIRAT 2.0 dataset [19] to perform our experiments. This dataset contains videos in the surveillance domain with temporally inverse events with the same concepts. These concepts are *person*, *car*, *other vehicle*, *object* and *bike*. The values of these concepts can be represented as (p, c, v, o, b), in which the variables are the values for each of the concepts. Instead of extracting the visual features and applying concept classifiers on the videos, we use the ground truth information of these concepts. For each (predefined) time point, we have binary values in each video for each concept. As explained in the previous section, our method can also handle concept classifier values between zero and one.

We focus on eight events, which can be temporally represented as:

- *person loading an object to a vehicle*: (1, 1, 0, **1**, 0) - (1, 1, 0, **0**, 0)
- *person unloading an object from a vehicle*: (1, 1, 0, **0**, 0) - (1, 1, 0, **1**, 0)
- *person opening a vehicle trunk*: (1, 1, 0, 0, 0) - (1, 1, 0, 0, 0)
- *person closing a vehicle trunk*: (1, 1, 0, 0, 0) - (1, 1, 0, 0, 0)
- *person getting into a vehicle*: (**1**, 1, 0, 0, 0) - (**0**, 1, 0, 0, 0)
- *person getting out of a vehicle*: (**0**, 1, 0, 0, 0) - (**1**, 1, 0, 0, 0)
- *person entering a facility*: (**1**, 0, 0, 0, 0) - (**0**, 0, 0, 0, 0)
- *person exiting a facility*: (**0**, 0, 0, 0, 0) - (**1**, 0, 0, 0, 0)

The bold digit indicates the temporal difference for each event. In two events, which are *person opening a vehicle trunk* and *person closing a vehicle trunk* no difference is present using these five concepts. We, therefore, cannot distinguish these events in this experiment.

For the training, we compared a manually created graph with the trained graph and no difference was found. To distinguish one event from another event (which are the negative training examples), only three concepts are relevant: *person*, *car* and *object*. Each graph consists of one ROOT node, one BEFORE node connected to two WHILE nodes. Each WHILE node is connected to three LEAF nodes, which are the relevant concepts.

We used the standard scene independent process presented by Oh et al. [19], so that the training and testing sets are composed by videos extracted from multiple scenes. For each video, we calculate the root node score and compare that score to the score for each of the other events. We use the Mean Accuracy, based on the confusion matrix among the events, to report performance. This is the standard approach for this dataset [19] and calculated by taking the amount of correctly classified videos divided by the total amount of videos per class and averaging over all classes / events.

We compare the results of our model with an (RBF) SVM trained on the mean pooled keyframes, an (RBF) SVM with the feature vectors of two time sequences concatenated and an HMM. The results for the methods are shown in Table I.

TABLE I. MEAN ACCURACY SCORES ON VIRAT 2.0 DATASET

Method	Mean Accuracy
SVM_{mean}	0.39
HMM	0.45
SVM_{concat}	0.60
Graph	0.61

The SVM with mean pooling has the lowest performance. This is an expected result, because the temporally opposite events cannot be represented by this type of SVM. Creating a longer feature with the time information increases performance. The HMM has slightly worse results compared to the proposed graph model and the SVM with concatenated time sequences. This is due to the fact that three events have the same end state (11000). These events are, thus, confused using the HMM.

V. Dicussion, Conclusion and Future Work

This work explores a graphical model that makes directly clear which concepts and which relations play a role in a certain event. We propose a model in which BEFORE and WHILE nodes are used as well as ID and NOT nodes. The temporal nodes show the temporal relation and the ID and NOT nodes show which concepts are important and in which polarity (present or not present). Initial experiments on a simple surveillance dataset using ground truth annotations show that our model seems slightly, but not significantly, better than state of the art methods. In future work, it is important to create an improved training process, upgrade the model in a way that it can handle multiple BEFORE nodes and test our model on a difficult dataset with noisy concept detectors. Our model should also be compared to other AND-OR graph based models in the event retrieval field. We, however, provided a solid base for an insightful graph model that can model temporal relations and is transparent, which makes it easy for users to create temporal queries in graphical format.

References

[1] Y.-G. Jiang, S. Bhattacharya, S.-F. Chang, and M. I. Shah, "High-level event recognition in unconstrained videos," Int. J. of Multimedia Information Retrieval, 2012, pp. 1–29.

[2] A. Krizhevsky, I. Sutskever, and G. E. Hinton, "Imagenet classification with deep convolutional neural networks," in Advances in neural information processing systems, 2012, pp. 1097–1105.

[3] Y.-G. Jiang, Z. Wu, J. Wang, X. Xue, and S.-F. Chang, "Exploiting feature and class relationships in video categorization with regularized deep neural networks," in arXiv preprint arXiv:1502.07209, 2015.

[4] D. Tran, L. Bourdev, R. Fergus, L. Torresani, and M. Paluri, "Learning spatiotemporal features with 3d convolutional networks," in ICCV. IEEE, 2015, pp. 4489–4497.

[5] Z. Xu, Y. Yang, and A. G. Hauptmann, "A discriminative CNN video representation for event detection," in Proc. of CVPR, 2015, pp. 1798–1807.

[6] H. Zhang et al., "VIREO-TNO @ TRECVID 2015: Multimedia Event Detection," in Proc. of TRECVID 2015, 2015.

[7] Y. Kim, J. Chen, M.-C. Chang, X. Wang, E. M. Provost, and S. Lyu, "Modeling transition patterns between events for temporal human action segmentation and classification," in Int. Conf. on Automatic Face and Gesture Recognition, vol. 1. IEEE, 2015, pp. 1–8.

[8] W. Li, Z. Zhang, and Z. Liu, "Expandable data-driven graphical modeling of human actions based on salient postures," IEEE Transactions on Circuits and Systems for Video Technology, vol. 18, no. 11, 2008, pp. 1499–1510.

[9] K. Tang, L. Fei-Fei, and D. Koller, "Learning latent temporal structure for complex event detection," in Proc. on CVPR. IEEE, 2012, pp. 1250–1257.

[10] H.-S. Chen and W.-J. Tsai, "A framework for video event classification by modeling temporal context of multimodal features using HMM," J. of Visual Communication and Image Representation, vol. 25, no. 2, 2014, pp. 285–295.

[11] D. L. Vail, M. M. Veloso, and J. D. Lafferty, "Conditional random fields for activity recognition," in Proc. Int. Conf. on Autonomous agents and multiagent systems. ACM, 2007, p. 235.

[12] P. Hanckmann, K. Schutte, and G. J. Burghouts, "Automated textual descriptions for a wide range of video events with 48 human actions," in European Conference on Computer Vision. Springer, 2012, pp. 372–380.

[13] G. Sanromà, L. Patino, G. Burghouts, K. Schutte, and J. Ferryman, "A unified approach to the recognition of complex actions from sequences of zone-crossings," Image and Vision Computing, vol. 32, no. 5, 2014, pp. 363–378.

[14] K. Schutte et al., "Long-term behavior understanding based on the expert-based combination of short-term observations in high-resolution cctv," in SPIE, vol. 9995. International Society for Optics and Photonics, 2016.

[15] K. Tang, B. Yao, L. Fei-Fei, and D. Koller, "Combining the right features for complex event recognition," in Proc. of the Int. Conf. on Computer Vision, 2013, pp. 2696–2703.

[16] B. Li, T. Wu, C. Xiong, and S.-C. Zhu, "Recognizing car fluents from video," arXiv preprint arXiv:1603.08067, 2016.

[17] K. Tu, M. Meng, M. W. Lee, T. E. Choe, and S.-C. Zhu, "Joint video and text parsing for understanding events and answering queries," MultiMedia, IEEE, vol. 21, no. 2, 2014, pp. 42–70.

[18] M. Pei, Y. Jia, and S.-C. Zhu, "Parsing video events with goal inference and intent prediction," in ICCV. IEEE, 2011, pp. 487–494.

[19] S. Oh, A. Hoogs, A. Perera, N. Cuntoor, C.-C. Chen, J. T. Lee, S. Mukherjee, J. Aggarwal, H. Lee, L. Davis et al., "A large-scale benchmark dataset for event recognition in surveillance video," in Conf. on CVPR. IEEE, 2011, pp. 3153–3160.

Resolution Enhancement of Incomplete Thermal Data of Earth by Exploitation of Temporal and Spatial Correlation

Paolo Addesso, Maurizio Longo and Rocco Restaino

Dipartimento di Ingegneria dell'Informazione, Ingegneria Elettrica e Matematica Applicata
Università degli Studi di Salerno
Via Giovanni Paolo II, 132 I-84084 Fisciano (SA), Italy
Email: {paddesso, longo, restaino}@unisa.it

Gemine Vivone

North Atlantic Treaty Organization (NATO)
Science and Technology Organization (STO)
Centre for Maritime Research and Experimentation
I-19126 La Spezia, Italy
Email: vivone@cmre.nato.int

Abstract—**Many remote sensing applications require the availability of radiometric surface temperature information with both high acquisition rate and high spatial resolution, but unfortunately this requirement is still not achievable through a single sensor. However, the huge amount of remote sensed data provided by several heterogeneous spaceborne sensors allows to use data fusion in order to overcome this issue. In this paper, we propose a method for sharpening thermal images in a nearly real-time scenario, also capable to deal with missing data due to cloudy pixels. Moreover, we analyze the robustness of the method with respect to cloud mask misclassifications and assess its effectiveness via numerical simulations based on SEVIRI (Spinning Enhanced Visible and InfraRed Imager) data.**

Keywords–Thermal Sharpening; Cloud Masking; Multitemporal Analysis; Bayesian Smoothing; Robustness.

I. INTRODUCTION

In remote sensing applications, such as agriculture, forest management and coastal monitoring [1], remote sensed Brightness Temperature (BT) images acquired with sufficient *high temporal resolution* (*htr*) and *High Spatial Resolution* (*HSR*) could be of paramount importance. Due to physical constraints of spaceborne sensors, the strategy for achieving images with high spatial and temporal resolutions relies on fusing *low temporal resolution/High Spatial Resolution* (*ltr/HSR*) and *high temporal resolution/Low Spatial Resolution* (*htr/LSR*) data [2]. This possibility is guaranteed by the huge amount of remotely sensed data acquired by the many satellites in operation [3].

In previous research studies [4]-[6], the authors have investigated several smoothing techniques for possible use in non-real time scenarios. The most promising one relies on the fusion of images obtained by temporal interpolation of *ltr/HSR* data with others obtained by spatial interpolation of (*htr/LSR*) data (see Figure 1). This technique has the advantage of being simple enough while catching the temporal and spatial correlation that real data exhibit [7]. Unfortunately, the scenario is complicated by the presence of clouds, that is a serious issue for multitemporal techniques [8]. Simply using a cloud mask, as can be obtained via several strategies [9] [10], could not be sufficient. Indeed, the incompleteness of the images sequence may compromise the functionality and the effectiveness of most fusion algorithms. To circumvent this problem, a possible strategy is to fill the gaps in the image sequences due to clouds by estimating the BT of the cloud covered areas. Such a strategy may take advantage of the temporal correlation present in the image sequence, but must also take into account the unavoidable events of misclassified pixels. To deal with these issues, in this paper we consider several approaches to implement the said fusion strategy, focusing on different methods of spatial and temporal interpolation whose accuracy and robustness with respect to pixel misclassification in the cloud map is compared via a simulation setup based on the use of SEVIRI data [11].

The paper is organized as follows: Section II presents the formalization of thermal image sequences enhancement; Section III reports the numerical results; finally, conclusions and future developments come in Section IV.

II. METHOD DESCRIPTION

As stated before, the BT of the ground surface is masked by the top of cloud, thus contaminating the data. The solution we propose (depicted in Figure 1) relies on the availability of sufficiently accurate cloud masks, both for htr/LSR and ltr/HSR data, and is described by the following steps.

1) *Temporal Interpolation* (*TI*): the first step is applied to both the htr/LSR sequence $\mathcal{L} = \{\mathbf{L}_k : k \in T_L\}$ and the ltr/HSR sequence $\mathcal{H} = \{\mathbf{H}_k : k \in T_H\}$.

1.1) $\mathcal{H} = \{\mathbf{H}_k : k \in T_H\}$ is upsampled to the same time resolution of $\mathcal{L} = \{\mathbf{L}_k : k \in T_L\}$ and the cloudy pixels are estimated via a TI algorithm to obtain a sequence $\widehat{\mathcal{H}} = \{\widehat{\mathbf{H}}_k : k \in T_L\}$ (see, e.g., images $\mathbf{H}_4$ and $\widehat{\mathbf{H}}_4$ in Figure 1);

1.2) cloudy pixels in $\mathcal{L} = \{\mathbf{L}_k : k \in T_L\}$ are estimated via a TI operator $I_T(\cdot)$ to obtain a sequence $\widetilde{\mathcal{L}} = \{\widetilde{\mathbf{L}}_k : k \in T_L\}$ (see $\mathbf{L}_k$ and $\widetilde{\mathbf{L}}_k$ for $k = \{2, 3, 4\}$ in Figure 1).

2) *Spatial Interpolation* (*SI*): $\widetilde{\mathcal{L}} = \{\widetilde{\mathbf{L}}_k : k \in T_L\}$ is upsampled to the same spatial resolution of $\mathcal{H}$ via an SI operator $I_S(\cdot)$ to obtain the sequence $\{\widehat{\mathbf{L}}_k : k \in T_L\}$. In our setup, we choose to use a bicubic interpolator $\mathcal{B}(\cdot)$.

3) *Data Fusion*: in this step the two intermediate sequences $\widehat{\mathcal{L}}$ and $\widehat{\mathcal{H}}$ are combined, instant by instant, to obtain the estimated sequence $\mathcal{E} = \{\mathbf{E}_k : k \in T_E\}$, where, for sake of simplicity, $T_E = T_L$. More in detail, two fusion sub-steps are performed.

3.1) *Sharpening Fusion* (*SF*): the two intermediate sequences $\widehat{\mathcal{L}}$ and $\widehat{\mathcal{H}}$ are combined, instant by instant,

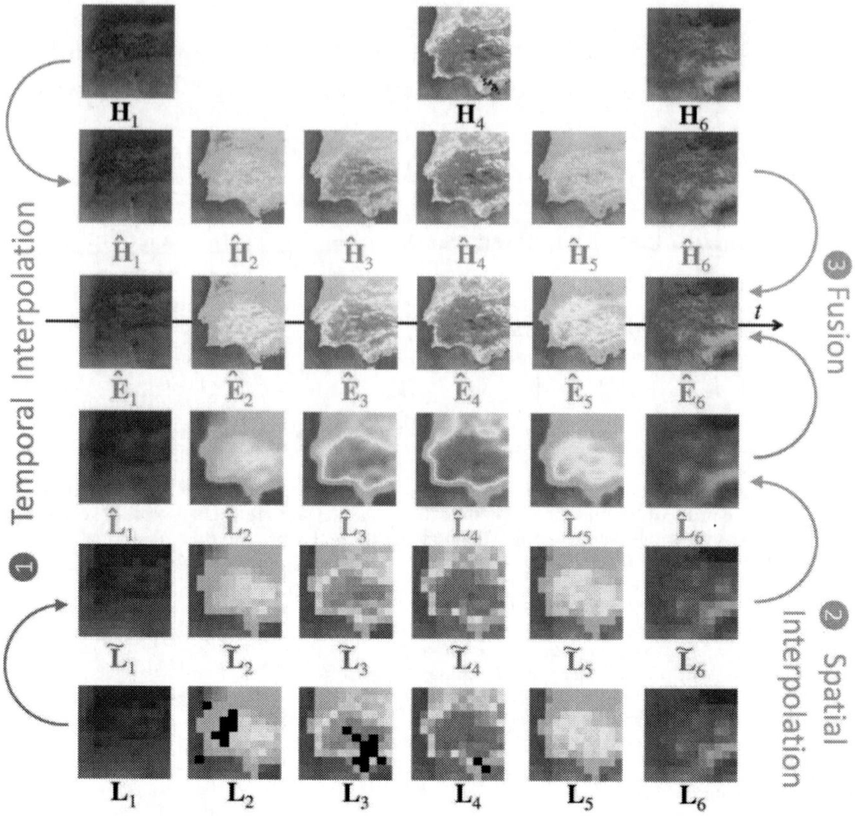

Figure 1. Pre-processing steps for BT enhancement. The image sequences are: $\{\mathbf{L}_k\}$ =*htr/LSR*, $\{\widetilde{\mathbf{L}}_k\}$ = temporal interpolation of *htr/LSR*, $\{\mathbf{H}_k\}$ = *ltr/HSR*, $\{\widehat{\mathbf{H}}_k\}$ = temporal interpolation of *ltr/HSR*, $\{\widehat{\mathbf{L}}_k\}$ = spatial interpolation of *htr/LSR*, $\{\mathbf{E}_k\}$ = target *htr/HSR*. Dark spots in images $\mathbf{H}_4$ and $\mathbf{L}_2$,$\mathbf{L}_3$,$\mathbf{L}_4$ are the cloudy pixels.

through a sharpening rule $F_S(\cdot,\cdot)$, producing the estimate of an htr/HSR sequence $\mathcal{S} = \{\mathbf{S}_k : k \in T_L\}$. For its appealing sharpening features [12] the *High Pass Modulation* (*HPM*) (or *High Frequency Modulation - HFM*) injection scheme [13] is employed in the data fusion along with an undecimated wavelet decomposition (see also [5] for further details).

3.2) *Bayesian Smoothing* (*BS*): Bayesian smoothing allows to obtain the final estimated sequence $\mathcal{E}$ by using (for example) the *Rauch-Tung-Striebel* (*RTS*) algorithm [14], using the sharpened sequence as observation, as explained in [15].

III. Numerical Results

In this section, we consider: *i*) the accuracy of the proposed estimators in terms of Root Mean Square Error (RMSE), defined as $\sqrt{E[(\mathbf{I}-\mathbf{J})^2]}$ where $\mathbf{I}$ is the ground truth, $\mathbf{J}$ is the estimated image and $E[\cdot]$ indicates the sample average over the pixels; *ii*) the design of the TI operator $I_T(\cdot)$ under a criterion of robustness with respect to cloud masking error.

As test set, we employ sequences of thermal images acquired by the SEVIRI sensor in the band IR 10.8, characterized by the a spatial resolution of about 6 km and a temporal rate of 4 images per hour. In particular, the presented results are related to data collected on 16 August 2014 on the Iberian peninsula (latitude between 35.7 and 41.4 degrees North, longitude between 4.1 and 9.8 degrees West). The simulation setup is as follows. The original dataset plays the role of the estimating htr/HSR sequence $\mathcal{E}$. $\mathcal{H}$ is simulated by selecting a subset of $\mathcal{E}$ with a temporal interval $\Delta^H = 8$ between each couple of ltr/HSR images. $\mathcal{L}$ is simulated by generating a spatially degraded version of $\mathcal{E}$, with spatial resolution ratio $R = 6$ between $\mathcal{E}$ and $\mathcal{L}$.

Given the unavailability of a ground truth for the soil (or sea) temperature under the clouds, we use clear sky images and artificially change the BT of the whole image in order to mimic a temperature decrease which is typical when clouds are present. The top of the cloud is supposed to have a BT of 270 K, and the initial and final transition phases, modeled via a raised cosine function, are completed in 1 hour (see Figure 2, panel (a)). The time duration of each period of cloud coverage is indicated with $\Delta^c = \{2, 4\}$, and the cloudy images are chosen to be in the midpoints between two HSR images, that are the most critical point for our algorithms. More in detail:

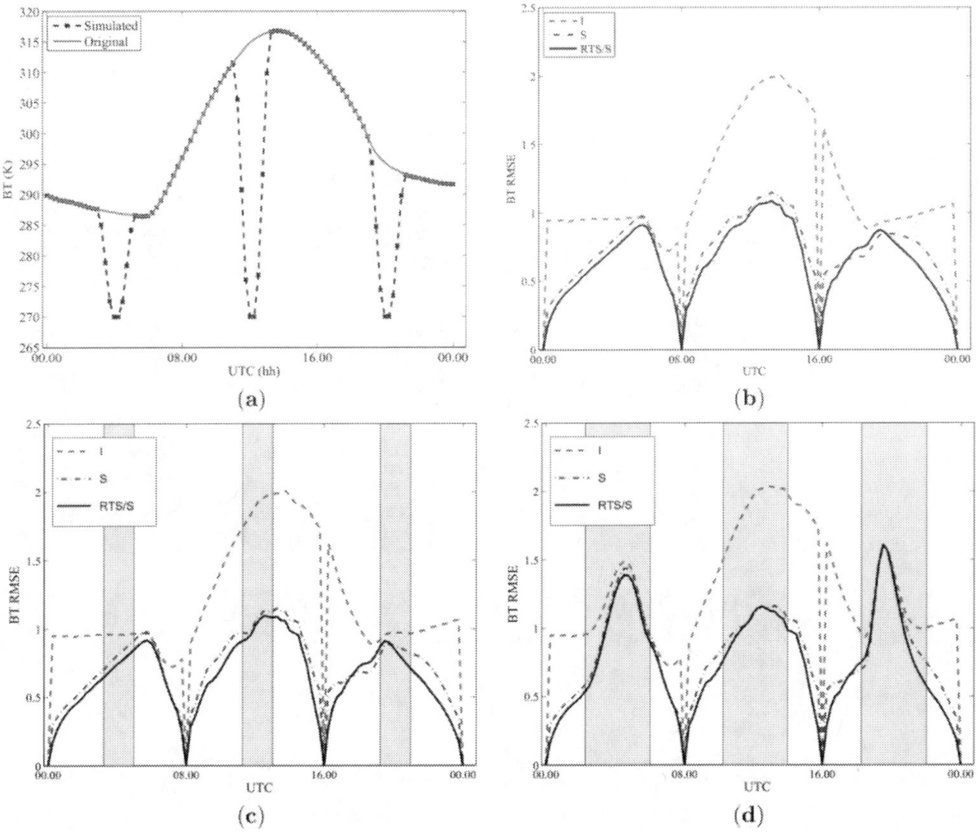

Figure 2. Panel **(a)**: BT time evolution for cloud simulation (black dashed line) and original data (red continuous line) when $\Delta^c = 2$ hh. Panels **(b)**-**(d)**: RMSE computed between the forecast of thermal SEVIRI image and the actual value for the simulated Spain dataset in the PCC case. The panel **(b)** refers to the case in which the clouds are absent. Panels **(c)** and **(d)** refer to cloud data periods (highlighted by the gray-shaded areas) with time duration $\Delta^c = 2$ hh and $\Delta^c = 4$ hh respectively.

TABLE I. RMSE RELATED TO SIMULATED PCC SCENARIOS. RELEVANT PARAMETERS ARE $R = 6$ AND $\Delta^H = 8$ hh.

	Type	Δ^c [h]	I	S	RTS/S
Whole	Cloud	2	1.251	0.759	**0.697**
	Cloud	4	1.332	0.883	**0.832**
	Clear-sky	[2,4]	1.249	0.756	**0.692**
Cloudy	Cloud	2	1.346	0.916	**0.875**
	Clear-sky	2	1.337	0.905	**0.859**
	Cloud	4	1.475	1.099	**1.061**
	Clear-sky	4	1.319	0.887	**0.834**

- when $\Delta^c = 2$ hours, we put the cloud coverage in the intervals $[03.00 - 05.00]$, $[11.00 - 13.00]$ and $[19.00 - 21.00]$ UTC (Universal Time Coordinated);
- when $\Delta^c = 4$ hours, we put the cloud coverage in the intervals $[02.00 - 06.00]$, $[10.00 - 14.00]$ and $[18.00 - 22.00]$ UTC.

The approach has been assessed in two cases: *i) Perfect Cloud Classification (PCC)*, in which perfect cloud/no cloud pixel classification is assumed; *ii) Non Perfect Cloud Classification (NPCC)*, in which misclassifications are considered.

A. Perfect Cloud Classification

In the scenario of error-free cloud mask, we use a *TI* scheme based on a blockwise Cubic Interpolation (CI) to compute $\widetilde{\mathcal{L}}$ and $\widetilde{\mathcal{H}}$ sequences and then we compare the following three algorithms.

- *Interpolated image estimation (I)*: this method is used as a yardstick, since it does not involve any data fusion (the estimate at time k is given by the bicubic interpolation bicubic interpolation of the LSR sequence $\widehat{\mathcal{L}} = I_S(\widetilde{\mathcal{L}})$).
- *Sharpened image estimation (S)*: The estimate at time k is produced by performing a *SF*, as described in Sect. II, namely it coincides with the sequence $\mathcal{S} = F_S(\widehat{\mathcal{L}}, \widetilde{\mathcal{H}})$.

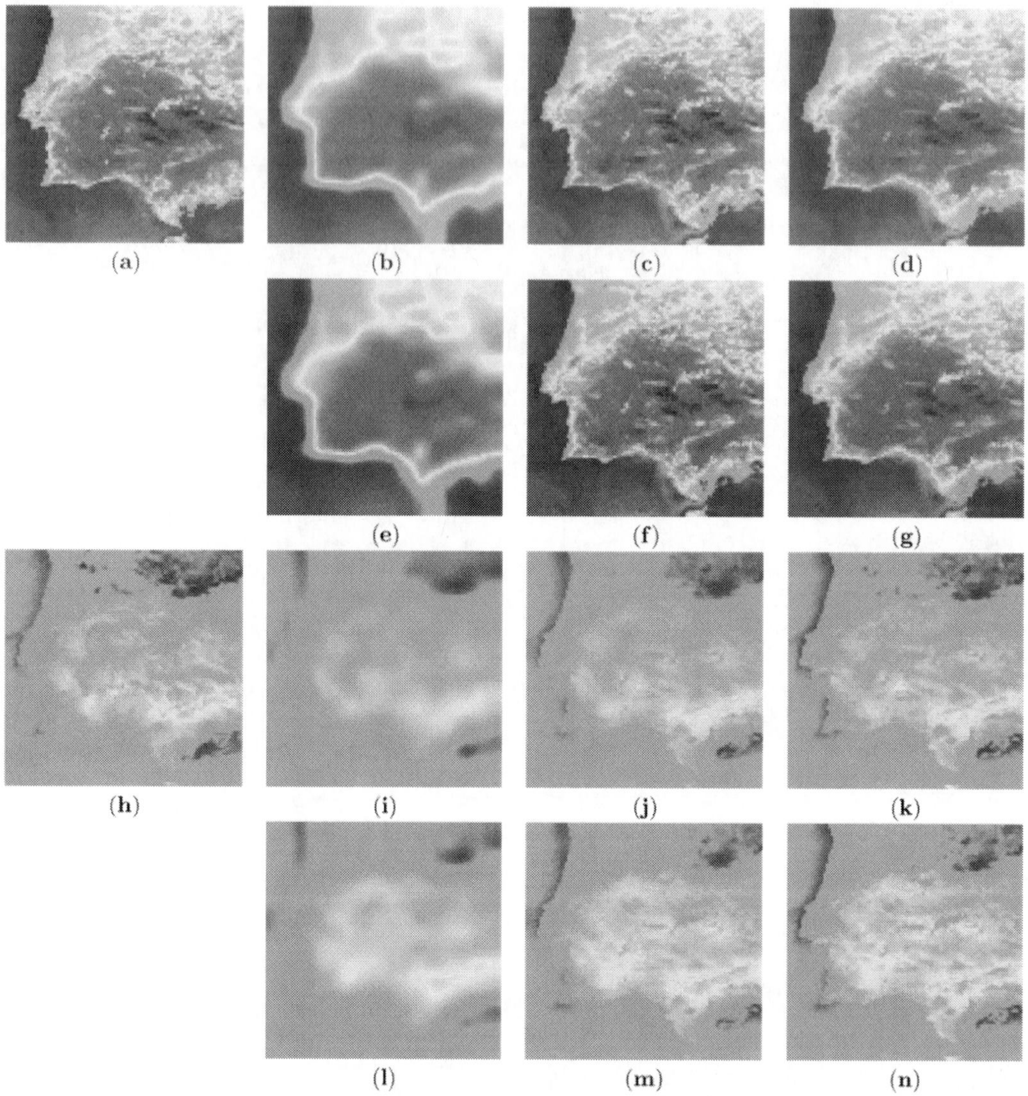

Δ^c	t = 12.00 UTC			t = 20.00 UTC		
	I	S	RTS/S	I	S	RTS/S
2	1.898	1.054	**1.026**	0.970	0.878	**0.864**
4	1.968	**1.099**	1.110	1.471	1.448	**1.427**

Figure 3. Example of estimation with missing data. Panel **(a)**: missing image to be estimated (acquired at 12.00 UTC on 16 August 2014). Panels **(b)**-**(d)**: images estimated at 12.00 UTC on 16 August 2014 for $\Delta^c = 2$ by algoritms I **(b)**, SI **(c)** and RTS/S **(d)**. Panels **(e)**-**(g)**: images estimated at 12.00 UTC on 16 August 2014 for $\Delta^c = 4$ by algoritms I **(e)**, SI **(f)** and RTS/S **(g)**. Panel **(h)**: missing image to be estimated (acquired at 20.00 UTC on 16 August 2014). Panels **(i)**-**(k)**: images estimated at 20.00 UTC on 16 August 2014 for $\Delta^c = 2$ by algoritms I **(i)**, SI **(j)** and RTS/S **(k)**. Panels **(l)**-**(n)**: images estimated at 20.00 UTC on 16 August 2014 for $\Delta^c = 4$ by algoritms I **(l)**, SI **(m)** and RTS/S **(n)**. At the bottom, RMSE values for the estimated images.

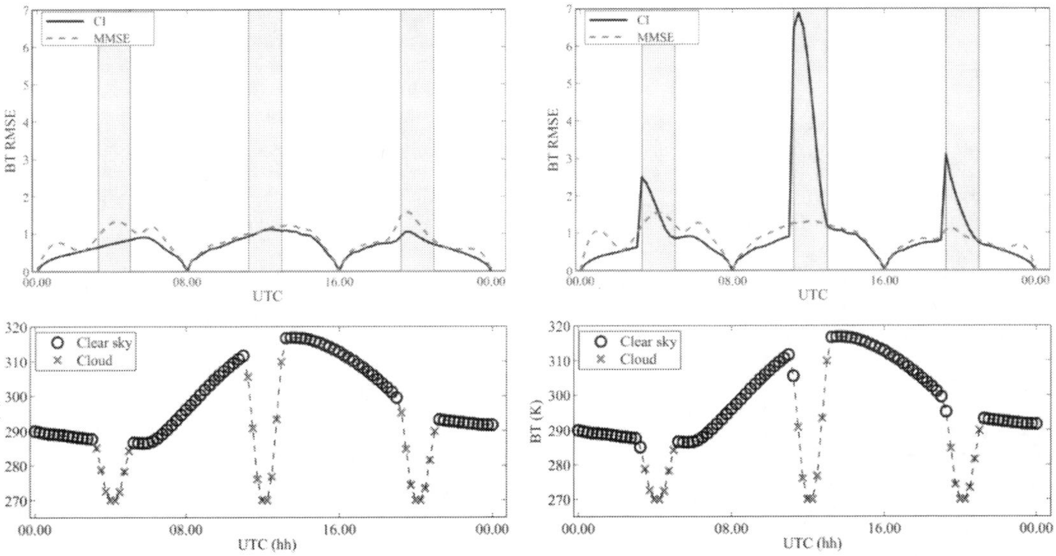

(a) (b)

Figure 4. RMSE computed between the forecast of thermal SEVIRI image and the actual value for the simulated Spain dataset (top plots) and related cloud mask (bottom plots). The gray-shaded areas in top plots are referred to the true cloud data periods with time duration $\Delta^c = 2$ hh. The panel **(a)** refers to PCC case, while the panel **(b)** refers to NPCC case.

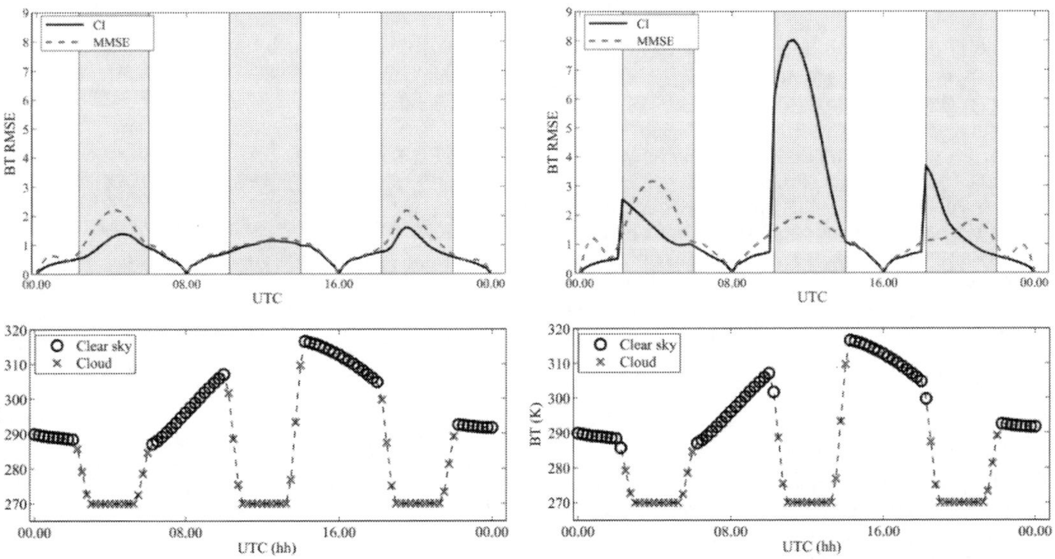

(a) (b)

Figure 5. RMSE computed between the forecast of thermal SEVIRI image and the actual value for the simulated Spain dataset (top plots) and related cloud mask (bottom plots). The gray-shaded areas in top plots are referred to the true cloud data periods with time duration $\Delta^c = 4$ hh. The panel **(a)** refers to PCC case, while the panel **(b)** refers to NPCC case.

- *RTS smoother with Sharpened observation (RTS/S)*: in this method, we employ a *BS* algorithm, i.e., the RTS one, that is fed by observations constructed upon the sharpened images.

The results are summarized in Figures 2-3 and in Table I. More in detail, in Figure 2, plots (c) and (d), it is shown the RMSE vs. time for the cases $\Delta^c = 2$ hours and $\Delta^c = 4$ hours, respectively. We can see that the error in estimating the htr/HSR sequence slightly increases in the first case during missing data intervals (i.e., the gray-shaded areas), with respect to the case without missing data (i.e., Figure 2, plot (b)), while the performance significantly degrades for $\Delta^c = 4$.

The performance trend is made evident looking at the RMSEs in Table I, computed over all time frames (Whole) and over the cloudy frames only (Cloudy), and more precisely comparing over the HSR images estimated in the cloudy frames (Type = "Cloud") with the RMSEs of the HSR images estimated in the same frames when no clouds have been added (Type = "Clear-sky"). Finally, in Figure 3 we present some image useful for a visual appreciation of the effectiveness of both the S algorithm and (even more) the RTS/S algorithm in producing satisfactory estimated HSR images (Figure 3, panels (c) and (d) for $\Delta^c = 2$ and panels (f) and (g) for $\Delta^c = 4$), in comparison with the missing HSR original image (Figure 3, panel (a)) acquired at 12.00 UTC. A similar comparison can be carried out looking at panels (i)-(n) of Figure 3, that are the estimated HSR images of a missing HSR original image (Figure 3, panel (h)) acquired on the same area, in the same day, but at 20.00 UTC. In any case, in the average, the best algorithm is RTS/S because it is the most stable one, though it is not uniformly the best one in every instance.

B. Non Perfect Cloud Classification

In dealing with the effects of cloud/no cloud misclassification, but limiting ourselves to the RTS/S rule, we focus on two possible *TI* interpolation strategies: (i) CI and (ii) MMSE, namely a polynomial fitting obtained via a Minimum Mean Square Error.

The results are summarized in Figure 4 and Figure 5 that refers to the cases $\Delta^c = 2$ hh and $\Delta^c = 4$ hh respectively. We can see that CI strategy outperforms MMSE one in PCC case, but it is less robust than MMSE when a single cloudy pixel is misclassified, as shown in panel **(b)** of both Figure 4 and Figure 5. Note also that the misclassification of a clear-sky pixel (not shown in this contribution) is by far less dangerous, because both techniques are not very sensitive to this kind of error, as evident by the analysis carried out in the previous subsection. Accordingly, these results give some hints for the design of the cloud detection algorithm, that should aim to minimize the probability of a miss.

IV. Conclusion

High spatial resolution thermal maps, collected with an elevate acquisition rate, are often required for several applications about the monitoring of rural and urban areas. In this paper, we present a framework that is able to perform a non real-time sharpening of thermal images encompassing the presence of missing data. It combines techniques of temporal smoothing and spatial enhancement by taking advantage of a Bayesian smoother relied upon the Rauch-Tung-Striebel algorithm and a pansharpening method belonging to the multi-resolution analysis family (an undecimated wavelet decomposition with a high pass modulation injection scheme). The experimental results using real data acquired by the SEVIRI sensor (band IR 10.8) demonstrate the ability of the proposed approach to reach better performance with respect to techniques based on either temporal interpolation or spatial sharpening and, in particular, the ability of the proposed technique to deal with missing data (e.g. due to the presence of clouds).

This work deserves further investigations towards the introduction of *a priori* knowledge about the surface (such as its Digital Elevation Model) or of the physical model of the incoming solar radiation.

References

[1] W. Zhan, Y. Chen, J. Zhou, J. Li, and W. Liu, "Sharpening thermal imageries: A generalized theoretical framework from an assimilation perspective," IEEE Trans. Geosci. Remote Sens., vol. 49, no. 2, Feb. 2011, pp. 773–789.

[2] F. Gao, J. Masek, M. Schwaller, and F. Hall, "On the blending of the landsat and MODIS surface reflectance: predicting daily Landsat surface reflectance," IEEE Trans. Geosci. Remote Sens., vol. 44, no. 8, Aug. 2006, pp. 2207–2218.

[3] M. Chi et al., "Big data for remote sensing: Challenges and opportunities," Proceedings of the IEEE, vol. 104, no. 11, Nov 2016, pp. 2207–2219.

[4] P. Addesso et al., "Enhancing TIR image resolution via Bayesian smoothing for IRRISAT irrigation management project," in Proc. SPIE Remote Sensing, no. 8887, 2013, pp. 888 710–1–888 710–13.

[5] P. Addesso, M. Longo, A. Maltese, R. Restaino, and G. Vivone, "Batch methods for resolution enhancement of TIR image sequences," IEEE J. Sel. Topics Appl. Earth Observ., vol. 8, no. 7, July 2015, pp. 3372–3385.

[6] P. Addesso et al., "Robustified smoothing for enhancement of thermal image sequences affected by clouds," in IEEE Geoscience and Remote Sensing Symposium (IGARSS), 26-31 July, Milan, Italy, 2015, pp. 1076–1079.

[7] A. Kallel, C. Ottle, S. L. Hegarat-Mascle, F. Maignan, and D. Courault, "Surface temperature downscaling from multiresolution instruments based on markov models," IEEE Transactions on Geoscience and Remote Sensing, vol. 51, no. 3, March 2013, pp. 1588–1612.

[8] X. Li et al., "Recovering quantitative remote sensing products contaminated by thick clouds and shadows using multitemporal dictionary learning," IEEE Transactions on Geoscience and Remote Sensing, vol. 52, no. 11, Nov 2014, pp. 7086–7098.

[9] P. Addesso, R. Conte, M. Longo, R. Restaino, and G. Vivone, "MAP-MRF cloud detection based on PHD filtering," IEEE J. Sel. Topics Appl. Earth Observ., vol. 5, no. 3, June 2012, pp. 919–929.

[10] G. Vivone, P. Addesso, R. Conte, M. Longo, and R. Restaino, "A class of cloud detection algorithms based on a MAP-MRF approach in space and time," IEEE Trans. Geosci. Remote Sens., vol. 52, no. 8, Aug 2014, pp. 5100 – 5115.

[11] F. Pasternak, P. Hollier, and J. Jouan, "Seviri, the new imager for meteosat second generation," in Geoscience and Remote Sensing Symposium, 1993. IGARSS '93. Better Understanding of Earth Environment., International, Aug 1993, pp. 1094–1099 vol.3.

[12] G. Vivone, R. Restaino, M. Dalla Mura, G. Licciardi, and J. Chanussot, "Contrast and error-based fusion schemes for multispectral image pansharpening," IEEE Geosci. and Remote Sens. Letters,, vol. 11, no. 5, May 2014, pp. 930–934.

[13] R. Schowengerdt, Remote Sensing: Models and Methods for Image Processing, 3rd Ed. Elsevier, 2007.

[14] H. Rauch, F. Tung, and C. Striebel, "Maximum likelihood estimates of linear dynamic systems," AIAA Journal, vol. 3, no. 8, 1965, pp. 1445–1450.

[15] P. Addesso, M. Longo, R. Restaino, G. Vivone, and A. Maltese, "An interpolation-based data fusion scheme for enhancing the resolution of thermal image sequences," in IEEE Geoscience and Remote Sensing Symposium (IGARSS), 13-18 July, Quebec, Canada, 2014, pp. 4926–4929.

Extraction of Periodic Features from Video Signals

Davide Alinovi and Riccardo Raheli

Department of Engineering and Architecture
Information Engineering Unit
University of Parma
Email: {davide.alinovi, riccardo.raheli}@unipr.it

Abstract—**In a number of application scenarios, proper video signals may exhibit simultaneous correlation characteristics over the space and time dimensions which jointly describe periodic features or behaviors. Examples of such scenarios may be found in video monitoring of physical systems, sport and athlete coaching with automatic video supervision, biomedical applications to newborn video monitoring for the detection of epileptic seizures or apnea episodes, surveillance systems and others. A general Maximum Likelihood (ML) approach to the detection of common periodic features possibly present in a set of video signals and the estimation of their characteristics, such as the fundamental frequency and the local amplitude, is proposed. Application examples in various scenarios are presented and the performance of the proposed ML solutions is shown to be effective.**

Keywords–Features extraction; periodicity analysis; video processing; maximum likelihood estimation.

I. Introduction

A video signal is characterized by a multidimensional domain in which two space dimensions specify the pixel position within a frame and a time dimension describes the evolution of the frame image (3D). An additional space dimension may come from the simultaneous use of multiple cameras framing the same scene from different viewpoints, bringing the overall dimensionality to 4D. This paper discusses the extraction of periodic features from video signals obtained by one or multiple cameras—a topic which has been the subject of a large body of literature, e.g., see [1] and references therein.

A first approach considered in the literature uses spatial matching to identify an object or a portion of the image, follow the evolution of its trajectory over time in successive frames and analyze this trajectory to extract possible periodic features [1], [2]. Despite being very general, this approach is impacted by the reliability of the spatial matching step, which is largely affected by the quality and resolution of the video sequence, as well as possible optical effects, including illumination variations, reflections, occlusions and others.

As nicely pointed in [2, Figure 1], the fundamental ability to recognize periodic features in a sequence of frames does not require high quality or resolution, as demonstrated by an example of a significantly blurred low-resolution sequence of images in which the human brain can still appreciate the periodic feature of a man waking on a treadmill.

A second approach discussed in the literature avoids the critical spatial matching step and uses suitable projections of the video sequence in the spatial domain to extract compact representations of the video variations in the time domain, which can then be easily analyzed in the frequency domain to recognize possible periodic features. In this category, [1] projects each frame onto the x and y dimensions to obtain two signals $x[n]$ and $y[n]$, in the time index n, that can be jointly analyzed to extract possible periodic components. Another example within this approach is [3], where each frame is projected onto the single space dimension represented by the average luminance signal, which can be easily processed along the time domain to extract the frequency components of interest and detect possible periodic features.

These approaches, despite being general and reasonable, are based on specific initial assumptions—spatial matching in the first one and frame projection in the second one—which may possibly limit their effectiveness and efficiency. To avoid these specific assumptions and their possible consequences, in this paper, we wish to take a more basic and radical approach by considering the direct application of fundamental estimation and detection criteria to the multidimensional video signal. To this purpose, we have selected the sound and trustable Maximum Likelihood (ML) principle, which is very well studied, documented and widely applied [4], [5].

As in all applications of the ML criterion, a key part of the problem is the selection of a suitable observation model. To this purpose, we propose to base the estimation and detection process on the direct observation of the 3D or 4D video sequence, possibly affected by noise. The proposed solutions are then considered in a few application examples and their performance is analyzed and discussed.

The remainder of this paper is organized as follows. In Section II, the model of periodic variations and the extraction of related features in multidimensional video signals are described. Section III presents some applications in specific fields of the proposed technique. Finally, conclusions are drawn in Section IV.

II. Analysis of Periodic Variations

A. Preliminaries

A digital video signal consists of a series of digital images, also known as frames, properly captured over time. Precisely, a video can be defined as a multidimensional signal which describes the evolution over time occurring in the framed area. Moreover, digital frames are bidimensional projections of the real world on the camera sensor and a loss of information about the full 3D motion has to be considered. Therefore, a physical 3D displacement in the space corresponds to spatio-temporal variations in the structure of the multidimensional signal; such movements affect to some degree the pixel intensity values in the video signal captured by the camera sensor.

Periodic variations can be of particular interest: in fact, they can represent specific events and need to be properly detected

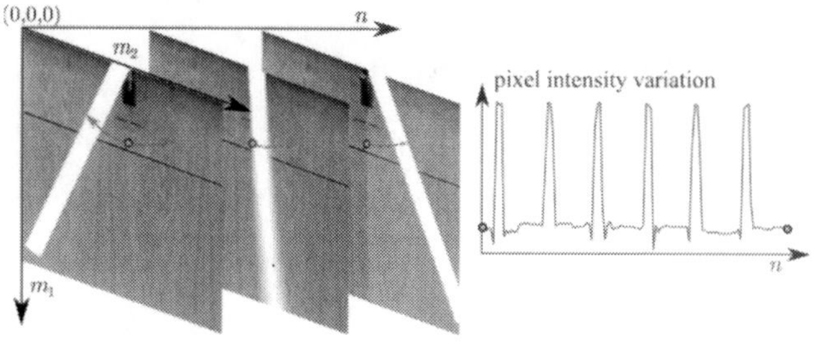

Figure 1. An example of periodic motion and the variations it causes in a multidimensional signal: a physical pendulum swinging from left to right.

and analyzed. In the specific case of periodic movements or recurring events, the pixel intensity values in the video stream may exhibit periodic features. As an example, in Figure 1, some frames extracted by a video capturing the motion of a physical pendulum are shown, with a spatio-temporal reference system describing the spatial plane (m_1, m_2) and the temporal dimension (n). Considering a reference pixel, specified by the highlighted point, the intensity variations which affect it are also shown: these periodic pixel-wise variations can be exploited to analyze spatio-temporal movements.

Before detailing the model of multidimensional periodicity and the approach to detection and estimation of periodic features, some preliminary considerations have to be introduced. The model proposed in the next subsection is valid under the following assumptions:

1) the camera is still or is moving solidly with the framed subject;
2) the subject of interest is not affected by translation or superposed motion.

The first condition is related to the considered scenario: as the main goal is to extract periodic features of subjects in the scene, global movements are not considered.[1] The second condition assumes that no large movements or intensity variations affect the subject: the only main motion components are expected to be the periodic variations.

B. Model of Periodic Variations

For the presented assumptions, the model of periodicity in a multidimensional signal is now defined. Consider a video signal acquired by a camera sensor with a sampling period T_s, namely with a frame rate $f_s = 1/T_s$. A gray-scale frame captured at the sampling instants nT_s can be described by a matrix $\mathbf{X}[n]$ composed of $M_1 \times M_2$ pixels, where M_1 and M_2 are the numbers of rows and columns of the matrix, respectively, and $X[m_1, m_2, n]$ is the intensity of the pixel with coordinates (m_1, m_2) in the n-th frame. For color videos, a proper number of channels has to be considered: as an example, for standard Red, Green and Blue (RGB) cameras each frame is composed by three matrices, one per color channel.

To simplify the notation for the following steps, the operator of vectorization of a matrix and its inverse are now introduced. Let $\mathbf{X}[n]$ be the matrix representing the video signal: the vectorized version $\mathbf{x}[n]$ is defined as

$$\begin{aligned}\mathbf{x}[n] = &\ \mathrm{vec}(\mathbf{X}[n]) = \\ = &\ [X[0,0,n] \cdots X[0, M_2-1, n] \\ &\ X[1,0,n] \cdots X[1, M_2-1, n] \\ &\ \vdots \\ &\ X[M_1-1, 0, n] \cdots X[M_1-1, M_2-1, n]]^{\mathsf{T}}\end{aligned} \quad (1)$$

where the column vector $\mathbf{x}[n]$ has size $M_1 M_2 \times 1$, its element $x[p, n]$ denotes the intensity value of the p-th element of the n-th vectorized frame and $(\cdot)^{\mathsf{T}}$ denotes the vector transpose. Accordingly, the inverse operator is defined as

$$\mathbf{X}[n] = \mathrm{vec}^{-1}(\mathbf{x}[n]) \quad (2)$$

where the frame sampled at discrete time nT_s is retrieved to the original size $M_1 \times M_2$.

Another useful representation is given by the variations of the single p-th element over time. Starting from the vector $\mathbf{x}[n]$ introduced in (1), the evolution of the signal relative to the pixel in position p is denoted by the vector

$$\tilde{\mathbf{x}}[p] = [x[p,0]\ x[p,1]\ \ldots\ x[p, N-1]]^{\mathsf{T}} \quad (3)$$

which has size $N \times 1$, where N is the total number of considered frames.

Relying on the assumptions introduced at the beginning of Section II, the video frames are recorded by still cameras and contain pixel intensity variations related only to the periodic motion. In order to extract periodic features from the video signal, a proper model of the multidimensional structure is needed. Considering the scenario in which movements are driven by a single common periodicity, a useful model, including noise on the sequence of frames, may be given as

$$\mathbf{X}[n] = \mathbf{B} + \mathbf{A}\cos(2\pi f_0 n T_s + \mathbf{\Phi}) + \mathbf{W}[n] \quad (4)$$

where all the matrices have size $M_1 \times M_2$ (equal to the resolution of the involved camera sensor), $\mathbf{B}$ describes the pixel-wise continuous components, $\mathbf{A}$ is the matrix of the amplitudes, f_0 is the common fundamental frequency, T_s is the video sampling period, n is the frame index, $\mathbf{\Phi}$ is the matrix of the initial phases, $\{\mathbf{W}[n]\}$ are matrices of independent and identical distributed (i.i.d.) zero-mean Gaussian noise samples. In (4) and the following equations, the $\cos(\cdot)$ operator and the addition of a scalar to a vector or matrix are applied element-wise. The vectorized version of equation (4), according to (1), is given by

$$\mathbf{x}[n] = \mathbf{b} + \mathbf{a}\cos(2\pi f_0 n T_s + \boldsymbol{\phi}) + \mathbf{w}[n] \quad (5)$$

where the definition (1) is applied to the matrices $\mathbf{X}[n]$, $\mathbf{B}$, $\mathbf{A}$, $\mathbf{\Phi}$ and $\mathbf{W}[n]$.

Given this multidimensional model, the aim is to efficiently extract periodic features, such as the fundamental frequency f_0 and the amplitudes $\mathbf{A}$, which are useful to check the presence/absence of periodicity (or measure its repetition period) and identify the position of periodic variations in the video, respectively. In order to achieve the estimation of these parameters, it will be shown that the application of the ML approach to the model (5) is a reliable solution.

[1]Motion compensation algorithms could be used to limit this effect [1].

It can be noticed that extensions to a full RGB video, considered analyzing jointly the three color channels or multiple camera sensors, can be an application example of this approach, as shown in [6].

C. Generalized Maximum Likelihood Estimation

The approach consists of a generalized version of ML estimation applied to multidimensional signals. The parameters to be estimated are: the fundamental frequency f_0, the relative local amplitudes $\mathbf{a}$ and possibly the phases $\boldsymbol{\phi}$. These parameters can be collected in a vector $\boldsymbol{\theta} = [\mathbf{a}, f_0, \boldsymbol{\phi}]$. Following standard methods in [5], the likelihood function to be minimized in order to obtain the ML estimate $\hat{\boldsymbol{\theta}}$ is

$$J(\boldsymbol{\theta}) = \sum_{p=0}^{M_1M_2-1} \sum_{n=0}^{N-1} \Big[x[p,n] - a[p]\cos(2\pi f_0 n T_s + \phi[p]) \Big]^2 \tag{6}$$

where NT_s is a suitable observation window and $x[p,n]$ represents the observed video signal in the p-th position at discrete time nT_s.

The ML estimation of the parameters of interest is now derived, following proper steps similar to the ones in [5], [7]. Using trigonometric identities in (6), it is possible to obtain

$$J(\boldsymbol{\theta}) = \sum_{p=0}^{M_1M_2-1} \sum_{n=0}^{N-1} \Big[x[p,n] - \alpha[p]\cos(2\pi f_0 n T_s) - \beta[p]\sin(2\pi f_0 n T_s) \Big]^2 \tag{7}$$

where $\alpha[p] = a[p]\cos(\phi[p])$ and $\beta[p] = -a[p]\sin(\phi[p])$. As $a[p]$ and $\phi[p]$ are strictly related with $\alpha[p]$ and $\beta[p]$, it is possible to substitute the vector parameter $\boldsymbol{\theta}$ with $\boldsymbol{\theta}' = [\boldsymbol{\alpha}, \boldsymbol{\beta}, f_0]$. By properly combining the variables in the temporal dimension, it is possible to obtain a simplified version of the likelihood function:

$$J(\boldsymbol{\theta}') = \sum_{p=0}^{M_1M_2-1} (\tilde{\mathbf{x}}[p] - \alpha[p]\mathbf{c} - \beta[p]\mathbf{s})^{\mathsf{T}} \cdot (\tilde{\mathbf{x}}[p] - \alpha[p]\mathbf{c} - \beta[p]\mathbf{s}) \tag{8}$$

$$= \sum_{p=0}^{M_1M_2-1} (\tilde{\mathbf{x}}[p] - \mathbf{H}\boldsymbol{\gamma}[p])^{\mathsf{T}} (\tilde{\mathbf{x}}[p] - \mathbf{H}\boldsymbol{\gamma}[p]) \tag{9}$$

where

$$\mathbf{c} = \left[1 \ \cos(2\pi f_0 T_s) \ \ldots \ \cos(2\pi f_0 (N-1) T_s)\right]^{\mathsf{T}}$$
$$\mathbf{s} = \left[0 \ \sin(2\pi f_0 T_s) \ \ldots \ \sin(2\pi f_0 (N-1) T_s)\right]^{\mathsf{T}}$$

are vectors of size $N \times 1$ associated with the cosine and sine components over time. In (9), the parameters $\alpha[p]$ and $\beta[p]$ and the vectors $\mathbf{c}$ and $\mathbf{s}$ are grouped by defining: $\boldsymbol{\gamma}[p] = [\alpha[p] \ \beta[p]]^{\mathsf{T}}$, with size 2×1, and the matrix $\mathbf{H} = [\mathbf{c} \ \mathbf{s}]$, with size $N \times 2$.

A formulation in terms of a simple linear model [5], [8], can be obtained using a suitable notation which groups the involved vectors and matrices as

$$\tilde{\mathbf{x}} = \left[\tilde{\mathbf{x}}[0]^{\mathsf{T}} \ \tilde{\mathbf{x}}[1]^{\mathsf{T}} \ \cdots \ \tilde{\mathbf{x}}[M_1M_2-1]^{\mathsf{T}}\right]^{\mathsf{T}},$$

$$\mathbf{Z} = \begin{bmatrix} \mathbf{H} & \mathbf{0} & \cdots & \mathbf{0} \\ \mathbf{0} & \mathbf{H} & \cdots & \mathbf{0} \\ \vdots & \vdots & \ddots & \vdots \\ \mathbf{0} & \mathbf{0} & \cdots & \mathbf{H} \end{bmatrix} \text{ and}$$

$$\mathbf{d} = \left[\boldsymbol{\gamma}[0]^{\mathsf{T}} \ \boldsymbol{\gamma}[1]^{\mathsf{T}} \ \ldots \ \boldsymbol{\gamma}[M_1M_2-1]^{\mathsf{T}}\right]^{\mathsf{T}}$$

where $\tilde{\mathbf{x}}$, $\mathbf{Z}$ and $\mathbf{d}$ have size $N(M_1M_2) \times 1$, $N(M_1M_2) \times 2M_1M_2$ and $2M_1M_2 \times 1$, respectively. Equation in (9) can now be expressed in the form

$$J(\boldsymbol{\theta}') = (\tilde{\mathbf{x}} - \mathbf{Z}\mathbf{d})^{\mathsf{T}} (\tilde{\mathbf{x}} - \mathbf{Z}\mathbf{d}). \tag{10}$$

Following the classical theory of estimation for multiple parameters in linear models [5], the function (10) can be minimized over $\mathbf{d}$ for

$$\hat{\mathbf{d}} = (\mathbf{Z}^{\mathsf{T}}\mathbf{Z})^{-1} \mathbf{Z}^{\mathsf{T}} \tilde{\mathbf{x}} \tag{11}$$

so that its minimum with respect to $\mathbf{d}$ is

$$J(f_0) = \left(\tilde{\mathbf{x}} - \mathbf{Z}\hat{\mathbf{d}}\right)^{\mathsf{T}} \left(\tilde{\mathbf{x}} - \mathbf{Z}\hat{\mathbf{d}}\right) = \tilde{\mathbf{x}}^{\mathsf{T}} \left(\mathbf{I} - \mathbf{Z}(\mathbf{Z}^{\mathsf{T}}\mathbf{Z})^{-1}\mathbf{Z}^{\mathsf{T}}\right) \tilde{\mathbf{x}} \tag{12}$$

where $\mathbf{I}$ is the identity matrix, $\hat{\mathbf{d}}$ in (11) has been used and the dependence of $J(\cdot)$ on the remaining variable f_0 has been emphasized. This optimization is effective for $\mathbf{d}$, which includes only information relative to the amplitudes $\mathbf{a}$ and the phases $\boldsymbol{\phi}$; in order to obtain the estimation of f_0, the last equation has to be minimized over f_0 or, equivalently, maximized over the term

$$\tilde{\mathbf{x}}^{\mathsf{T}} \mathbf{Z} (\mathbf{Z}^{\mathsf{T}}\mathbf{Z})^{-1} \mathbf{Z}^{\mathsf{T}} \tilde{\mathbf{x}}. \tag{13}$$

After the maximization of (13), the estimation of the parameters in $\hat{\boldsymbol{\theta}}'$ is obtained, from which the parameters $\mathbf{a}$, f_0 and $\boldsymbol{\phi}$ can be computed.

A proper approximation and simplification of the matrix $\mathbf{Z}(\mathbf{Z}^{\mathsf{T}}\mathbf{Z})^{-1}\mathbf{Z}^{\mathsf{T}}$ can lead to an *approximate* ML estimator. Following [5], [7], [9], the ML estimator of the frequency f_0 can be obtained by maximizing the periodogram $I[k]$ over the overall p positions. More precisely, this can be obtained as

$$\hat{f}_0 = \frac{f_s}{N} \underset{k_{\min} \le k \le k_{\max}}{\arg\max} \ I[k] \tag{14}$$

where, assuming regular periodicity, the $\arg\max$ search is limited to the discretized frequencies set $[k_{\min}; k_{\max}]$, related to the real frequencies $f_{\min} = \frac{k_{\min}}{N} f_s$ and $f_{\max} = \frac{k_{\max}}{N} f_s$, and the periodogram is defined as

$$I[k] = \frac{2}{N} \sum_{p=0}^{M_1M_2-1} \left| \sum_{n=0}^{N-1} x[p,n] \, e^{-j2\pi \frac{k}{N} n} \right|^2. \tag{15}$$

This simplified estimator is approximately ML if the real frequency f_0 is not close to 0 or $f_s/2$, only.

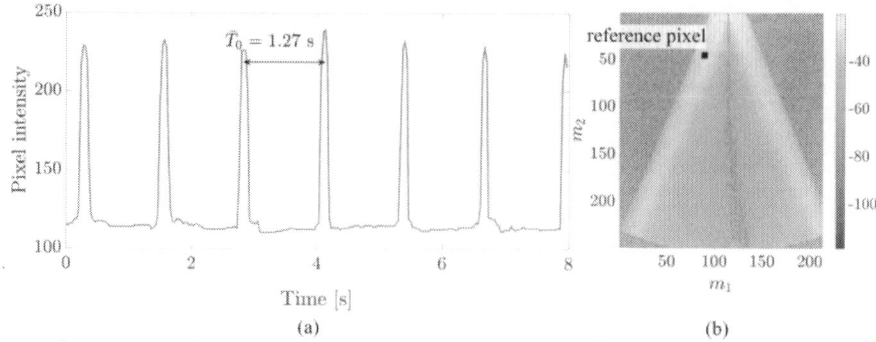

Figure 2. Example of periodicity analysis for the video of a pendulum. In (a) the intensity variations on the reference pixel and (b) the estimation of $\text{vec}^{-1}(\mathbf{a})$ i.e., the amplitudes at the position of the various pixel.

III. APPLICATIONS

In this section, the performance of the ML approach is discussed, showing its effectiveness in the extraction of periodic features. In particular, we discuss the importance of estimating the fundamental frequency f_0 in the framed image variations and the capability of localizing them inside the frame by the estimation of local amplitudes $\mathbf{a}$. The first feature is attractive, because it may be very useful in several tasks that involve the monitoring of some events or movements related to a periodic variation. The second one is equally important, since the localization of such variations may be a key feature to increase computational efficiency in some applications or video signal analysis for surveillance purposes.

In order to show the efficiency and the simplicity of the ML approach, three examples in different scenarios are reported, describing the capabilities of the approach and focusing on its properties in each application. Specifically, the examined scenarios are related to:

1) analysis of physical oscillations
2) analysis on movements of athletes and people doing gymnastic activity
3) monitoring of vital signs in animals and humans.

A. Physical Oscillations

As a first application example, we analyze the periodicity of the oscillations of a physical pendulum captured by a still camera positioned in front of the pivot. This example demonstrates the effectiveness of ML estimation on multidimensional signals.

The recorded video sample, where few frames were preliminarily depicted in Figure 1, shows an oscillating plank, with the pivot hooked on a border of a desk. Selecting a proper reference pixel, it is possible to show the intensity variations over time connected with the periodic passage of the pendulum on the involved pixel.

In Figure 2(a), these variations over the time dimension of the multidimensional signal are displayed: the peaks inside the signal correspond to the passage of the white pendulum on the reference position, which has higher intensity values than the dark background. By measuring the distance between the peaks, it is possible to estimate the average rate of the oscillation: by inspection of the signal in Figure 2(a), an average oscillation time of $\bar{T}_0 = 1.27$ Hz can be obtained, corresponding to a fundamental frequency $f_0 = 0.787$ Hz: this value is used as reference and can be compared with the estimate extracted by the video estimation system. Applying the approximate ML approach (14) on the considered sample video, a frequency $\hat{f}_0 = 0.77$ Hz is estimated, with a relative estimation error equal to 2.16%.

The influence of the periodicity on every pixel is computed by the estimation of $\hat{\mathbf{a}}$. Using (11), the amplitudes are obtained and shown in Figure 2(b), where the results are shown as an image with size equal to that of original video frames. It can be noticed that in the area directly below the pivot the estimated amplitudes have lower values: this effect is due to the fact that in this area the pixel intensities are stressed by variations with a rate doubled with respect to the fundamental one. Differently, the areas on the left and right of the axes of the pivot are mainly affected by the fundamental periodicity: therefore, the intensity of the estimated amplitude is higher. It is remarked that the estimated amplitudes are reported in a logarithmic scale, with the purpose to enhance and make more visible the difference between the various areas.

B. Athlete Monitoring

As a first realistic application example, the scenario of monitoring of physical activity made by people or athletes is presented. In fact, many physical exercises involve periodic movements or repetition of a single gesture: examples of these movements are given by weight-lifting, sit-ups and stretches. These repetitive movements are expected to involve specific body parts without a global motion of the gymnast, as they are performed on a fixed position.

To show the effectiveness of the ML approach in this environment, we consider a video sample of a man doing a series of push-ups. The duration of the video sample is about 26 s, it is recorded with a frame rate $f_s = 30$ Hz and has a frame size of 516×216 pixels. By visual inspection, the man was able to do about 19 push-ups during the whole video, with an approximate average frequency of $\bar{f}_0 = 0.73$ Hz. In Figure 3(a), a sample frame of the considered video is shown.

Initially, the analysis of the local amplitudes is clarified: after an estimate by video processing of the fundamental frequency with an average push-up rate of $\hat{f}_0 = 0.725$ Hz, the parameter $\text{vec}^{-1}(\hat{\mathbf{a}})$ is computed and shown in Figure 3(b). As in the example of the pendulum described in Subsection III-A, pixels with higher value are those mainly affected by the periodic motion of the push-ups. On the other side, the background has lower intensity value, since pixel variations are modified only by random motion on the scene or noise. In Figure 3(b), the estimated amplitudes are reported in logarithmic scale. It

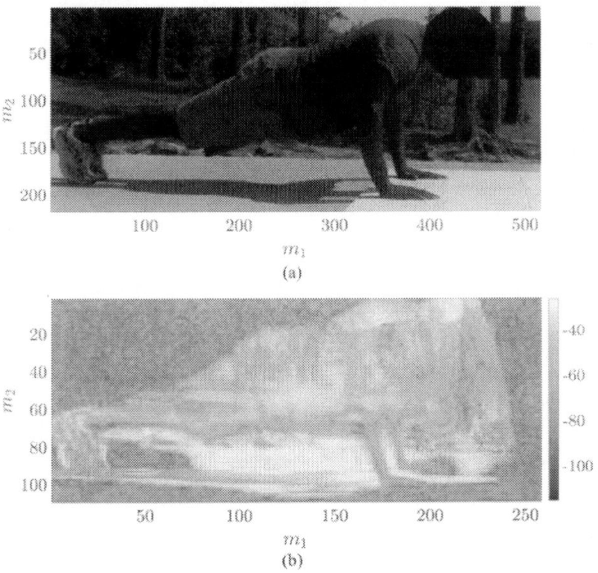

Figure 3. Example of athlete monitoring: (a) sample frame of a man doing push-ups and (b) amplitude estimation for $\hat{f}_0 = 0.725$ Hz.

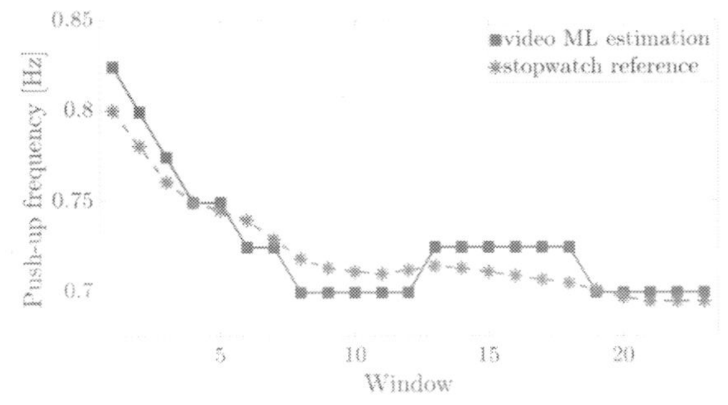

Figure 4. Performance evaluation in the estimation of the fundamental frequency f_0, related to the push-up rate of an athlete.

is clear that this analysis can be used to localize the periodic motion and, as an example, create a mask for further video processing algorithms.

Afterwards, a deeper analysis of the fundamental frequency estimation is performed. The repetition times of the athlete doing push-ups were measured by the use of a stopwatch and computing a curve fitting of the evolution of the push-up rates over time. The video was analyzed with temporal windows of $NT_s = 10$ s and an overlapping parameter of 90%, obtaining an estimation of the fundamental frequency for every second. In Figure 4, the stopwatch reference compared with the rates estimated by applying the ML approach proposed in Section II is shown; the quality of the estimation is clear, exhibiting also a pattern similar to that of the original rates.

As further evidence of the effectiveness of the proposed approach in the estimation of the periodic features of the video signal, the error on the estimation of f_0 is also reported. Considering the results shown in Figure 4, a Root Mean Squared Error (RMSE) of 0.0128 Hz is obtained, which, normalized to the average value of the reference, gives an average relative error of 1.8%.

C. Monitoring of Vital Signs

As last example of the reliability of the ML approach for periodic feature extraction, an application in the biomedical scenario is proposed. In particular, monitoring of vital signs is a key tool to asses the health condition of a patient. Recent studies [9]–[13] report that some of the vital signs, such as hearth and respiratory rates, can be evaluated by contactless systems employing video cameras and multidimensional signal processing. Among vitals signs, the Respiratory Rate (RR) plays a very important role as indicator of the health of a patient. It is now demonstrated that the proposed ML approach can be used for both tasks of estimating the RR of a framed patient and localizing the areas mainly affected by respiratory movements. This last feature may be very useful in order to reduce computational complexity of video processing-based algorithms by localizing Regions of Interests (ROI), as shown in [9].

A first test is performed on monitoring the respiration of a sleeping cat. The animal was completely still and breathing with a constant RR $f_0 \in [0.28, 0.35]$ Hz, obtained by a chronograph. The RR reference measurements were obtained by live inspection during video recording by careful observation of the animal. These measurements can be easily converted to breaths per minute (bpm) if desired. In Figure 5(a), a sample frame of the video sequence is shown: the video signal has a total duration of 1 min and 13 s with a sampling rate of 15 Hz and a camera resolution of 320×240 pixels.

In Figure 5(b), the likelihood function $J(f_0)$ used for the estimation of the fundamental frequency is shown. The periodicity related to breathing movements obtained by processing the variation of pixel intensity is clear. Taking the $\arg\max$ of the likelihood function, the frequency $\hat{f}_0 = 0.3$ Hz can be estimated, according to the frequency range used as reference. As discussed in Section II, after the estimation of the fundamental frequency, the parameter $\text{vec}^{-1}(\hat{\mathbf{a}})$ can be computed. In Figure 6, the estimated pixel-wise amplitudes are shown. Higher values are obtained in the pixel positions mainly involved in breathing movements that are near the chest and the abdomen of the cat. By selecting this area as a possible ROI, it is feasible to develop algorithms that are robust against possible large random movements [9], excluding other areas that are involved in useless movements or random noise.

As a last test, relying on the work presented in [9], the estimation of the RR on a real newborn patient and the localization of breathing areas are performed. The video was recorded in the University Hospital of Parma, by video cameras with resolution of 720×576 and sampling rate $f_s = 25$ Hz, with an overall duration of 3 min and 3 s. As in the push-up example, the RR is here estimated over time and compared with the pneumographic reference, the gold-standard system for monitoring of respiration mainly used by clinicians. Using windows of analysis of length $NT_s = 20$ s and an overlapping parameter of 90% (i.e., with RR estimation obtained every 2 s), the comparison between the reference and the estimation by video processing is depicted in Figure 7. Excluding the first five windows, where the algorithm has startup issues, the correspondence of the estimated RRs with the pneumographic ones is very good.

As described in Subsection III-B, also for this example a thorough analysis is performed, reporting the RMSE and the average relative estimation error on the RR. A RMSE equal to

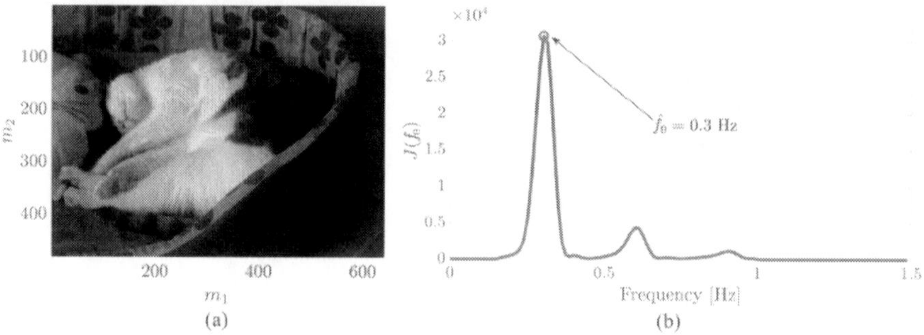

Figure 5. Monitoring of a sleeping cat: (a) frame sample from the video recording and (b) the likelihood function $J(f_0)$ for the estimation of the RR.

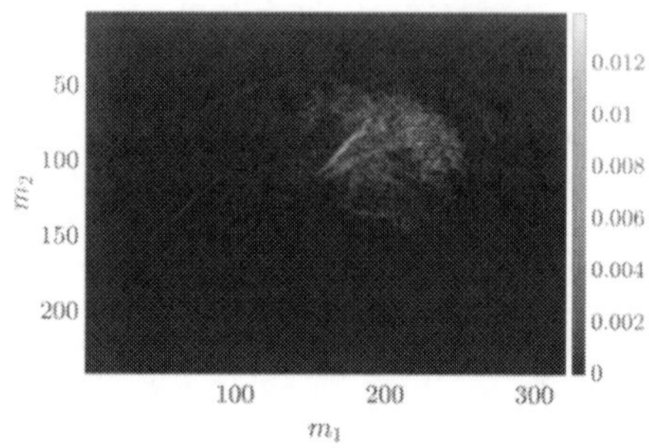

Figure 6. Estimated amplitudes for the video example of a sleeping cat: maximum values of $\text{vec}^{-1}(\mathbf{a})$ can be noticed near the chest of the animal.

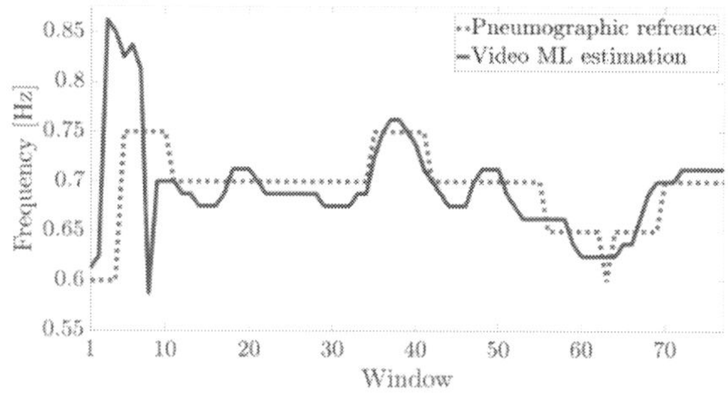

Figure 7. Estimation of the RR in monitoring of a newborn: comparison of the estimation from video signals and the pneumographic device.

0.051 Hz is obtained with an average relative error of 7.5% An in-depth analysis on the performance for RR estimation of the technique introduced in Section II is beyond the scope of this paper. The interested reader is referred to [9]. Nonetheless, the presented results highlight the usefulness of the ML approach applied to multidimensional video signals for the extraction of periodic features.

IV. CONCLUSION

In this paper, we proposed a method for the extraction of periodic features in video signals. Under the assumptions of still camera and that the framed subject is not affected by translation or superposed motion, we introduced a model of periodicity in multidimensional signals; then, we applied the ML criterion for the estimation of the periodic features of interest. Finally, we demonstrated the effectiveness of this approach, showing three different application examples: monitoring of physical oscillations, athlete movements and vital signs. The advantage in the localization of periodic variations and estimation of the fundamental frequency has been demonstrated by comparing the obtained results with suitable reference values.

REFERENCES

[1] A. Briassouli and N. Ahuja, "Extraction and analysis of multiple periodic motions in video sequences," IEEE Trans. Pattern Anal. Mach. Intell., vol. 29, no. 7, July 2007, pp. 1277–1261.

[2] R. Cutler and L. S. Davis, "Robust real-time periodic motion detection, analysis, and applications," IEEE Trans. Pattern Anal. Mach. Intell., vol. 22, no. 8, Aug. 2000, pp. 781–796.

[3] G. M. Kouamou Ntonfo, G. Ferrari, R. Raheli, and F. Pisani, "Low-complexity image processing for real-time detection of neonatal clonic seizures," IEEE Trans. Inf. Technol. Biomed., vol. 16, no. 3, May 2012, pp. 375–382.

[4] H. L. Van Trees, Detection, Estimation, and Modulation Theory (Part I), 1st ed. New York, NY, USA: John Wiley & Sons, Inc., 2001.

[5] S. M. Kay, Fundamentals of Statistical Signal Processing: Estimation Theory. Upper Saddle River, NJ, USA: Prentice Hall, 1993, vol. 1.

[6] L. Cattani et al., "Monitoring infants by automatic video processing: A unified approach to motion analysis," Comput. Biol. Med. (Elsevier), vol. 80, Jan. 2017, pp. 158–165.

[7] N. Patwari, J. Wilson, S. Ananthanarayanan, S. Kasera, and D. Westenskow, "Monitoring breathing via signal strength in wireless networks," IEEE Trans. Mobile Comput., vol. 13, no. 8, Aug. 2014, pp. 1774–1786.

[8] C. M. Bishop, Pattern Recognition and Machine Learning, 1st ed. New York, NY, USA: Springer-Verlag, 2006.

[9] D. Alinovi, G. Ferrari, F. Pisani, and R. Raheli, "Respiratory rate monitoring by maximum likelihood video processing," in Proc. IEEE Int. Symp. Signal Process. and Inf. Technol. (ISSPIT), Limassol, Cyprus, Dec. 2016, pp. 172–177.

[10] D. Alinovi, L. Cattani, G. Ferrari, F. Pisani, and R. Raheli, "Spatio-temporal video processing for respiratory rate estimation," in Proc. IEEE Int. Symp. Med. Meas. and Applicat. (MeMeA), Turin, Italy, June 2015, pp. 12–17.

[11] L. Tarassenko et al., "Non-contact video-based vital sign monitoring using ambient light and auto-regressive models," IOP Physiol. Meas., vol. 35, no. 5, May 2014, pp. 807–831.

[12] R. Janssen, W. Wang, A. Moço, and G. de Haan, "Video-based respiration monitoring with automatic region of interest detection," IOP Physiol. Meas., vol. 37, no. 1, Jan. 2016, pp. 100–114.

[13] C.-W. Wang, A. Hunter, N. Gravill, and S. Matusiewicz, "Unconstrained video monitoring of breathing behavior and application to diagnosis of sleep apnea," IEEE Trans. Biomed. Eng., vol. 61, no. 2, Feb. 2014, pp. 396–404.

AUTHOR INDEX

Abrardo, A. 79
Addesso, P. 89
Alinovi, D. 95
Barni, M. 79
Boer, M. 85
Carrive, J. 16
Chbeir, R. 32
Dhamodaran, A. 20
Doukhan, D. 16
Eggeling, E. 10
Endo, M. 38
Escher, C. 85
Gatimu, K. 20
Hatano, K. 73
Hayashi, T. 67
Hirota, M. 38, 44, 51
Hwang, E. 26
Ishikawa, H. 32, 38, 44, 51, 57
Kallas, K. 79
Kato, K. 51
Kawai, Y. 67
Kikuchi, S. 44
Kim, H. 26
Kim, W. 26
Krispel, U. 10
Kume, I. 73
Kusu, K. 73
Lee, B. 20
Lee, J. 1
Longo, M. 89
Ohno, S. 38
Raheli, R. 95
Restaino, R. 89
Schinko, C. 10
Schutte, K. 85
Shoji, Y. 38
Sumiya, K. 67
Tanaka, T. 57
Tondi, B. 79
Ullrich, T. 10
Vivone, G. 89
Wang, Y. 67
Yamada, R. 44, 51
Yamamoto, Y. 44, 51
Yan, W. 1
Yokoyama, S. 44, 51
Yu, C. 1

International Academy, Research,
and Industry Association (IARIA)
412 Derby Way
Wilmington, DE 19810

ISBN 978-1-5108-4318-9

CURRAN ASSOCIATES INC.
proceedings.com

IARIA Annual Congress on Frontiers in Science, Technology, Services, Applications (IARIA Congress 2022)

Nice, France
24-28 July 2022

IARIA